Singer and lead guitarist **Francis Rossi** is a founder member of Status Quo as well as the co-writer of most of their fifty-plus hit singles, including 'Paper Plane', 'Caroline' and 'Down Down'. He lives in Surrey with his wife Eileen and his children, where he now eschews the rock 'n' roll lifestyle in favour of 'going to the gym, then coming home, putting my slippers on and doing the cross-word'. He also continues to release chart albums and play more than 200 shows around the world each year with Quo.

Rick Parfitt joined Status Quo in 1967, and has been a key member of the band ever since, singing and playing rhythm guitar and co-writing many of their biggest hits, including 'Whatever You Want', 'Rain' and 'Living on an Island'. These days he lives overlooking the Thames in Teddington along with his ex-wife and partner Patty and young son Harry, his Mercedes CL600, his Mercedes CL65 AMG Bi-turbo and his motor cruiser.

Mick Wall is one of Britain's best-known music journalists, broadcasters and authors. Currently writing for *Mojo*, he was formerly the editor-in-chief of *Classic Rock* magazine and he has written for a number of newspapers and magazines around the world. He has also presented his own shows on Sky TV, Radio One and Capital Radio. More recently, he has become a regular face on VH-1's Behind the Music series, plus several Channel Four and BBC1 documentaries. His books include the recent bestselling biography of John Peel, *Mr Big* – the ghosted auto-biography of Don Arden, *Guns N' Roses: The Most Dangerous Band in the World*, and his much-acclaimed semi-fictionalized memoir *Paranoid: Black Days with Sabbath and Other Horror Stories* – described by *The Times* as 'dark, twisted and frequently hilarious'.

THE STATUS QUO AUTOBIOGRAPHY

FRANCIS ROSSI AND RICK PARFITT

WITH MICK WALL

PAN BOOKS

First published 2004 by Sidgwick & Jackson

This edition published 2006 by Pan Books
an imprint of Pan Macmillan
20 New Wharf Road, London N1 9RR
Associated companies throughout the world
www.panmacmillan.com

ISBN 978-1-5098-5943-6

9 8 7 6 5 4 3 2 1

A CIP catalogue record for this book is available from
the British Library.

Typeset by SetSystems Ltd, Saffron Walden, Essex
Printed and bound by CPI Group (UK) Ltd, Croydon, CR0 4YY

Visit wwwpanmacmillan.com to read more about all our books and
to buy them. You will also find features, author interviews and news
of any author events, and you can sign up for e-newsletters so that you're
always first to hear about our new releases.

XS All Areas is dedicated to all
Status Quo fans throughout the world
with our appreciation and thanks
for your fantastic and loyal support
over the past thirty-nine years.
We couldn't have done it without you . . .

Francis Rossi and Rick Parfitt
September 2004

Picture Credits

Acknowledgements

Francis Rossi and Rick Parfitt would like
to acknowledge the following people
and contributors who have helped
to make *XS All Areas* possible:

Nigel Angel   Joe Bangay
Peta Blewett   George Bodnar   Paul Cox
Ingrid Connell and all at Pan Macmillan
Fin Costello   Steve Murray
Simon Porter   Jeany Savage   Persha Sethi
Simon Trewin and Claire Scott at PFD
Mick Wall   Bob Young

ONE

Even though my roots are Italian-Irish, I have always thought of myself as a South London boy, through and through. It's where I was born, where I grew up and where I still live today. As far as I'm concerned, whenever I'm anywhere in South London, I'm home.

In reality, however, my family origins are more complicated than that. Born on 29 May 1949, I was the first of two sons to an English-born Italian father, Dominic Rossi, and Anglo-Irish mother, Anne – or Nancy, to her friends. There had been a daughter, Arselia, who had died a couple of years before I was born because of a hole in the heart. Consequently my mother, a staunch Catholic, swore that if she ever had another baby she would name it Francis – after St Francis of Assisi, the founder of the Catholic Franciscan order. Just to make sure, she also threw in the names of every other saint she could think of that day and I ended up as Francis Dominic Nicholas Michael Rossi. I was two when my brother Dominic was born, by which point they'd obviously given up trying to think of new names. He's my accountant now and he's a pain in the arse, as the best accountants are wont to be from time to time.

It sounds ancient now, but believe it or not, being born in 1949 sounded young once. Even the world back then seemed to be young – to be starting out again. Four years after the end of the Second World War, rationing was still in place and money and food were in pitifully short supply for most working-class people. We always did all right though, because of the family business, which was primarily ice-cream. Rossi's ice-cream vans were well-known in that part of London in the fifties.

Both my parents were Catholic, which meant I was Catholic too – Holy Communion, confirmation, confession, the full monty. Boys and girls always had their first Holy Communion separately, but I missed my first Communion for some reason – I think I had a cold – and ended up having my big day out with all the girls from the local convent instead. It was great! We used to go to mass every Sunday at the church of Our Lady and St Philip Neri in Forest Hill. People I meet in the music biz often look at you a little bit strangely if you tell them something like that, and I under-stand why, but of course it wasn't at all strange to me as a child. I had never known any different, so as far as I was concerned it was all perfectly normal. Just something we all did, the same way we all ate breakfast.

I had a wobbly period, in terms of my Catholicism, when the band first took off in the seventies. I was always away on the road and had all the excuses I needed to stay away from church. But it never left my mind – nor did the Catholic guilt in various weird forms – and I started going again in my thirties and became a regular attendee at Sunday mass at my local church in Purley, John the Baptist, until I was nearly fifty. I even went as far as having my own kids confirmed into the church as well, poor blighters! I only finally managed to shrug the whole thing off, in fact, just a few years ago when I read a very interesting book called *Conversations with God*. But we'll get to that later . . .

My mother was born in England but her family were among the millions of Irish who emigrated to Liverpool before and after the war. They lived in a place called Crosby, and we used to go there sometimes for family holidays. I can't say I liked it much. Getting from London to Liverpool in those days was like getting to America is now. There was no motorway you could take, no direct trains, and it would take a whole day just to get there. So it wasn't a journey we made often – thank God. My main memory was that it was all gaslights and darkness. My dad used to enjoy swimming in the nearby canal in Birkenhead until we found out it was a sewage outlet! Talk about swimming in your own shit . . .

Mainly we stayed at home in South London. My parents didn't really go out a lot because they were always working, and any socializing they did was usually at the house. My dad was never a drinker, but people often used to think he was drunk because he was one of those real life-and-soul-of-the-party types; never down, always had something to say for himself. He was also a great cook and a horny little git. Many years later he told me how he would get my mother to dress in stockings and suspenders and put lipstick on her nipples. But then the man was Italian, what could he do? It was in his genes. He was a wonderful family man, though. He had this sort of Italian-cockney accent, and one of his expressions when he got annoyed was 'Arseholes!' Except the way he said it in his mangled Italian-cockney it always sounded more comical than threatening. He died a few years ago and I find myself imitating him sometimes, walking round the house going 'Arseholes!' at everything in that same funny voice.

For some convoluted reason we called my paternal grand-mother Mummy. Even people that weren't strictly family but who had become part of the larger extended family through working for them called her Mummy. Mummy was originally from a small Italian island called Atina. She was a Coppola; very good stock, apparently. I think my Italian grandfather, whom we called Pop, was the rabble element. As a result, my father, even though he was born in London, was supremely Italian in his ways. Family and business were inextricably linked. Part of the family seemed to own most of Deptford at the time, through the ice-cream business. Apart from the vans, there was also a shop on Catford Broadway called Rossi's Ice Cream, which the family still owns and now rents out to a betting shop.

There was my dad and all his brothers and their wives, then all the grandparents and children. When one of my uncles died, I remember being at the funeral and all the men talking afterwards about different ice-cream routes, saying this street now belonged to this one, and that street now belonged to that one. He'd barely been in the ground five minutes and they were already divvying up the parts of the business he'd left behind.

Because of that, people tend to assume that I come from quite an affluent background. But while it's true that I don't remember us ever being poor, there were certainly enough times over the years when money was tight. It was a large extended family, a lot of hungry mouths to feed, and all anybody did was work. My parents did own their own house, and that made a big difference in those days. It still does now, but back then it was like the difference between the haves and have-nots. In those terms then, even though we were never rich, I was definitely from a family of haves.

Whatever my family had, though, you could be sure they'd worked hard for it. My mother and father used to be out on the ice-cream van all day. Then in the evenings they used to turn it into a mobile fish-and-chip shop and go out on another round. Times were tough after the war, but plenty of people still managed to fork out for ice-cream and chips; it was like their one treat amid all the doom and gloom. My dad would get to my grandmother's to load up at six every morning. He'd get home a couple of hours later and have breakfast with my mother and then they would go off in the van together. They would come home at about six o'clock and my mother would make us all a meal, and afterwards they would go out again on the fish-and-chip round. I'd be in bed by the time they came home again that night. It was a long day, but that was just the way they were – very enterprising. You see it with a lot of immigrant communities.

It was Mummy who actually owned the ice-cream business. Pop was a parquet-floor layer, and my dad had originally learned that as a trade too. It all came to a bad end, though, when he had an accident in which he nearly lost his hand. They were somewhere up north, doing a job. Pop had stayed in London, working on another job, and had sent my dad and his younger brother, Albert – or Chas, as he was always known. Unfortunately my dad decided to let Chas drive, to give him some practice, and the next thing he knew the car had jumped a crossroads and collided with a bus! My dad, who was in the back seat, went flying out of the window and the bus ran over his hand and crushed it. They had to pull bits of his fingers out of the road and he ended up having nearly forty different operations on the hand to try to save it. It was in the pioneering days of surgery, and when I went to visit him in hospital one day I couldn't believe my eyes –

they'd sown his hand inside his stomach! To help it heal, they said. For a while it left him with this big pouch on his stomach, like a kangaroo. They tried all sorts of stuff. He ended up with this ugly-looking thing for a hand. I was about five at the time and just accepted it, the way kids do. He got used to it pretty quick too. It was no big deal until, years later, I suddenly noticed he had become self-conscious about it for some reason. I think someone must have said something unkind, or something had happened that made him feel differently about it. Which was strange after so many years. He used to show it off to us when we were kids but he wouldn't let his grandchildren look at it at all.

To begin with, we lived in a large house in Mayow Road, in Forest Hill. My main memory is that it was always full of people – uncles, aunties, cousins, grandparents and a whole host of extended family members. I was encouraged early on to take part in the business, too. I would go out on the van with my dad in the school holidays. It must have seemed like the dream job for a school kid, but it was just what my dad did, so it was no big deal. It's like with my kids now: their friends think it must be great having a famous dad, but my kids have never known it any other way, so it's totally unremarkable to them.

As a result, my whole sphere of reference as a small child was essentially Italian. Not that I knew it then. It wasn't until I started going to school and getting singled out by the other kids as 'different' that I began to appreciate that not every-body was the same; a fact I now cherish, but something that I didn't like one little bit back then. No kid wants to be different. So from that point on I did everything I could to play down the Italian side of my character, right down to the way I walked and talked. Now I'm proud of it, but as a kid, and for a while as an adult too, I now admit, I was almost ashamed to be Italian.

When we were growing up, the rule was that everyone in the house had to speak English. Nevertheless, the older members of the family did slip back into Italian quite often. I could understand a fair bit of it as a child but it's all lost on me now, which is a shame, because I would love to be able to speak and read Italian. The aggro I used to get in the school playground could be merciless, and so for years I tried to completely bury anything to do with being Italian. I had a messed-up accent, which got picked up on immediately – a mixture of my mother's sing-song Liverpudlian and my father's broad Italian-cockney. And they said I ate worms – that's what they called spaghetti – and that I stank of garlic. It was like that for me, my brother and our two cousins. We all grew up together at about the same time, and as far as the other kids were concerned we all stank of garlic, ate worms and talked funny . . .

The other thing I got picked on about was my name – everybody kept taunting me about 'Francis' being a girl's name. Which it is, as well as being a boy's name. Try telling that, though, to a gang of snot-nosed hoodlums intent on ritual humiliation. I could lose the funny accent and hide my worm-eating ways, but I couldn't do anything about my name, though that didn't stop me trying. At different times I tried to get people to call me Frank, or Franny, or even just Fran. I never liked any of those either, but anything was better than Francis. In the end, most of my school mates ended up calling me 'Ross', short for Rossi. And when Status Quo first started I was known for the first few years as 'Mike' Rossi. Even today I get called all sorts of things other than Francis. Rick, for example, always calls me Frame. (Because

I'm so skinny I look like the wire frame of a coathanger, apparently.)

I learned quickly, though, as kids do if they want to survive at school, and from then on I tried to turn myself into more of what I thought of as a real English kid – which meant being very cor-blimey-guvnor. I realized the transformation was complete a few years later when I was round at original Quo bassist Alan Lancaster's house one day: we were watching TV with his family when an obvious 'spick' came on and started speaking with the same sort of jingle-jangle Italian-cockney accent I'd once had. Alan came from a tough old South London family in Peckham – they had a black cat called Nigger – and his dad laughed and said, 'He talks funny, like Ross.' Alan's mum went, 'Naw, Ross is one of us now.' That made me so proud, to be accepted like that. 'One of us!' It was like the ultimate accolade. Better than 'stinks of garlic', anyway . . .

The odd thing was that to my own family I was definitely English. Or at least, not really Italian. Mummy used to call me Sangue-Bianco – white blood. She'd say in Italian: 'Here comes White Blood, watch what you say, he's like his mother.' Meaning that I could understand Italian better than they realized, but I wasn't really Italian and was therefore not to be totally trusted. She was a funny old woman like that. My brother was darker-skinned and more Italian-looking, so he and my cousins would get pasta to eat while I would be given a tomato sandwich – English 'white blood' food. But that's just how it was when I was a kid. I didn't know any better and so I just accepted it. I certainly wasn't unhappy. I was a bit weedy and cowardly as a teenager and that bothered me a bit, but most of my childhood memories are basically happy ones.

We lived at the house in Mayow Road for a few years after I was born, then we moved for a short time to another place in Forest Hill. As a result, I have always loved the area. Many years later I moved back there again, to a place next door to my aunt's, which I bought just after I got married to my first wife. It was quite a wrench when, at the age of eleven, the family moved from Forest Hill altogether, to a shop on Balham High Road.

Compared to what I'd been used to, Balham could be a rough old area. I vividly recall my mother stepping in to try to stop the fights of the prostitutes who would gather in our shop doorway sometimes. I didn't know the sordid details but I understood the general idea that prostitutes were 'bad'. I was still at that age, though, when sexuality is an almost indifferent thing, and I couldn't really see what all the fuss was about. I remember me and my mates being told by some bigger kids that the local barber in the high street liked to give young boys a wank under the sheet while he was doing their hair for them. They said he used to give them a fiver for letting him do it. We were all like, 'Great! Let's go!' A fiver! That seemed like a million quid to us back then! Six months later and we would probably have looked on that information completely differently. But we were at that tender age where our sexuality hadn't been boxed into compartments yet and a wank was a wank whoever gave it. To get a fiver on top of it . . . well, that was an offer you simply couldn't refuse.

Unlike most of the lads I used to hang around with, I was never into football or other sports. I did try rugby once at school but it was a disaster. It seemed obligatory to do rugby practice right after there had been a heavy rainstorm and the ground was so cold the mud had turned to jagged ice. Sure enough, I made my first – and last – appearance on the rugby field on just such a bitingly cold wintry day, and ended up with my arms and legs all cut to ribbons. I found the whole thing appalling. Some huge guy would be running straight at you and the sports master would be screaming, 'Hack him down, laddie! Hack the bastard down!' I said, 'Excuse me, sir, but if I pull his legs away from under him he's gonna fall down and hurt himself quite badly.' The sports master said, 'Yes, well?' I said, 'Well, that isn't sport, that's violence.' He flew into a rage. 'Get back out there, you fucking wimp!' he roared. 'Show us you're a man!' The trouble was, I already knew I was a man, I just didn't want to be that kind of a man. I have never been anywhere near a sports field again.

Even now, whenever I'm on the road with the band and it gets to Saturday, and the talk on the tour bus invariably turns to the football or whatever, I completely tune out. I'm just not interested. Which is maybe why I found it so easy to focus on music and learning the guitar when I was a kid. Up until then, everything was so geared towards the family business I didn't really have anything else. I liked films and comics, and listening to the radio. But mostly I liked watching my dad and my uncles sit there counting the takings at the end of each day. It wasn't so much the money they made, we were only kids and that wasn't important yet, it was more about how many ice-creams they had sold that day. Did they break the record? That was how we knew if it had been a good or bad day – by how many cones they had shifted.

I still love the idea of 'turnover'; the idea of selling 'pieces'. But again, not simply because of the money involved, but because that's the barometer I still use in my mind to judge whether a record or a tour has been successful or not; by how many 'pieces' we've sold – be it records or tickets – compared to previous times. That said, I freely admit that I always saw the music business as a way to make money. It was either that or selling ice-creams – in my case, quite literally! If I'd been Peter Pan and stayed a little boy all my life I'd have chosen the ice-creams. But I was fast becoming a big boy and had already decided I wanted something more exciting from life than that.

My mother always liked to boast to everybody that I got my musical side from her. But I realized after she died a few years ago and I got back together with my father again, that that wasn't necessarily the case. He came round once and I played him 'Still the One' by Shania Twain, a beautiful song that always makes the hairs stand up on the back of my neck. As soon as it came on, my father's whole body started contorting, which is exactly what happens to me when I hear a piece of music I really like. He was like, 'Oh, fuck! Oh, yeah!' and started wriggling in his seat. I thought: so *that's* where I get it from . . .

The earliest songs I consciously remember hearing and liking were on the records my parents would play at home. The first one I remember becoming absolutely besotted by was an old Italian song called 'Papa Piccolino'. My mother played it to me one day to try to soothe me after I had slipped and fallen down the stairs. I wasn't badly hurt, just a bit shocked and upset, but she put this 'Papa Piccolino' record on and I just fell in love with it immediately. Not just the song, I realize now, but the huge fuss my mother was making over me. I loved it so much, in fact, that I threw myself down the stairs again the next day! Just so my mum would play 'Papa Piccolino' again and make another big fuss. Then I did it the next day, only this time she cottoned on and threatened to break the record over my head if I did it again.

What I didn't realize at the time was how much of that

old Italian music that they used to play around the house I was actually soaking up as I vied for my mother's attention. For years I used to wonder where this fascination I had for shuffles came from, whether it was the blues-derived kind that bands like early Fleetwood Mac and Chicken Shack specialized in, or the kind you find quite often in country music. Wherever it came from, I had always been a sucker for that insistent, shuffling beat. If you listen to them you'll see it's all over the most famous songs I've written for Status Quo. In fact, it's become our musical trademark, to the point where even some of Rick's best-known songs like 'Whatever You Want' have that same shuffling rhythm.

It wasn't until the mid-seventies, however, when I saw the first *Godfather* movie and noticed this traditional old Italian band sawing away in the background during the opening wedding scene, that I finally realized where it all came from – it was that shuffling Italian rhythm all the time! Looking back, it seems obvious to me now that I should have been influenced by it. But it took me a long time to recognize that, maybe because I was so deeply involved in completely bury-ing my Italian side. That it would help make my fortune, however, is something that could not have been foreseen.

In terms of actually sitting down and learning an instru-ment, my first go at anything like that was with the harmon-ica, which I used to mess around with when I was four years old. At five, I had a little Hohner Mignon accordion, which I actually had a few lessons on. The trouble was we used to have them in the lounge and I could always see my brother and his mates through the French windows, playing in the garden, so I couldn't concentrate at all and soon gave them up.

I was nine when I got my first guitar. I had managed to

busk a few tunes on the harmonica and accordion, and now I wanted to take things a step further and had come up with what I thought was the brilliant idea of forming a duo with my brother. I was mad about the Everly Brothers; theirs were the first songs I ever learned how to sing properly all the way through. I think that must be why I never developed any interest in playing lead guitar – although that has always been my nominal job in Quo – because the Everly Brothers didn't go in for any of that. It was simple singing and strumming, but it was magnificently effective.

I spelled out my plan for world domination by teatime to Dominic and asked him what he thought. To my relief, he said he thought it was a great idea and so we asked our parents for guitars that Christmas. When they actually said yes, I thought this is it, we're on our way! Then Dominic changed his mind at the last moment and got a train set instead. I could have killed him! I would have killed him if my mum had let me! Because bang went my dream of us being the new Everly Brothers. (I got my own back a couple of years later, however, when I borrowed the train set – and promptly sold it.)

My dad told me to look on the bright side – at least I had a guitar. So I banged away on it on my own for a while and then I got taken to a shop in Lewisham called Len Styles Music that used to sell instruments and give guitar lessons. Len Styles Music was *the* place to hang out locally if you were an aspiring musician, so I had quite high hopes for what I might learn there. Instead, the whole thing was a washout. The only time I went there, the guy giving the guitar lessons looked at me and said, 'What do you want to learn then, laddie – foxtrots or waltzes?' Gym teachers call you 'laddie', so that sent out all the wrong signals straight away. And I had absolutely no interest whatsoever in learning foxtrots or waltzes. I said, 'Well, I would like to learn some Everly Brothers tunes and stuff like that.' He looked at me and scowled: 'We don't do any of that shit here, laddie!' I got up and walked out and vowed never to go back. Therein ended my formal education as a musician.

After that, for a long time I saw it as 'establishment' to even *try* to learn anything. Once I'd formed my own group, in fact, even the idea of practising went out the window. Once a gig was over, I didn't want to see the guitar again until it was taken out of its case at the next show. All because I got shut down the first time I expressed a serious interest in actually learning something. Which is terribly sad, I think. Now I want to learn all the time, but that first bad experience put me off for years – decades! In my case, it didn't stop me going on to become a professional musician because that's what I'd already decided I was going to do. But it makes me wonder how many kids must have gone there, or other places like that, over the years, and been put off the idea of learning an instrument altogether.

It's a mistake I think we still make today. Whenever a child expresses an interest in music – whatever it is that's sparked that interest, whether it be Britney or Beethoven – parents still have this tendency to say, 'Oh, you don't want to bother with that.' Because they don't see any immediate benefits from it. They certainly don't see a job at the end of it. Unless they themselves have a special interest in music or the arts, most families don't encourage their kids to learn about music at all. Or if they do, they want them to learn 'serious' music, which can be equally off-putting to a nine-year-old. Children decide to learn an instrument because they think it will be tremendous fun, which it is.

Instead, they immediately get the idea that this is something they have to knuckle down to like extra homework. No wonder so many kids give up before they even get started. Unless they like foxtrots, of course . . .

The opposite extreme is when they are taught to such a high standard that they think everything they play has to be as complicated as fuck to be any good. Which is another criminal misunderstanding of the joys of music. For example, there's a classically trained pianist I'm working with on an informal basis at the moment named Charlotte – or 'Charlie', as I call her. Charlie's tutor, a very dear friend of mine named Mrs Theobold, has nursed her through primary and secondary school, and decided recently that it might be an interesting idea to see what someone like me would make of her progress.

I gladly agreed, and as soon as Charlie started playing you could tell she was a brilliant musician. But she came in with this awful, pompous piece she'd written, and I just had to tell her straight: 'I'm sorry, my dear, but that's just bollocks.' She took it well. If you're going to be an artist of any kind, you've got to be prepared to take the brickbats. I've lost count of the number of times I've been told exactly the same thing by the critics and even by my own band about something new I've written that I thought was great or momentous.

In Charlie's case, it wasn't a bad or even an uninteresting piece she'd written, and of course she played it beautifully. It just sounded like something she had been taught to write; doing what she thought was expected of her rather than something she really felt. I told her: 'What I want to hear is something that comes more from your own heart. Something that says something about who you really are, not just some-one who's been taught well at college.'

Being more open-minded than most classically educated people, Mrs Theobold agreed and later sent Charlie back to me for guitar lessons – and she now plays better than I do! More importantly, she's also learnt to play the piano in a much more relaxed, freewheeling style, and she's started to come up with some really moving new pieces of her own. I get really excited when she comes round now because I can't wait to hear what she's come up with next.

To get back to my own earliest forays on the guitar, however, I travelled down a completely different road, receiving no formal education in music whatsoever. I learned simply by copying the few records we had at home, stuff like Guy Mitchell, who my mother had the hots for, and Connie Francis, who I had the hots for. I still go weak at the knees when I hear one of her old records and she does all that heart-wrenching stuff with her voice that makes her sound like she's crying. To me it was all just pop music, the same as the Everly Brothers. It wasn't until I first went to America years later that I realized it was actually country music I'd been listening to way back when. As a result, I still love country music, it just does something to me.

By the time I was twelve, however, I was into my full-blown rock'n'roll phase. My favourites were Little Richard, Jerry Lee Lewis, Gene Vincent, Eddie Cochran – all the original generation of American rockers. And then there was Cliff Richard and the Shadows, who I also really liked. Most of all, though, there was the Everly Brothers. Discovering them was definitely the turning point for me. It's why a lot of the stuff I have written has been based around three or four simple chords – and I write these words in the full knowledge that to some people they will only reinforce the image of Status Quo as 'three-chord wonders'. But as I always try to explain to the people who still think that joke is funny – usually people who don't actually know how to play an instrument themselves – certain pieces of classical music that people remember for ever are primarily based around three chords. And if I do move a finger and put an extra chord in there, which I'm perfectly able to do, does it make it a better song?

How many chords did the Beatles use? They were the most inventive pop group of all time, and they certainly used more than three chords along the way. But they could go from 'I Am the Walrus' to 'Yellow Submarine' and nobody batted an eye. It was always the simplicity that made their songs so memorable, whatever changes their music went through, and that's the reason why so many of us still sing and play those songs today.

The pity is that after the Beatles it was like you had to be in pockets – rock group, pop group, soul group, whatever. You could never have imagined Deep Purple doing 'When I'm Sixty-Four' or the Bay City Rollers doing 'Lucy in the Sky with Diamonds'. Whereas the Beatles proved that it was being able to do all those things that people loved best. Because at the end of the day it's all about melodies – catchy tunes. The things that make the milkman whistle in the morning. If you can come up with one of those you've cracked it. But be warned: it's not as easy as you think. In my case, I may not have been any good at practising scales and notes, but I was great at just sitting there with the guitar and bashing out tunes. It required dedication to get good, that much was apparent to me. But it took hardly any effort at all to get started – you can learn the bones of a tune on the guitar in one lesson – and once I got started I didn't want to stop.

When the Beatles first exploded they reminded me of the Everlys, only they were a full-on electric band and sounded even more powerful and exciting. Their arrival proved that a British group could be as good as an American one and made me even more determined to try to form some sort of group of my own. Not having the first idea how you actually went about that, though, I joined the school orchestra instead. Unfortunately there was no requirement for a guitarist, so I started to learn the trumpet. Which sounds about as un-rock'n'roll as you can get, except to add that if I hadn't made the effort to learn the trumpet and join the school orchestra I would never have got to know Alan Lancaster and Alan Key, the two guys I would eventually form my very first group with: the first step towards the formation just a few short years later of the original Status Quo line-up. Which only goes to show how these things work out. There's a saying: aim for the sun and you're sure to land on the moon. I'd go along with that.

We all played in the school orchestra but we were all into rock'n'roll as well, which is how we struck up a friendship. I liked Alan Lancaster but he was a very domineering, very outspoken character. He always saw the group as his group, and the rest of us were forced to go along with it, if just to keep the peace. Once or twice I did confront him about it and say, 'Look, you're not the leader here. No one is.' Because we'd decided early on that there weren't going to be any leaders. But he just wasn't having it and we would end up having terrible arguments about it, sometimes even fights. I hadn't learned yet that Alan Lancaster never backed down about anything. He just kept on being ... well, Alan.

The truth is, Alan Key is the one I think of now as the real instigator of the group. It all began when he and Alan Lancaster started messing around trying to put their own little outfit together, outside the orchestra. They were looking for a third person to join; someone who could play but also sing. Which is how I managed to get my face into the picture. Despite knowing the words to every single Everly Brothers hit, I hadn't until then actually considered myself a singer. But I was desperate to join the group – any group – and so there and then I decided I was a singer. Needless to say, Frank Sinatra I wasn't. But there was no one else around with the bottle to get up and give it a go, so they had no choice but to let me join. Suddenly, out of nowhere, I was the singer in a group! Look ma, no hands!

Connoisseurs of heavy rock might wish to skip the following paragraph, but in the very beginning we were actually a brass group. Alan Key and I both played the trumpet and Alan Lancaster played the trombone. Occasionally I'd stop playing long enough to sing a verse or two. We were very much in the style of Kenny Ball & his Jazzmen, who were always on telly at the time, right down to an exact copy – or as exact we could manage it – of their big hit, 'When the Saints Go Marching In'.

The trouble was we never really got beyond rehearsing in Alan Lancaster's bedroom, and we soon grew bored with marching the bloody saints in and the talk turned to trying other sorts of songs, more pop and rock'n'roll-type stuff. For that, though, we knew the trumpets would be pretty useless. So I mentioned that I had a guitar and the next thing I knew Alan Lancaster had gone out and got a guitar, too! He bought a blonde Hofner bass which was lovely to look at, except he couldn't afford a guitar case as well so he used to carry it everywhere in this see-through polythene bag. Classy, like. Meanwhile, Alan Key's older brother was actually in Rolf Harris's backing group, the Diggeroos, and because of that Alan had the use of his brother's spare Fender Stratocaster, jammy git. And that's when we first became a rock'n'roll group, doing all these big guitar instrumentals we'd learned from the Shadows, like 'F.B.I.' and 'Wonderful Land'.

We called ourselves the Scorpions but we never actually played a gig, we just used to rehearse together a couple of times a week. That went on for a year or so, until we were all about fourteen. Then, just as we'd decided we were ready to take on the world, Alan Key announced he was leaving. He could see how committed the rest of us were to really trying to make something of the group, he said, but he had decided he was going to marry the girl next door as soon as they were legally able to, and so he thought it best if he stepped down now, before things got really serious. A man of his word, sure enough, as soon as he turned sixteen he did marry her, bless him. I later discovered that that was something that happened to almost every professional musician – being faced with the choice between marrying the girl of your dreams and settling down, or giving your all to your music and hoping that that takes off instead. Alan Key chose one option and I chose the other. The wonderful thing is we both appear to have made the right choice. I still hear from him occasionally and he's still with the girl of his dreams, happy as can be; and I suppose you could say the same for me. Most of the time.

At that point, though, Alan leaving was a blow to me. He was someone I always looked up to; just a really nice guy. Anybody that was nice and quiet and wasn't aggressive was always all right by me. I grew up surrounded by so many psychos, meeting him was like coming across an oasis in the desert. The school we all went to – Sedghill Comprehensive in Beckenham – housed all the kids from some of the roughest council estates in the area. The biggest thing most of the kids there aspired to was being able to knock a teacher through a classroom window. If you could do that you were a kingpin. Anybody even slightly studious was treated as a dickhead. The thicker and the more aggressive you were, the freer you were from victimization.

Alan Lancaster was one of the toughest kids there. He had to be, because where he grew up in Peckham if you weren't super-tough you got shat on. I was lucky in that living with the Italians I didn't really go out at all until I was a teenager – and what an awakening that was! Alan Lancaster, though, was a fierce fighting character from the off: hard as nails. In all the years I knew him, I never saw anybody beat Alan Lancaster, and there have been some punch-ups over the years. But nobody ever got close to Alan. Nobody. That's some feat, I'll tell you. As time wore on, however, and we all got older, I did begin to wonder how much of it was really him, and how much of it was what he thought *should* be him. The whole permanently aggressive stance began to seem put on to me, and once that happened it made it harder to take so seriously. He was always going on about being a family man. I'm a family man too, but it doesn't mean I have to knock somebody out if things don't go my way.

After Alan Key left, it was sink or swim time for the group. It would have been very easy just to forget the whole thing. That's when Alan Lancaster's toughness actually came in handy. Alan simply refused to give in on anything and he made me vow to carry on. We already had a keyboardist by the name of Jess Jaworski, a kid from school who played accordion and who we more or less forced into learning keyboards for us. And we'd found a drummer called Barry. I don't remember where he came from. I don't think I even knew his surname, just that he was called Barry and he played the drums a bit.

By then we had moved out of Alan Lancaster's bedroom and used to rehearse in Lordship Lane, Dulwich, in a disused garage next door to the South London headquarters of the Air Training Corps (ATC) – better known locally as the air cadets' base. I think Barry's dad had somehow arranged it for us, which was nice of him. Unfortunately, I also seem to recall messing about on the quiet with Barry's girlfriend, which wasn't very nice of me, but then there wasn't much I could do about it. She was a very stout girl and could be quite scary if she didn't get what she wanted. I was still completely naïve sexually, and the first time she tried to give me a blowjob I had no idea what she was doing and ran away from her in fright. I thought she was trying to bite my knob off!

Anyway, we were rehearsing at the garage in Lordship Lane one day when we heard this terrific racket coming from somewhere and realized that there must be another band playing nearby. We went off to investigate and it turned out the ATC had its own little outfit, called suitably enough, the Cadets, who were rehearsing in a room on the base. They were like us in that they hadn't really done many gigs yet, but it was clear they were already really good. In particular, the drummer. As we stood there watching them, listening, it was obvious he was the one holding it all together and really driving it on. Fast and steady and not too many frills – that is, until he saw us watching and started to show off. I was impressed, though. Even though he was just a kid he already played like a pro.

Afterwards we went over and introduced ourselves. The drummer's name was John Coghlan. They were all real air cadets, John was very into that back then. When he heard we were a band too, he decided to come back to the garage with us to take a look. He ended up having a quick blast on the drums with us, and he was fantastic! Easily the best drummer we'd ever played with. After Barry went home that night we talked about it. Poor old Barry, I felt sorry for him. But as a drummer he just wasn't in the same league as John. And so we snuck off behind his back, as bands are wont to do in these situations, and offered his job to John.

We didn't offer him the job straight away, though we were sorely tempted to. At first we tried to play it cool and just invited him to come and have an audition. But John was already two steps ahead of us in the coolness stakes, and I'll never forget the day he turned up for his first rehearsal with us. He arrived in a chauffeur-driven car! We thought, bloody hell! Turned out his dad was dead shrewd and had paid for a cab service to bring him to us. 'Make it look good, son,' he'd told him and it did. It impressed the hell out of us! Even his drum kit was cool: a second-hand Slingerland that had once been owned by Duke Ellington drummer Louie Bellson, whose initials 'LB' were still on both the bass drums. I think we'd played about two numbers before we finally broke down and pleaded with him to join us.

As a person, thankfully, John wasn't really very flash at all. If anything, he seemed unnaturally quiet sometimes, almost too down to earth. So far down, in fact, he seemed to be almost underground sometimes. As we found out, John was a very moody, dark character who never felt obliged to laugh at anybody else's jokes – unless of course he thought they were funny, which he rarely did. He was kind of a loner, even as a teenager. But he played fantastic drums, and with him in the band we now felt truly set to go. We even had a great new moody name for ourselves: the Spectres.

Our first proper gig together as the Spectres was at Samuel Jones' Sports Ground, which was arranged for us by

Alan Lancaster's dad, Harry. It sounds quite grand, but it was actually just a drafty little shed on the edge of a ropy old sports field. But we began to play there fairly regularly over the next few months and started to build up confidence in ourselves. There was never much of a crowd, but all our friends and family would always be there. My dad used to drive us and all our equipment there in the back of his ice-cream van. I would never allow the band to go on until I knew for sure they were all there, particularly Alan's mother, May, who I thought was just wonderful. Harry was great too. He was an ex-boxer who had been around, and I just loved them both; they were always so good to me, treating me as one of their own.

We just used to play covers to begin with, mainly instru-mentals by the Shadows and the Tornados; the stuff in the charts, basically. We would play for about twenty minutes then make a run for it. One night after one of our first shows there this guy came up to us and said, 'I want to manage you.' 'If you like,' we said, and suddenly we had a manager. His name was Pat Barlow; a gas fitter by trade who had worked his way up to the point where he owned his own gas showroom. He wasn't a millionaire but he had a few bob, as they say, and he fancied, as he put it, 'getting into this rock'n'roll game'. Neither of us had ever done anything like that before, but Pat took a chance on us with his money and we took a chance on him with our fledgling careers. That's how it worked for a lot of groups back then. It was the start of the sixties and they were different, more innocent days. People were taking chances left, right and centre.

What Pat lacked in experience he more than made up for with thick-skinned persistence, and he quickly became another father-figure to us. Because he had done well in his own business he was a confident man on the phone and in person, and he badgered the hell out of people about us. In that way he started getting us various different gigs at well-paying but out of the way places like the El Partido club in Catford. His biggest coup at the time was getting us a regular Monday night residency at the Café des Artistes in Chelsea. We were only fourteen, but we would play until two in the morning, then Pat would drive us home, where we'd grab a few hours sleep before getting up to go to school.

Some money started coming in, not much but enough to suddenly be able to afford better equipment, and I got myself a nice Guild semi-acoustic guitar while Alan became the proud owner of a flashy-looking Burns bass guitar. And we started becoming very clothes-conscious. It was the beat group era and you had to have an identity, like the Beatles, so we all wore the same blue suits. We had them made for us by this guy in Lambeth Walk who used to charge us £12 a suit. All except for Alan, who had a 'special' suit made for £25. They were all blue, it's just that Alan's was a more expensive sort of blue, I suppose.

Once we had some regular gigs on the table and the look sorted out, the next thing on the list, of course, was to try to get a record out. We hadn't made a demo tape yet, and at first we tried just getting people from record companies to come to the shows. Fat chance! It seemed like the record company people only went to shows by groups that already had a name or a buzz of some kind going for them. To get over this hurdle, Pat hit on the idea of having us perform a showcase gig supporting the Hollies, who were massive at the time. It was at Orpington Civic Hall in Kent, some time in early 1965, and several leading figures from the music business were supposed to be there in the audience. At least, that's what we were told just before we went on. Big mistake! We were so rattled with nerves we turned in a really poor performance, which was rare for us by then. Needless to say, if there was anyone there from the biz who saw us that night they never bothered to get in touch the next day. Or the day after that . . .

We did, however, make what we saw as a big break-through when Pat got us an audition for a summer season at Butlin's in Minehead, Somerset – which is where the story of Status Quo really began, in many ways. I thought we had no chance at the audition because at the time anyone who went to Butlin's usually went on to bigger and better things. But we were fairly well polished by then for a bunch of schoolkids and, lo-and-behold, we got the gig! We couldn't believe it! It was like saying we were a proper group at last, like we had reached another level. Which I suppose, in retrospect, we had.

Jess certainly saw it that way and immediately quit the group. Like Alan Key before him, Jess could see what a commitment the rest of us were now ready to make – being at Butlin's meant being away from home for four months – and, in his case, he just decided he wasn't up for it. He wanted to continue his studies and go on to university and so he did the decent thing and declared his hand. We wished him well and hurriedly set about finding a replacement. In the end, Pat found us a guy called Roy Lynes, who he'd come across playing organ in a pub. Roy was a car parts inspector by trade and was seven or eight years older than the rest of us; a huge chasm when you're just fifteen. But he had his own equip-ment, he was immediately available and he could play. With our big break at Butlin's looming, that was all we needed to know. Roy was in.

We couldn't wait to get to Butlin's. Not only was it steady paid work but we thought we could look forward to an entire summer of running around a holiday camp chasing birds. Although it's fair to say that we did manage to squeeze in a fair amount of the latter, once we got there we soon realized what a treadmill we were on. We had to play every afternoon for two or three hours and then again in the evening for two or three hours. We ended up playing something like fifty songs a set, twice a day, six days a week. It was insane. I still don't know how we managed it. After about the third week I think we just went onto autopilot. One thing it did do for us, though, was toughen us up as musicians. Performing that many hours a day, every day, you either collapse under the weight of it or you get really, really tight. We got so tight that when we came back to London a few months later we were literally a different band.

When we first got to Butlin's we found we were expected to play in a camp pub called the Pig & Whistle. It was a huge old place, with a big stage, but it was still a pub full of tables and chairs. Not our scene at all. We had noticed they also had this venue at the camp called the Rock'n'Roll Ballroom, and so we kicked up a fuss until they put us in there instead. It wasn't until we'd been there for a few weeks and the season was in full swing that the awful truth dawned – hardly anybody bothered with the so-called Rock'n'Roll Ballroom. They were all down the pub! It was even worse in the afternoons, when at best you might get a few curiosity-seekers in, but we'd play most of our evening sets to about a dozen people. It wasn't until the last twenty minutes, when the pub had closed, that the place would suddenly fill up with 'happy campers', all wildly drunk and ready to rock.

Even then we had a job on our hands trying to please them. We were still terribly naïve when we arrived at the camp, and at that point we had this thing in our heads about not playing anything too contemporary. We thought it made us more hip to do older covers by the Everly Brothers, Bill Haley, Chuck Berry, all that sort of stuff. Which was fine for what it was, but not really what a holiday camp crowd expects; they just want a jukebox of the hits of the day. Consequently, most nights we went down like a lead balloon. The only part of the show that always went down well was when Roy stepped up to do his one and only song in the set, 'I Can't Help Falling in Love with You'. He used to sing it in this cod-Elvis voice and afterwards the applause would be deafening! We'd think, right, we're off . . . But no, the very next number, whatever it was, and we tried everything, it would go dead again.

That was where we learned that playing the songs *we* liked best didn't always guarantee success with a live audience. Playing before a live audience, whatever the size or the venue, and we must have played them all – twice – it's a very different chemistry to making records. On an album, you can kickback and do your own thing if you want to. Live, you have to keep your antennae open to whatever moves and excites the crowd at that moment. There's no room for any bullshit and you can lose them in one song if you're not careful. The set has to be balanced just right. But we were still learning that back then, and in that respect playing at Butlin's proved invaluable. Not just in how we performed but in how we saw other acts perform, too. There was another band on with us called the Olympic Five and they used to do this one number called 'The Hucklebuck' and the pissed punters would go absolutely mad for it. When things were going badly for us at first, I used to stand there at the side of the stage watching the Olympic Five doing this bonkers 'Hucklebuck' thing, thinking, hmmm . . .

By the end of the season we had learned a few tricks, and I definitely think now that if we hadn't been through that – similar, say, to when the Beatles were performing multiple sets a night at the Star Club in Hamburg – we wouldn't have been half the band we were about to become. We not only came back tighter as a band, we also came back more knowing. We really knew how to work an audience now and we felt ready for anything.

We didn't know we hadn't even got started yet . . .

ONE

For someone who would later develop a taste for fast cars, flashy speedboats and even flashier-looking women, the closest I ever got to anything like that as a child was a toy wind-up train that I used to love. In fact, my earliest memory is of sitting in the street playing with this little tinplate train, winding the key in its side and watching it go round and round on its little circular track. In my memory, if I look up from the train, I can still see the bomb-damaged houses across the street. This was only a few years after the Second World War and you could look right through the holes into their living-rooms and see their wallpaper.

We lived in Colliers Wood, in south-west London, in a road called Cottage Grove, which I've since tried to go back to but can no longer find. Which is a great pity, as I love going back and looking at my past. It's practically a hobby of mine. For example, I frequently go back to the place the family lived in when I was ten years old because it still looks exactly the same now as it did then. I sit there in my car and ask myself whether I could ever have believed as a kid that I would one day be doing this: playing guitar and singing in a hugely successful rock band?

Unfortunately, however, the streets I lived in until I was four are all long gone. It's just flats and new estates now. Had Cottage Grove still been there, though, you would have found me on many occasions over the past few years just sitting there savouring the memories. I still look out for Colliers Wood tube station whenever I drive past, even now. There's a church there, and when I was three we used to climb over the church steps to sit on top of a telephone-box that stood next to it. In those days nobody told you off. They knew you meant no harm; that it was just great fun to be a little kid perched on top of this phone-box watching the world go by. I still think of that whenever I drive by there now. The phone-box is still there, only now it's a modern BT box, but the church is the same and every time I see it, it takes me back fifty-odd years . . .

My family has always given its children princely names – a tradition I have continued with my own two boys, Richard and Harry – and so when I was born on 12 October 1948 I was named Richard John Parfitt. I don't know if it was a conscious decision they made or just the ways things turned out, but my parents didn't have any more children and so they tended to spoil me, which is something I still enjoy – a bit of spoiling.

My mum's name was Lillian, or just plain Lil to her friends. She and her four sisters and three brothers had been born in Stepney, in the East End of London, where her family had lived for generations. They were real-life Eastenders; tough and resourceful but much more cheerful than the depressing bunch depicted on the TV show of the same name.

My dad's name was Richard, known to his mates as Dick, and he was originally from Newmarket, in the heart of what they now call York Region. He came from an even larger family than my mum's: one of twelve brothers and two sisters! Newmarket was, and remains, a horse-racing town, but apart from the odd job as stable boy, the only involvement my dad's family had with the gee-gees was when they backed them.

I didn't know it then, but I have since had it looked up and it turns out that the origins of the name Parfitt actually go back to some French noblemen from the eleventh century. Apparently Parfitt derived from Parfait, which was the French for 'the Perfect One'. There is even a family coat-of-arms that I now have at home with the words *En. Tout. Parfait.* on the crest, which roughly translated means: perfect in everything. I look at that sometimes and think back on my life and ... well, you've got to laugh! That sort of historical information does fascinate me though, so I kept digging and discovered that the name Robert Parffette was first recorded in England, in Lincolnshire, in 1273. According to the Yorkshire poll tax, by 1379 there was already a Richard Parfite living there. The earliest reference to the name in English literature, however, is in Chaucer, who wrote back in the fourteenth century of 'a veray parfit gentil knight'. That's me, all right ...

Cottage Grove was a cul-de-sac. We lived on one side and I remember my mum telling me not to go round to the other side to play with what she called 'those snotty-nosed kids'. She didn't mean they were snobs but that they were, literally, snot-running-down-their-noses kids, and she didn't want me playing with kids like that. I was her only child and I think she wanted what she thought of as 'better things' for me. Not that that stopped me going over there and playing with them anyway. I couldn't see what all the fuss was about, they were just kids like me, and without any brothers and sisters to play with it was either that or play on my own and no kid wants that.

My maternal grandmother, whose name was Maude but who was known to everybody just as Nan, owned a string of cafés – the working man's greasy spoon variety – all called Miller's, which was my mum's maiden name. There was one in Colliers Wood, one in Clapham, and two in Woking. Both my mum and my dad worked in the family business, running the café in Colliers Wood. A fact I never let anybody forget. Whenever anything to do with restaurants or catering comes up even now I always say, 'Don't worry, leave it to me, I was brought up in cafés.' As a result, I suppose we were doing all right money-wise when I was first born. We all lived in the same house as Nan, and from what I can remember it was quite a substantial property.

Then came what seemed to me, as a child, a massive upheaval when we suddenly upped sticks and moved out to Harlow. Dad must have decided he wanted to get out of the family business, because he gave that up and became an insurance salesman instead. Maybe he wanted to prove he could make it on his own, or maybe there was some sort of temporary falling out, I don't know, they never told me, but the next thing I knew we were living in Harlow, away from my mum's family and much closer to my dad's sister Ivy and all of his brothers.

It was in Harlow that I had my first major accident. I say 'first', because from this time on I was known throughout my childhood as accident-prone. I can still see my mother standing there frowning and saying, 'If anything's going to happen, it's going to happen to Rick.' The first time was when I was about five years old and I crushed my finger in the garden gate. I was watching my mate swing on it but I had my hand in the hinge and when he swung the gate to it sliced most of my finger off! I remember running round the corner crying, 'Mummy, mummy, mummy!' As chance would have it, she was just on her way out the door to go shopping. Next thing was she saw me running towards her covered in blood with half my finger hanging off!

We didn't have a telephone, not many people did in those days, so she couldn't just phone an ambulance. She had to literally run me up the high street to the chemist's shop, in what they called Harlow's Old Town. She was in a state of hysterics, but the old chemist just clamped the finger back on, smothered it in iodine, bandaged it up and sent me to the hospital to get it stitched properly. God, what an ordeal that was! I can still remember the noxious smell of the iodine, and whenever I walk into a hospital now it still takes me straight back to that day.

Not long after that I hurt my arm and ended up with it in a sling. But it affected my balance and I tripped and fell on to a brick and split my head open. A bit of brick also got lodged into my face, which I had to have snipped out. I have since paid to have it fixed but it left a bloody great dent in my face for years. Another time I fell off some scaffolding I shouldn't have been playing on but was, and took a chip out of my cheekbone, which I've also now had fixed. Then there was the time I got knocked down by a car outside Saturday morning pictures and ended up with six stitches in my chin, which I've also still got the scars of. To make matters worse, a few days later I collided in the playground with a kid at school and split my chin open again. Yet another time I ran into an iron spike hanging from the bottom of a bridge and needed fourteen stitches across the top of my skull. We didn't have a car so my dad had to literally carry me to the hospital in his arms. I got so used to wearing bandages as a child I used to put on a pair of sunglasses and pretend I was the Invisible Man.

We were only in Harlow for a year or so, however, before we moved again – this time to Woking, in Surrey. I don't know how happy my parents were in their new life, but when Nan sold the café in Colliers Wood and opened a new one in Woking, and offered my parents the chance to come back and run it, they gladly accepted.

Woking has changed a great deal now, of course. It's on the main Portsmouth-to-London train line and it's gone from being the quiet, leafy little suburb of my childhood into a booming satellite town for London businessmen. A lot of the shops and cinemas from my childhood are gone too; it's all new developments. And it's a great shame, because I remember Woking when we first lived there as a beautifully unruffled little town.

I went to Goldsworth School in Goldsworth Road. The new café was also in Goldsworth Road and I remember feeling very content there. It was also at Goldsworth that I met my first girlfriend, Josephine Tickner. I couldn't have been more than six but I fell madly in love with her. We would walk home from school together sometimes. She never had any books to carry, but if she had I would gladly have done so for her. I remember kissing her once and hoping she didn't have a baby . . .

Mainly, though, I hung out with the boys. On the way home from school each day we used to pass an old canal, with a bridge going over it. My mum used to say, 'Don't go near the canal,' but of course we would be straight down there every afternoon to play on it. Bridges and canals are very exciting to young boys. They spell adventure. And then there was the canal itself. The water was covered with green algae and was dead still. The whole thing was such a temptation. Until, of course, one afternoon accident-prone Rick fell in!

I didn't actually hurt myself, but the thought of going home and admitting I'd been down to the canal – and actually fallen in it! – was far worse than any physical pain I had ever endured. I thought I was a dead boy. But to my surprise my mum was quite kind about it. I think she was so relieved I hadn't drowned she forgave me at once and we just forgot about it. I was probably back down there again the very next day . . .

I wasn't a naughty child, though. All children test the limits of their parents' endurance, to an extent, but I wasn't unruly or anything like that. I was just cheeky. Because I used to socialize with people a lot in the café, I always found it easy to get on with everybody. For pocket-money I used to carry the plates of food to and from the tables sometimes, then go around afterwards with a toy post-box asking if anyone could spare a penny or a halfpenny. A lot of them would succumb to this sweet-looking blond boy who'd brought them their tea and put a penny in the box. By the end of the week I'd have amassed three or four shillings, an absolute fortune to me as a child.

The café is now a motorbike shop. It wasn't so long ago that I was outside there on a Sunday afternoon, sitting in the car just taking it all in and remembering. Peering through the window, I could see the door leading to the back of the shop, where we used to go through into what was then our scullery. Then I looked up to the window of what used to be my bedroom. It looks so tiny now.

It's not visible from the shop window, of course, but in my mind's eye I could still see the garden out the back where I used to build camps. I used to drag bits of corrugated iron and any old scraps I could find into the garden in order to build secret hideaways for myself, where I could re-enact some battle from the war that I'd just seen on TV or in some comic. I used to love it when it rained because I would sit inside my camp, nice and dry, listening to the sound of the rain beating down on the corrugated iron roof, and I would think: I'm safe. I'm in my camp, my army all around me . . .

There was a bakery at the bottom of our garden, too. They used to provide a lot of the stuff for the café and I used to love the smell of the freshly baked bread that wafted over the garden wall each morning. I used to go in there some-times and make jam cakes and just generally help out. They were such lovely days. All my memories of those days are so innocent and beautiful.

We lived in a flat above the café and my nan lived in a really nice house in nearby Maybury Road. I've been dying to go back there for a good look, too, some day, but there's a family living there now and I'm a bit wary of just knocking on the door and asking if I can come in for a mooch about. I'm sure if I explained why they wouldn't mind, but it's the explaining I can't face. I drive past the house frequently but I've never been able to pluck up the courage. The weird thing is I remember the house as *huge*, because it had five bed-rooms and Nan used to have lodgers there. Now when I go past it looks quite modest to me, though it does still have a lovely big garden with an orchard.

The most exciting thing I remember about going round to my nan's house in those days was that she was the first person I ever knew that had a remote control for the TV. This was in about 1955, so it must have been one of the first that came on the market. All it was, in fact, was a long white wire attached to the TV with a single button on it that allowed you to turn it on and off, but I thought it was just the most fantastic gadget I'd ever seen.

The next most exciting thing I remember from those days was getting my first two-wheeled bicycle. It was an Elswick Hopper that I had begged my parents to get for me one Christmas. I was almost sick with excitement as I came downstairs that morning and saw it standing there by the Christmas tree. Later on I had a racing bike, a real beauty with drop handlebars and five-speed gears. I used to let other kids have a go on it in exchange for a couple of marbles, which was our currency as kids. Marbles and conkers.

Christmas was always a great time anyway, of course. My main memories revolve around cap-guns and toy cars. Somewhat prophetically, for a while my most prized possession was this silver toy Mercedes the size of a shoebox. It was what they called a 'friction-action' car. You would drag its wheels backwards on the floor and it would rev up and shoot forward when you let it go. Absolutely fantastic! I also had a green-and-blue McLaren toy racing car that I loved, too. Is it any wonder that when I grew up I wanted to own the real things?

Ironically, however, we didn't have a real car in the family until I was a teenager. Not many people we knew did. In the street where we lived, in fact, there were virtually no cars parked at all. Then one day, completely out of the blue, my dad came home and announced that he had bought a car! I scampered out to see it and it was this little black Standard 8 with the Union Jack on the front of the bonnet. A nice, shiny thing, I can still remember the number plate – DHO 455. I've been trying to find that plate for years, in fact, but it either isn't out there any more or someone is hiding it from me. Which is a shame, because the car was made in 1954, I believe, and the memories it would bring back for me would be precious.

It turned out my dad had been taking driving lessons from a mate of his who owned an Anglia. He'd passed his test first time, but the first we knew about it was when he actually came home one day with this car. Later he traded it in for a big Rover 12, but when he sold that he soon went back to the Standard 8. They were magic little cars for their day. I don't know where he got that first one or how much he paid for it, but it was lovely. It had the chrome headlights on top of the mudguards and I was just thrilled with it. I'll always remember the smell of the interior as well – sumptuous. I still like to sniff the interiors of cars now, I'm a real car-sniffer – there's a lot of us about. As soon as I get into a new car, the smell just hits me and it's better than perfume, I'm gone.

Anyway, Dad said 'Jump in' and he took us all for a spin round the block. I remember him saying, 'Look at that, son – thirty miles an hour!' It was a marvellous moment. From then on, after guitars, cars have been my number one passion. It's a wonder I didn't become a racing driver or a mechanic. I was always interested in the engines and how much power they had in them. In those days the most common sights on the road in Britain were small six- or eight-horsepower engines: either an Austin 6 or a Morris 8. If you had told me then that I would one day own a car with *six hundred* horsepower, I simply wouldn't have been able to believe you. It would have been like saying that one day I would own a magic flying carpet.

When my nan died we had to move out of Maybury Road

and suddenly family life was full of turmoil again. Both the house and the café in Woking were sold and we were virtually thrown out on the street. Why that happened I don't know. Just before my own mum died a few years ago, I asked her where the money went, and she just shook her head sadly and said that Nan had a lot of debts that had to be settled when she died. She didn't say any more but I knew what she meant. Nan loved to back the horses. She'd sit in a room with the curtains drawn watching the gee-gees on TV, making bets over the phone. Anything with the name 'Tudor' in it or any other name connected with royalty, she would back it, regardless of form. Needless to say, it hardly proved to be a winning formula and when she died the rest of the family was left virtually penniless.

Dad went back to being an insurance salesman and for a while we were forced to live in digs. We moved in with another family on a council estate, crammed into their spare room upstairs. The other family had two kids of their own, so there were four adults and three kids all trying to get by together in this one house, with us pretty much confined to our one room. It didn't really bother me but it must have been a terrible wrench for my poor parents. We lived there for a while, then we moved in with another family in another council house on the other side of Woking called the Elm Bridge Estate: into another upstairs room in a house on a road called Queen Elizabeth Way. Thankfully, we were only there a few weeks before we were given our own house in the same street – at number 101.

It's now become an almost mythical place to anybody who knows me well, because once you get me on the subject of 101 Queen Elizabeth Way you can never get me off it again. To me it was, and will always remain, a magical place.

The first time I went there I found these bamboo sticks that had been left there on the floor for some reason, and I remember picking them up and just looking around and thinking how unusual and fantastic this place was. We had a front lounge, an entrance hall, a kitchen, a large dining room, three bedrooms, a bathroom, a separate toilet, an airing cupboard, plus a fantastic garden out the back, with a shed with a flat roof where a boy could spend hours defending the fort from Red Indians – and it was all ours!

I could tell how happy it made my parents, too, and so to me it just became the most amazing place ever. Indeed, I would go as far as to say that pretty much everything that has happened to me since – all the stuff that has made me who I am today – can probably be traced back in some way to those wonderful days at 101 Queen Elizabeth Way.

I even wrote a poem about it once at school. It went as follows:

> *My name is Richard Parfitt*
> *I'm four-foot seven high*
> *I play the guitar, sing la-la*
> *And say: What a good boy am I.*
>
> *I live at Queen Elizabeth Way*
> *The number is one-oh-one*
> *I'm not really a naughty boy*
> *Just cheeky to my mum . . .*

I won the school poetry competition with that! It was the first prize of any kind I had ever won, and though it was just a small thing I got as much, if not more, pleasure out of that than I did being awarded any of our gold records later on in Quo. Mainly because it was about 101 Queen Elizabeth Way. The place just cast a spell on me.

To top it off, the house had a large, overgrown wood at the back of the garden with a swamp in it. Beyond the swamp was a river with a hump jutting out of it like the back of a partly submerged whale, which we called Moby Dick. On the other side of the house we were surrounded by playing fields with football and cricket pitches marked out on them. I could see the cricket field from my back garden. It belonged to the local club, the rather wonderfully named Oddfellows Cricket Club – which is still going strong today.

Once again we were in a cul-de-sac, with us on the corner of it. I still go back there sometimes. I just sit in the car and look at the old place and it's amazing the things, the people, the adventures that come back to me. If it's quiet enough and I close my eyes I can actually see it and hear it. Because I was so, so happy there. My main interests were sports and mucking about with my mates. I watched a bit of telly as a kid – I used to like typical boy stuff like *Have Gun Will Travel* – but there were only a few programmes broadcast in the fifties for children, so most of my playing time was spent outdoors with my mates. My best friends were Freddy Wellbeloved, Terry George, Edward Brogan, Philip Stead and Nicky Gunter, to name but a few. We all lived in the cul-de-sac, went to the same school, Highlands County Secondary, and played together each day. We weren't bad kids, by any means. But it makes me shudder when I think back now on some of the scrapes we used to get into. One game we made up involved getting a stick and nailing another smaller stick to the bottom of it with a rusty nail so that it looked sort of like a hockey stick. Then you would put your tin-wheeled roller-skates on and go chasing after this little wooden ball with it in your hand. There was a drain with a lamp-post next to it down one end of the street, which we used as a goal, and handily placed at the other end was another drain with a lamp-post which was the other goal. Have Ball Will Travel, we called it, and how none of us ever ended up with concussion after being bashed around the head with these sticks is a mystery.

And of course we used to play in the woods. We were always told not to go near the swamp because you could literally get sucked in and drown. But I was shown the way across it by the other kids: two steps forward, one to the left, that sort of thing. How they originally figured that out, I don't know, but it was like the secret of our gang – the path across the swamp. There was a bunch of kids from another part of the estate called Ryden's Way and they were our great enemies. If ever they dared come into our woods, we'd just hop across the swamp, knowing they would never try to follow us or that if they did they would come a cropper. We would make our own bows and arrows from the branches and twigs of the trees, then run around the woods firing them at each other. Or we'd be hanging from sixty-foot trees, firing marbles from catapults. It's amazing none of us ever lost an eye or broke a limb.

When we were bored with trying to maim each other, we used to make our own rafts by tying bits of wood to these old oil drums we'd found and push them out on to the river. Lethal contraptions they were, but great fun at the time. The river current would just carry you along, but if you so much as touched the side of one of the riverbanks the oil drums would roll to the surface and send you and your raft into the water.

Every Guy Fawkes night we would have a big communal bonfire. Because we had our own wood we always had plenty of stuff to burn. We had never heard of the words 'conservation' or 'environment'. We just used to go in there and chop down a few trees, then drag them over to the playing field and build a big bonfire. And then of course we'd set off all the fireworks. Jumping Jacks and bangers were my favourite because they made the most noise. Anything that made a noise and caused a commotion was good in my book. When the mums and dads weren't looking we used to light fireworks and throw them at each other like grenades.

The hole in the ground where we had the bonfire was actually an old bomb crater. The rest of the year we used to drag this ratty old carpet we'd found over it, stick a washing pole up the middle and have what we used to call the Carpet Club, all the kids under the big carpet together like a tent. To be in the gang you had to pass an initiation test. This involved going up the sewage tunnel and having to traverse the Four Irons, which is what we called the remains of the old bridge that had once run across the river but had now disintegrated into four old beams that led from one side to the other like rusty rails. To be in the gang you had to walk across the water using only these four iron beams, no more than an-inch-and-a-half wide. It was like walking an iron tightrope. What they didn't tell you was that once you got across you were in a field occupied by one of the fiercest bulls in the county! The only way out was a gateway on the other side of the field and it was like something out of a *Tom and Jerry* cartoon: you had to get across to the gate with the bull chasing you. All the other kids would have run round to wait for you at the gate, hoping to see the bull get you. If you got through all that you were in.

It was all such fun we never wanted to come home at night. Especially when we were playing football, which we would stay out there doing until it got so dark we couldn't see the ball any more. It got so bad we actually tried to get a few of the parents who had cars to bring them over to the field and switch their headlights on so that we could keep playing, though we never quite managed to persuade them. It was a proper, old-fashioned brown leather ball with laces that we used to play with. Horrendous to head, and murder to try to kick any distance when it was muddy and wet, but brilliant all the same. We used to play football summer and winter, day and night. Until the shout used to go out from my mum on the doorstep. "Ricky! It's time for tea!" When, very regretfully, I would slope off home. Until music came along it was all I wanted to do. Get outside and play . . .

My mum knew everything that went on, I think. But my dad was blissfully unaware of most of it, which was just as well. Instead, he spent most of his spare time in the local Working Men's Club listening to everyone else's problems, then saying: 'You don't wanna worry about that. Come to the bar and have a drink.' That was his favourite saying: 'You don't wanna worry about that.' He would come home three sheets to the wind most nights, but you didn't want to worry about that . . .

101 Queen Elizabeth Way was also where I became a teenager; a young man. It was where I first got into winkle-picker shoes and mohair sweaters; and where I gradually left sports behind and started to get more interested in music. And cars. And girls.

I first became aware of music at Saturday morning pictures, which I used to go to every week at the old ABC theatre in Woking. There was that song that they made all the kids sing at the start of the show: *'We are the boys and girls together / Minors of the ABC . . .'* We were all ABC Minors, and got to wear a special triangular badge to prove it. I started going there every Saturday morning when I was about nine or ten. I loved it, it was so riotous, all these kids going mad in the dark together. It was like going to a gig. There would be Superman movies, Flash Gordon, the Lone Ranger ... The funniest thing was the guy who used to walk on at the start to introduce the show. He used to wear a dress suit and bow-tie and come out bellowing. 'Good morning, Minors!'

Flash Gordon was so cool. The cliffhanger endings used to do my head in, though. At the end of every episode Flash would be falling out of his rocket ship into the mouth of some gigantic space dragon, and you'd have to come back the next week to see whether he survived certain doom or not. I used to fall for it every time and think, well, this time he *must* be done for! But he never was. Good old Flash.

My favourite, though, was Superman. I was a big fan! I used to get the comics, too. There was one classic episode where you saw people listening to news reports on the radio saying that the moon had moved its orbit. Then you saw Superman doing a handstand in some field and realized the moon hadn't moved at all, it was just Superman shifting the Earth off its axis! Well, that cemented Superman for me. If he could lift the world then he could do anything! And I just loved all that business about green Kryptonite sapping his strength. Even then he was still able to summon what little power he had left to stop a speeding train just by spinning in a circle and creating a whirlwind. Fantastic stuff! I used to love those ads you got in the back of the comics, too. The ones for X-Ray specs. Having a pair of those, I thought, would be the greatest thing in the world. But the prices were always in dollars and the addresses to write to were in America, so I never got around to it. Shame. I'd still like a pair now, actually.

My other favourite comic was *The Tiger*, which had Roy of the Rovers on the cover every week. Roy played for

Melchester Rovers and his best mate was Blackie Grey, the goalkeeper. They were the ones that led the team; the partnership that worked on and off the pitch. You could get all wanky and say that, in retrospect, it's easy to see why that idea held such appeal for me. But I won't, because it's simply not true. The fact that Francis Rossi and I have ended up being the partnership that fronts Status Quo has nothing to do with Roy of the Rovers. For a start, Roy never lost an important match. Quo have . . .

But I'm jumping the gun. I was ten when I first became interested in music. Out of the blue, I suddenly wanted a guitar. My parents loved Lonnie Donegan, and his were some of the first records I remember listening to where I became aware of what the guitar was actually contributing to the sound. Kenny Ball & his Jazzmen were also popular in the house, and for a while I took a few piano and saxophone lessons. But it was Lonnie Donegan who really got me thinking about the guitar. I'd also seen Bert Weedon, who was on television a lot in those days, and he made it look so easy. He had this beautiful shiny, blonde Hofner guitar with ornate machine-heads and mother-of-pearl facing – oh, it was beautiful!

Just as I had done with my first bike, I pestered my parents until they bought me a guitar for Christmas. It was an acoustic Framus, bought from Maxwell's Music Shop in Woking High Street, and to this day I still have no idea how much my parents paid for it, though I like to think I did my best to repay them for it later. Just like the first time I stepped into my dad's first car, I will never forget the smell the first time I opened up the guitar case. It was brand new and the odour of the varnish was so intoxicating it almost made me swoon. That's how guitars have smelt to me ever since –

utterly intoxicating. It not only looked fantastic but it smelt fantastic, which embedded it even more into me that this was the thing for me.

The strap that came with it was a gold-coloured cord about as thick as my little finger and it used to cut into your shoulder as you played, even though the guitar had very little weight to it. I didn't care. I just loved that guitar. It had this sash that came with it, too, where you had the pom-pom hanging down from the machine-heads. I thought that was just so stylish! Ten years old and up-and-running with my own flash-looking guitar. I was made up. And then I tried to play it . . .

I'll never forget the dismay I felt, the guitar hanging dolefully around my neck for the first time, and realizing suddenly that I couldn't actually play anything on it yet. Until that moment it had never occurred to me that I didn't actually know how to play a guitar. I tried it out for size anyway, though, and it was like a miracle. I didn't even know how to tune the damn thing yet but I was bashing out songs on it practically straight away! The first song I actually managed to pick my way through was 'Mary's Boy Child' by Harry Belafonte. It was Christmas and the song was on the radio all the time, so I felt like I already knew it backwards and, bizarrely, it turned out I did. The piano lessons obviously helped; I knew the rudimentary stuff, scales, notes and so forth. But I'd never actually laid my hands on a guitar before that day. I thought: this is *easy* . . .

To begin with, playing the guitar was just a hobby. Something I did on rainy days when I wasn't out wreaking havoc with my mates. By the time I was twelve, however, I had worked up a small repertoire of songs on the guitar like 'Baby Face' and 'Living Doll'. I still didn't know how to tune it properly, and I remember having tremendous difficulty getting my hands to bend into the right shapes to do barre chords. But for some reason I could always pick up melodies and learn tunes. I had the ear for it long before I had the hands – a talent I think inherited from my mum, who played the piano.

Nevertheless, if it hadn't been for my dad, I probably wouldn't have taken it any further than that; a party-piece for the family to enjoy. It was my mum who brought me up properly as a child – she was a beautiful woman, both in her head and her heart – but it was my dad who was the driving force behind me becoming a professional musician, no question. He desperately wanted me to try to turn whatever talent I had into something more than just a wonderful hobby. He really wanted me to go for it.

My second guitar was another Framus, but a red-and-black one this time, highly polished, beautiful, in a soft case. Every Saturday night me and my parents would go to the Working Men's Club together, and my dad would always encourage me to bring the guitar with me. I never used to want to but he'd say, 'Just put it in the boot in case you change your mind.' Invariably, of course, once we were there and Dad had had a few drinks, he would tell me to go and get the guitar. Before I knew it I would be up there singing and playing 'Baby Face'. Those were my first real public performances.

When the club held a talent contest one night my dad entered me into the draw. I remember being very nervous and apprehensive before I went on, but once I was actually up there, bashing out 'Baby Face' as I had so many times before for my dad and his mates, all the nerves left me and I really enjoyed myself. Best of all, I won! The prize was a cheque for five pounds. I was only twelve but I felt like a millionaire. I couldn't believe I had actually won this money from singing and playing the guitar! Not that I actually saw any of it personally. My dad took the cheque and it was drinks all round all night. Not that I minded: the money was great but it was the winning that really gave me a buzz.

It was around this time that my family entered me for a talent contest at Butlin's holiday camp in Cliftonville. My nan used to love going to Butlin's and we stayed in the place she had always stayed in, the Queen's Hotel. It's now gone, sadly, but my first impression of the place was that it was like a fantasy island; the sort of place that had stuffed parrots hanging over the pool. When I won my heat in the contest it just completed the picture I had in my mind of this utterly dreamlike place where wishes could come true. The prize for winning was a free holiday for two people later in the year when they had the Grand Final. I did this for two years running and two years running I won my heat and we got a free holiday.

When it came to the Grand Finals, I did almost as well, coming second both years. I was pipped to first prize both times by this bloke who used to sit and sing at the piano, a good-looking lad who always used to do the same song. I can still hear him now ... *'If you could buy all the stars in the sky then you could buy Killarney...'* He was pretty impressive, I must admit, in his cummerbund and his bow-tie, and I like to think I accepted defeat gracefully.

By then it didn't matter whether I won or not. I already knew deep down that playing the guitar and singing was what I really wanted to do. As a result, academically I became a bit of a layabout at school, because I just didn't care any more. I knew it would have very little bearing on what I did once I left there, and my parents didn't put me under any pressure to believe otherwise. Somehow we were all just convinced that I was going to be in show business. I don't know that we felt I would ever actually be *famous*, just that I was going to be in show business in some capacity.

After my success at the various talent shows, I used to do occasional spots at the Nuffield Centre in London, a Variety Club for the Forces, where I met some very strange characters indeed, theatrical types from a world I didn't belong to yet but couldn't wait to join. As a result, I was getting more professional now and had put together a new look for myself: a silk cravat, which was all the rage at the time, some black-and-white chequered trousers, and lacquered hair. I used to spend all day looking in the mirror, trying to perfect it.

One person who helped me out a lot back then was a local comedian named Johnny, who my dad had become friendly with. Johnny was well known on the Working Men's Club circuit, and through him my dad was able to get me some spots at some of the other clubs that Johnny performed at outside Woking. Johnny would be booked and he would allow me to turn up and do a quick opening spot for him.

I later found out that there was an ulterior motive behind his generosity, when we were travelling home in my dad's car one night. Johnny was in the front passenger seat while my dad drove, and I was in the back. Suddenly a hand came creeping round the back of the passenger seat and started to grope my knee. I didn't know what to do so I just let him get on with it. I must have only been about twelve and I didn't know about gay or straight yet, I just thought it was really strange.

It never went any further than that, thank goodness, and it's still fair to say that if it hadn't been for Johnny I probably wouldn't have been sitting here now recalling my life in this book. Johnny was a member of something called the MEA – the Metropolitan Entertainers Association. It was through his patronage that my dad and I were also able to become members – and it was through that that I ended up getting my first big break.

The offices were in Goodge Street, in the West End – in a smoky room above a pub called the Feathers, just by Goodge Street tube station. Over time, my dad actually ended up as Treasurer there. We used to meet upstairs at the Feathers every Thursday night, where we would all gather together and discuss what was going on in show business. The membership was a mixture of established cabaret acts, singers and comedians, and some not so established wanna-be artists like myself, trying to get a career started. There would also be various talent agents and club bookers there too, so it was a good excuse to mingle with the biz. You would get a chance to do what was called a 'shop window', where you aired your new material, and the various agents and bookers that were there could get a look at you and maybe throw a bit of work your way, or perhaps some good advice. It was a huge room and you would stand in the middle and do your stuff while everybody looked on, drinking and smoking.

I'd been going for a couple of years, I suppose, when one night, after I'd done a shop window, this guy came up to my dad and asked him when I turned fifteen. I was fourteen at the time and so my dad said, 'Soon. Why?' The guy's name was Gordon Mitchell, and he introduced himself as – inverted commas – 'the mayor of Hayling Island!' What he meant was that he was the guy who ran Sunshine Holiday Camp, a sort of scaled-down Hayling Island version of Butlin's. He had a

broad northern accent and a typically straightforward northern manner and so he came straight to the point. He said:
'I want to know how old he is because I want this lad for a
summer season at my holiday camp. When does he leave
school?'

The earliest age you could leave school and begin working full-time back then was fifteen. As luck would have it I
was fast approaching my fifteenth birthday, so Gordon said,
'Good, because I'd like to hire him!' And that was it – my first
proper job in show business, working at Sunshine Holiday
Camp on Hayling Island! Dad thrashed out the details with
him. Every evening I was to sit on a stool in the bar and sing
and play the guitar, and during the day I was to help out with
all the other entertainments and activities at the camp. If it
had been Butlin's you would have called me a Redcoat. But
this was Sunshine and we wore yellow coats and were called
Canaries.

It was my first job and I couldn't have been more thrilled.
It was fingers up to school! Once I knew I had a definite job
to go to, I stopped turning up for half the lessons and those
last few months at school dragged by excruciatingly slowly.
I would make excuses like I had to go and have my finger
looked at – the one I'd crushed in the garden gate back in
Harlow. It gave me the perfect excuse. I'd pinch some stuff
from the medicine cabinet at home and bandage up my finger
before I got to school. Anything to get out of Maths . . .

All I could think about was what I foresaw, basically, as
one long paid holiday. My wages were £5 a week. At first
Gordon offered me £10 a week, but my dad actually objected.
'We don't want to spoil the boy,' he said. So we made it a
fiver. (Smooth move, Dad!) After my insurance stamp, I used

to walk away each week with four pounds, sixteen shillings and four pence – about £4.80 in today's money – plus free bed and board.

Because of my previous holidays at Butlin's I had some experience of holiday camps, but I soon found out that Sunshine was on nothing like the grand scale of Butlin's. It was just an old-fashioned little holiday camp straight out of an old black-and-white *Carry On* film. I'd never been to Hayling Island before and didn't know anybody there, but I was too excited to worry about that. It didn't cross my mind that I was leaving behind all the comforts of home until I was actually down there living a completely different, much more grown-up sort of life.

I was given my official Canary uniform; yellow jacket, yellow jumper, white trousers and white shoes. I really felt the part. My digs were in a flat above the bar where I was scheduled to play, in one of several small single-room cells they called Treetops, where all the Canaries slept at night. They would wake us up at seven o'clock every morning – all the campers and Canaries – by playing the same corny song, 'Island in the Sun' by Harry Belafonte. It would be the first thing you heard every day, piped throughout the camp, and I grew to hate it. The Canaries all had to be up and dressed and looking smart, waiting at the door of the breakfast hall each morning to greet the campers. Then you had to sit down at the tables with them and be nice and chatty throughout breakfast. That could be hell sometimes, trying to be charming first thing in the morning, especially if it had been a late one the night before, which it invariably had.

Generally, though, I really enjoyed the job. I helped out with the sports and all the children's activities. I used to dress up as a pirate. The kids would be sitting down being told a story and I would suddenly jump out dressed as Captain Thunder! I had all the gear – tricorn hat, eye-patch, blacked-out tooth, the whole bit. They would end up chasing me over the sand-dunes. Eventually they had to catch me and the little bastards – some of whom weren't much younger than me – used to smack the shit out of me with their plastic cutlasses. Then I would be made to walk the plank, which meant being shoved off one of the diving-boards at the swimming-pool. And that's how the game would end, thank God.

I did enjoy it, though. I was so good with the kids they made me Children's Uncle, which is like chief children's entertainer. It was bizarre. There were kids there virtually the same age as me calling me Uncle Ricky, which took a bit of getting used to. But it was a wonderful, all-round grounding for a career in show business: from singing and playing to getting whacked over the head by the kids. I loved every minute of it. My sense of adventure was still strong and so there wasn't anything I didn't want to do. Being a holiday camp there was always a tremendous sense of camaraderie, too. Just walking round talking to the campers, being cheerful and cracking a joke, even that was good practice for what came later.

Saturday night would be the big show in the main ball-room. You'd have 300 people in there all hell-bent on having a good time. We would stage a big Variety show; all the acts performing at the camp that week would do a turn. I used to wear a blue lamé jacket for the show. That was my special Saturday night jacket because it used to sparkle under the spotlights. I had special black trousers, too, with a crimson stripe down the side, a crisp white shirt and a black bow tie. When I looked in the mirror in the dressing-room before I went on I felt immensely proud because I saw an entertainer looking back at me, which is exactly what I wanted to be right then. With the aid of a handful of Brylcreem I had a big blond quiff too. I thought I looked just great, especially with the guitar on. I'd gotten a new guitar to go away with – a blonde Hofner, like Bert Weedon's, with the mother-of-pearl trimmings and everything. It looked the business! I used to sing two songs, 'Baby Face' and something by the Four Pennies called 'I Think of You', and they used to go down a storm! The feeling was amazing, like nothing I'd ever experienced before.

The Saturday night shows would always feature special guests as the headliners, too. This was great for me because I got to see some acts I'd actually heard of performing up close. The best time of all was when Flanagan & Allen did it. The whole cast got up for the encore, and one of my most cherished memories is of being on stage next to Bud Flanagan in his fur coat and hat, singing 'Strolling', which was their big number, the old hand on the shoulder routine. Fantastic!

Things were going well at the camp but I had only seen half the season through before I started to get seriously homesick. I had never lived away from home before, never left school and taken a job before, and certainly never been a singer and a children's entertainer before. Now I had done all of those things in the space of a few short weeks and I think the impact of it all was starting to get to me. Outwardly, I couldn't have been happier. Inwardly, however, I longed to go home again, even for just a while.

I got one day off a week and I began getting the train home on those days. It was a long journey back to Woking, but it was worth it just to be with my mum and dad and my mates for a few hours. I used to leave at 6 p.m. on the Sunday and be back at the camp by six o'clock the following evening. My first visit home was a memorable one. Up until then I had never smoked a cigarette, never even taken a drink. But when I went home that first time I did so with a packet of fags in my hand and a few bob in my pocket, and the first thing I did was ask my dad if he fancied going out with me for a pint. I was wearing this porkpie hat, God knows where that came from, and I'd turned into a right little upstart.

Sunshine was also where I met these beautiful twin girls with jet-black, bouffant hair named Jean and Gloria Harrison – that was the name of their act: Jean & Gloria. They were seventeen – which is quite a bit older when you're a fifteen-year-old boy – very sexy and, it seemed to me then, very knowing and experienced. They used to sing and dance and do songs like 'Jeepers Creepers, Where'd You Get Those Peepers' and 'Won't You Charleston with Me', the latter in these dinky twenties-style outfits that really showed off their legs.

Unsurprisingly, I took an immediate liking to both of them, to the point where we would hang out together all the time, just me and the two girls. I fancied both of them like mad, but it was weird, being with two birds who looked exactly alike. As I got to know them better they began to look totally different to me, but when you first saw them it was like looking at two identical dolls.

There was another guy working at the camp who we were all friendly with called David Giles. It was he who suggested that me and the girls put together a little show of our own – things like 'Island of Dreams' by the Springfields and 'Doo Wah Diddy' by Manfred Mann. David had heard us rehearsing, getting this nice three-part harmony thing going on the vocals while I strummed on guitar, and he said: 'You've got the makings of a good trio there. Why don't we put a show on in the bar and see how it goes down with the punters?'

So we cooked up this act with David called Homespun. The first time we had intended just to go on and do two or three numbers, but it went down so well we stayed on and did a few more. From there, things snowballed and we started doing a regular Homespun set a couple of nights a week. We all started enjoying that more than what we were doing on our own. Suddenly we just felt like it was meant to be – we were complete, we were an *act* – and we started talking seriously about maybe joining forces full-time. We even came up with a flash new name for ourselves – the Highlights.

The idea was contrast: they were girls; I was a boy. Onstage, the girls would stand there looking fabulous in their skimpy costumes and dark hair, while I stood there to their left with my blond hair. To complete the image I pretended to be their brother. A bit like the Springfields, who had featured a real-life brother and sister in Don and Dusty (both actually born O'Brien) and their friend and other 'brother' Tim Field. I even took a new stage name: Ricky Harrison. Apart from my mum and dad, no one had ever called me Ricky before. To everyone else, even at school, I had always been Richard. But the twins just started calling me Ricky and it was like a symbol in my mind of the new and more exciting life I was busy forging for myself as a professional entertainer. I had always hated 'Parfitt' as a stage name anyway because as an anagram you could get 'fart' out of it, and I used to worry about things like that as a teenager. Ricky Harrison of the Highlights sounded much cooler, I decided, and the name Ricky stuck with me right up until I joined Quo.

It was agreed that as soon as the summer season was over and we had all left the camp I would go and live with the twins at their family home in Plumstead, in Kent, because the twins' dad, Sid, knew a lot of people in the biz and we could use that as a base to work from. This latest newsflash put my dad's nose right out of joint, unfortunately. Up until then, he had been the one directing my career. Now someone else's dad was taking over and he felt hurt. But we sat down and discussed it – it was definitely the hardest thing I'd had to do up until then – and he eventually accepted that I was doing the right thing. For a start, it would be more sensible having the three of us all living together, rather than them having to come and pick me up all the time. They had a much bigger house than us, too, with plenty of room for me. Plus, Sid had his own business – he owned a shoe shop in Plumstead High Street – and so he could afford to spend time looking after us. He had a three-litre Rover and was soon to get a Mark 10 Jaguar, and he would drive us to gigs in these beautiful cars, which I thought was great. Another symbol of my ever-growing success as a professional entertainer.

Sid knew an agent in London called Joe Cohen, who booked acts into places all over the country. Sid decided that Joe was the man to take us forward in our new guise as the Highlights. Which he did, and we ended up touring all over Britain, appearing in places like the Opera House in Belfast, the Floral Pavilion in Brighton, all the seaside theatres, as well as several shows abroad in places like Italy and France; mainly at US military bases.

We would start with 'Whole Lotta Shakin' Going On' and follow that with two or three similar sorts of numbers. Then the twins would go off to get changed into their Charleston outfits, and I would get the chance to do a song on my own, which was 'Baby Face'. Usually it went down a treat, especially with the mums and nans. Once, however, we were booked into this naval base in Naples and I suddenly found myself up there singing 'Baby Face' to 400 stony-faced American sailors. Where do you look?

Meanwhile, I had developed a serious crush on Jean. Initially I had preferred Gloria. I don't particularly know why, because they still looked exactly the same to me at that point – I just did. Then once I got to know them I swapped over to Jean, who I ended up falling head-over-heels in love with. This presented me with a serious problem. The trouble was, my feelings for Jean were never really reciprocated. We had a couple of attempts at getting it together but they always ended in disaster, and instead I became insanely jealous of her. She and Gloria both had different boyfriends for periods of time while the act was together, but nobody really steady. They were very attractive, popular girls, and it really did get to me sometimes when Jean went out with some other bloke. I was so upset I even smashed up a couple of hotel rooms. This was long before such behaviour was viewed indulgently as 'rock'n'roll', and I was given a right bollocking by Sid.

I couldn't help myself, though. I was really in a bad way. It was the on-off nature of it that drove me mad. Sometimes Jean would ask me to go out with her to the pictures and I would be so thrilled, because I'd have gone anywhere she asked back then. Nothing could have made me more happy. Sometimes the night would end with a kiss and cuddle and sometimes it wouldn't. On the few occasions we did go to bed together, though, it just wasn't happening. It had become such a huge deal in my mind I couldn't even get a hard-on. In a strange way, we had become *too* close. It was terribly frustrating because I really wanted it to work between us but it just wouldn't. Then seeing her go off with other blokes, it really did me in.

She didn't exactly help, either. I remember her turning round to me one time and saying, 'You're fucking useless, you are!' That devastated me. It scarred me, and I ended up having quite a problem with that sort of thing for years afterwards. I would get some bird I really fancied up to my room but wouldn't be able to go through with the wicked deed. It wasn't until a few years later, in fact, when I became involved with a beautiful older lady, that I rediscovered my sexual faculties, you might say.

But we'll get to that . . .

TWO

If the Butlin's experience proved, in many ways, to be the making of the band, that summer in Minehead was to be a life-changing experience for me in other ways, too. For a start, Butlin's was where we all met Rick Parfitt for the first time – or Ricky Harrison, as he was then. He was booked in there for the season with these twin girls in a cabaret act they had together called the Highlights. The girls were the Harrison twins, and Rick was supposed to be their brother, Ricky Harrison – that's how he introduced himself to us.

He and the girls were appearing each night in a Variety show at the camp's Gaiety Theatre, where the audience was mainly mums and dads. They used to do routines around songs like 'Baby Face' and 'The Sheik of Araby'. Then the girls would go off to change into another skimpy costume and Rick would crack a joke: 'My sisters are coming back on in a moment,' he'd say. 'I'm sure you're gonna enjoy them, they've been enjoyed a lot before.' Boom, boom!

As a result, to this day I still see Rick as this much more sort of rounded, showbiz figure than me. In fact, when we first knew him everyone assumed he was gay. I certainly did. Except of course we didn't use words like 'gay' back then, it would have been 'queer' or 'poof'. As I soon discovered, Rick wasn't gay, he was just more effeminate than us; very slim and slightly built, with fluffy blond hair. Truth to tell, he came across as a bit of a luvvy, and at that point I still had this stereotype in my mind of gay men being effeminate and a bit namby-pamby. It wasn't until years later when I met Freddie Mercury that I realized gay men could be masculine and assertive too.

Whatever he was, I liked Rick from the first time we spoke, mainly because he was so laid back and not at all aggressive. He was just very easy to have around, very funny, and from then on we always got on really well together. With Alan wanting everything to be so macho all the time it made a nice change to have someone else around who wasn't like that. If I cried, which I used to do quite easily when I was a teenager if I got angry or upset, Alan would shout: 'Stop it! You're showing me up!' Whereas Rick would put his arm round my shoulders and give me a hug. He's always been big on hugs.

We met when Rick wandered into the Rock'n'Roll Ballroom one afternoon while we were rehearsing, before the season officially started. I suddenly noticed this blond kid standing on his own out there on the dance floor, grinning from ear to ear. After we'd finished playing he came up and introduced himself and quite quickly we became friends. At first Rick was probably more matey with Alan than with me. An odd match on the surface perhaps, but then Rick is so non-confrontational even Alan felt relaxed around him. But then Alan was also after one of the twins. Rick was in love with the other one. It was a right caper . . .

The other big event triggered off by that fateful summer among the Redcoats was meeting the woman who would later become my first wife. The day we arrived at the camp was actually my sixteenth birthday. As 'concessionaires' – i.e. non-residential camp staff – we had to queue up with all the other camp workers at the office, where we would be given all the info about where we would be staying and what our official duties were. It took ages, but I got chatting to these two beautiful sisters who were also in the queue: Jean and Pat Smith. They were both lovely but Jean was the loveliest. They were from South London, like me, and we seemed to hit it off right away. In fact, the first time I laid eyes on Jean I remember saying to myself: 'I'm gonna marry her one day.' And two years later I did.

The relationship got off to a rocky start, however, when I got thrown out of my digs after the landlady caught us in bed together. The digs were run by a fierce Scottish woman. For £5 a week you got a bed, your meals, and all your washing done. It was great, like a home from home, only better. You'd still be lying in bed when she came in every morning to wake you for breakfast. She'd lean over and put her hand on my bum and go, 'Eh, Rossi, it's time to get up, aye!' If you had the presence of mind to turn over on your back before she came in, she ended up getting hold of your morning stiffy instead. Either way, she didn't seem to mind. You always got a little squeeze. When she came in one morning, however, and found me trying to give a little squeeze of my own to Jean, she didn't like it at all.

Mind you, I wasn't sure at first whether Jean liked it either. I don't know why people used to want to marry virgins, it's bloody hard work! It took me three nights of trying before I was even able to get it in there. Then finally it went pop one night and I thought: whey-hey, I'm in! We were trying again the next morning when the landlady walked in. Cue: utter pandemonium. First she threw Jean out and then she told me to pack my things and leave too. I went from heaven to hell in about five seconds. Worse still, suddenly I was homeless.

With the season in full swing it was almost impossible to find new digs at such short notice and I was reduced to sleeping rough for a couple of weeks. The rest of the band seemed nonplussed, but good old Ricky took pity on me and decided to keep me company until I could find somewhere else to stay. So for a couple of weeks Rick and I just bummed around together. We slept in phone-boxes, kipped on the beach. It was grim some nights but we didn't care. We were sixteen and it was all a big adventure for us.

When I did finally get myself in somewhere, Jean suddenly got cold feet and did a runner, quitting her job and taking off with a friend of hers, another gorgeous girl named Peta, to work at some other seaside place along the coast. I hated it when Jean left like that. It was the first time I really got cut up about someone. Then, two weeks later, just as I thought I'd lost her for ever, she came back! I didn't know it then, but it was a harbinger of what was to come when we were married. As I was to discover, she was always either running off or threatening to . . .

When we first got back from Butlin's, we found ourselves at a bit of a loss to begin with. Living for months on end in Minehead, you might as well have been living on the moon. You weren't just cut off from London, you were cut off from the whole universe. Back in 1965, Radio One hadn't been born yet and all the BBC had to offer 'young people' by way of pop music on the radio was the Light Programme. There was Radio Luxemburg if you could locate its signal for long enough to hear a song all the way through (very rare), and Radio Caroline and the other pirates were only just starting up, so you either totally got them or didn't even know they existed. It was very precarious. If you wanted to know what was really going on you literally had to go out there and find out for yourself.

Which is precisely what we did when we first came back to London, only to find that everybody was now into this soul thing. It was the beginning of the heavy-duty mod-era and our old rock'n'roll set sounded positively outdated. Suddenly gigs were hard to come by, and for a time I worked part-time in an optician's shop, where I got paid £3.10s. a day. Then I got a job as a gardener on the local council for £12 a week. Basically, I mowed lawns. That didn't last either, though, and we were faced with a stark choice: if we wanted to keep getting bookings and still sound contemporary, we would have to start incorporating some of these obscure soul and R&B numbers that people were now revelling in into the set. The trouble was we didn't have a clue about that sort of music. But we plugged away at it, doing our best to pretend we knew what we were doing.

We also worked, briefly, during this period as a backing band for various people, including P.J. Proby, who we went out on tour with not long after we got back from Butlin's. After Christmas, Pat managed to get us a job backing an American female vocal group called the Dixie Cups, who'd had a couple of hits with songs like 'Chapel of Love' and 'Iko Iko'. They were great girls to work for, talented and huge fun. They also had their own guitarist, this big black guy whose name I can sadly no longer recall but who was a tremendous character. He was the first person we ever met that took their drugs seriously. We had all been really straight until then and found the whole thing quite shocking at first. We learned quickly, though, and the mysteries of amphetamines and marijuana were soon unravelled for us. That was our only real experience of drugs, however, until we toured with the Small Faces in 1969. They were always doing so much speed and pot we started following suit, particularly the dope-smoking. Faces singer Stevie Marriott was a very charismatic figure, and it was also he that got me and Rick into sharing half-a-bottle of Scotch before we went on stage. We all kind of looked up to the Small Faces and I suppose we thought, well, if it works for them . . .

Pat would get these gigs for us and we would do them purely for the money. It wasn't ideal work but it paid the bills and kept us busy while Pat worked on getting us a record deal. The important thing was to try to remain visible. We weren't picky about where we played as long as it was in front of an audience. It was a policy that had already paid off once by getting us a manager. Now it worked again, as the band saved enough money from the shows to go in and record our first demo.

It was some time around the start of 1966 and we'd cobbled together enough dough to afford an afternoon in a small professional studio somewhere up in town. We just went in, played a few numbers exactly the way we would play them live, then packed up and left again – clutching the tape. Pat had copies made and mailed them out to anyone and everyone he could think of. As chance would have it, one of them found its way on to the desk of a music publisher in Soho named Ronnie Scott – not *the* Ronnie Scott, but a songwriter then running a publishing company called Valley Music. Somehow Ronnie got interested in our material – which was outrageous luck as there was nothing original about it, as I recall, just a fairly bog-standard recording of us doing a few of the covers from our live set – and Pat ended up doing some sort of deal with him that led to us recording a couple of singles with the new in-house producer at Pye Records, a guy named John Schroeder.

We signed to Pye on 18 July 1966 and got put into the studio immediately with John Schroeder. John had been in the business a long time, working as an A&R man, producer, even songwriter (penning hits for artists like Helen Shapiro, for whom he wrote 'Walking Back to Happiness'). He also fronted his own John Schroeder Orchestra, recording such classic sixties TV theme tunes as *The Fugitive*. With his droopy moustache and languid expression he even looked a bit like a character from another sixties TV show – *Jason King*. But he was someone we immediately respected. He was the first proper record man we'd ever met, let alone worked with. And he was a nice guy, too, always full of enthusiasm for the group. He used to say to Pat: 'The Spectres are *that* much away from greatness!' And he would snap his fingers theatrically. John was very old school like that and we loved him for it.

We all knew, though, that if we were ever to be thought of as truly great by anyone other than John (and our mums and dads) we had better start coming up with some original material of our own, like the Beatles and the Stones did. Up until then you went to Tin Pan Alley-based companies like Valley Music and bought songs from them like sweets from the tuck shop. The Beatles changed all that, and bless them for it. But then the Beatles changed everything: not just how people listened to pop music but how they thought and felt about the world.

None of the other guys in the group really picked up the songwriting baton, though. So just as when it came to finding a lead singer, I thought, well, if no one else is interested, I'll give it a go. I don't even know how I learned to write a song; I have no recollection of sitting down trying to do it, other than noticing little phrases and passages in other records that I liked, and trying to imitate them. I just sat down with the guitar one day and started to write.

That said, the first single we released as the Spectres was actually a cover of the old Ben E. King record, 'I (Who Have Nothing)', which had also been a hit for Shirley Bassey a couple of years before. Released on the Piccadilly label, a subsidiary of Pye, it was chosen because it had been the track on the demo that had most impressed both Ronnie and John. In retrospect, it seems like an absurd choice for a first single by a band like ours, but we didn't know what kind of band we were yet. We were still just kids doing what we were told. We did rev it up, though. It was all done four-to-the-bar, as we musos say, which means it was practically shuffling already. Needless to say, however, it was not a hit. A fact I admit I am now deeply grateful for.

Our second single was an original song – I use the word 'original' loosely – which Alan had written with a mate of his, called 'Hurdy Gurdy Man'. Yes, the same title as the later Donovan hit but not the same song and, sadly, not even half as successful. For our third single we went back to trying another cover version: a tune that had been a big Top 5 hit in the States earlier that year for the Blues Magoos called '(We Ain't Got) Nothing Yet'. It came out in January 1967 and just like its predecessors quickly sank without a trace – and along with it any last hope of making it as the Spectres.

People just weren't getting it, and after six months of trying Pye was ready to drop us. John Schroeder, however, still believed in us. Maybe he had a point to prove: he was the one who had agreed to sign us to the label, and he was the one who had produced the records. The last thing he wanted to do now was write the whole thing off as a failure. Instead, it was decided to try to wipe the slate clean with a change of name. First we decided to call ourselves the Traffic. But Stevie Winwood and Island Records beat us to it and so at the last minute we switched to the Traffic Jam.

Unfortunately, from that moment on the whole Traffic Jam project seemed doomed. The track we released as our first, and, as it turned out, last single came out in May 1967 and was something I had written called 'Almost But Not Quite There'. Yet another flop, that single at least had the distinction of getting banned by the BBC. It was 'too suggestive', they said. At which point I felt like throwing in the towel as a songwriter. I still believed in the band but I was starting to think we were never going to have a hit record. I was also under a lot of pressure from home to stop 'messing round' and 'settle down'. Pressure it might have been easier to ignore had I not by then been married with a kid.

Bizarre as it may seem now, it was also in the summer of 1967 – the summer of love, no less, and the very height of the so-called permissive age – that I finally married Jean. We were still just teenagers but I had wanted to do this from the moment we met. Because she was seven months pregnant at the time there was no way we could get married in a Catholic church, so we went and had a quickie ceremony at a registry office in Peckham instead. It was a very low-key affair, with just my mum and dad and a few friends there. My parents hadn't wanted to have anything to do with it at first. My mum was upset I wasn't getting married in a Catholic church. But they eventually agreed to be there. To add to their embarrassment I wore a green-and-yellow-striped blazer, pink shirt and white trousers – my stage outfit, basically. Jean wore this flowery pale green smock. Her belly was already huge but her hair looked fantastic.

We never had a honeymoon. Instead we went straight to live at Jean's mum's house in Dulwich. Jean's dad had died some years before and I think her mum was probably glad of the company. We slept in the spare room and, without meaning to sound ungrateful, it was hell. I could never understand why, before we were married, Jean didn't want me to meet her mother. Then after I moved in I realized why. She would sit there in the armchair with her skirts gathered up and her gusset hanging out, smoking a fag and farting. A real character, you might say, if you wanted to be kind.

The wedding was in June and my first son, Simon, was born in August. This was six months before we'd had our first hit, and the pressure was suddenly on big-time for me to seriously reconsider what I was doing with my life. At one point Jean actually uttered the immortal words: 'It's either me or the band!' I said, 'Right, well, in that case I'm off...' She said: 'You can be so cold.' I said: 'You knew about the band before we got married, you knew that's the way it was. If you want to change your mind now then fine, but I'm sticking to what I said I was gonna do.'

I sounded like I meant it, but each month that went by without success I felt myself being drawn closer and closer to quitting the whole thing and getting a 'proper' job, for the sake of Jean and Simon. I had to think about it because I took my duties as a father very seriously for a young man. Apart from the difficulties of living under the same roof as her mother, I was very happy to be married. I loved it when people used to ask if I wasn't a bit young to be married and be having children. These days they say the opposite and accuse me of being too old to have children! They're wrong on both counts. Thankfully, I'm a fit and healthy man with the financial means to give a child the right start in life – so why say I shouldn't have more children just because I'm middle-aged?

As a father, even though I have always loved the company of children, I was pretty strict. The sixties generation had this terrible belief in letting children run free, and that anything the child did was all right. Not in my book, it isn't. The way I see it, along with providing food and love for them, it is also your duty to guide them. A child by definition doesn't know any better until it's taught to do so, which means it's going to do things occasionally that it needs reprimanding over. Otherwise how is it ever going to learn right from wrong?

Jean, who was more influenced by the age, used to boast how 'my children will be able to do anything they want'. I used to think that was a hell of a sweeping statement and we used to argue about it a lot. I saw it as a total cop-out. It was just that sixties generation thing we were all caught up in. We wanted everything to be different because we were going to change the world. And we did. We messed things up a lot. Not just with drugs but with this whole attitude of always getting what you want when you want it. When I was a little kid my dream was to have enough money one day to buy all the sweets in the shop. But as you get older you realize that not only is that attitude unrealistic, it's down-right greedy. To me, the sixties attitude was about not getting past that sweetie-wanting stage; about not wanting to grow up; about being greedy. It's impossible to go forward without any pointers: this is good, this is bad. Suddenly, though, in the sixties, we were supposed to have thrown all the pointers out the window. And I suppose, for a while there, we did ...

Meanwhile, we were due to go in and have one last go at

making a hit, and suddenly I was pinning all my hopes on it. After four straight flops, we knew that our record deal was on the line and the next single was probably make or break for us. I really did feel that if it died that would probably be it for the band – or at least my own involvement in it.

By then, Pat Barlow and John Schroeder had also made what I saw as the rather bold decision to get another singer in. What Pat actually said was: 'Look, the voices in this band are useless. We need another guy who can sing.' I said, 'Thanks very much.' But when he told us who he had in mind – a certain blond-haired, poofy-looking friend of ours by the name of Rick Parfitt – I started to cheer up again. It was almost two years since we'd first met Rick at Butlin's and by then he was very much a friend. The others seemed equally at ease with the idea – even Alan, who surprised me with how laid back he was about the whole thing. Which leads me to believe now that Pat had probably already discussed it with him before telling the rest of us, because he took it all very calmly, which wasn't like Alan at all.

From my own point of view, I did wonder, I admit now, if it meant they didn't want me singing at all any more. But thankfully it never worked out like that. Because we already had an established set worked out, on stage Rick just started to play along on rhythm guitar and join in on the harmonies, and that's what seemed to do the trick. Over time he would start to sing lead on some of the songs, but it was the sound of our voices together that really made our music blossom now. Equally important to me, however, was the fact that he was like a kindred spirit. Rick always felt more like me than the rest of them did. That's no slant on the others, it's just how it was. Rick and I really could have been brothers.

His first show with us was supporting Episode Six, a

brilliant band that later became half of Deep Purple. He wore the same get-up I had got married in the month before – the green-and-yellow blazer, pink shirt and white trousers. I loaned them to him for the gig because he didn't have any decent clobber of his own to wear on stage yet.

By now we also had a new name – The Status Quo – Pat's other big idea to try to distance us from the Traffic Jam débâcle. I wish I could say that we had the foresight to come up with the name because it fitted our music so well, because to me it fits like a glove. But it was Pat who first thought of it. The name Traffic Jam was now problematic; first because of the fuss at the BBC about the 'Almost But Not Quite There' single; and second because Winwood's Traffic had now really taken off.

If we were going to change the name again, however, we decided we wanted something that sounded much more up-to-date this time, something like Amen Corner or the Pink Floyd. Hence the early suggestion of Quo Vadis, a name Pat had seen written inside a shoe. Then he changed his mind and suggested we call ourselves the Muhammed Alis, on the basis that we could use the slogan 'They're the Greatest!' Luckily, he couldn't get permission from Ali's people so that died a death too.

Eventually we came back to The Status Quo. It was kind of a hip phrase at the time, you seemed to hear people using it a lot. It was the dawn of the hippy age and talk of challenging the status quo was everywhere. Pat figured it meant people would be talking about us even when they didn't know they were talking about us – or some such. Anyway, it fitted and so now we were The Status Quo.

We had only done a few gigs with Rick in the band before

we found ourselves back in the studio, recording the tracks that would make up our first single under our new guise. The A-side was originally going to be another song we'd recorded called 'Gentleman Jim's Sidewalk Café' which, frankly, was a pile of crap. While the B-side was originally going to be a new song I'd written called 'Pictures of Matchstick Men'. Much to my surprise, and no little relief, John Schroeder decided to flip the songs at the last minute and make 'Pictures of Matchstick Men' the A-side instead. A decision that was to completely transform our careers.

Read whatever significance you like into it, but I first came up with the idea for 'Matchstick Men' while I was sitting on the toilet at home one day. I used to write a lot of songs in the loo in those days because it was the only place I could get away from the rest of the house and its permanent soundtrack of crying babies, screaming wives and barking dogs. Bloody grim it was too, this tiny cold toilet with a cold hard seat. It was so narrow in there I had to hold the guitar vertically. But I'd sit there for hours with my feet up against the wall, just strumming and crooning and trying to think of something other than what was going on outside. Jean would be banging away at the door going: 'What are you *doing* in there?' 'Nothing!' I'd cry. 'Go away!'

This particular day, however, they all went out and so I left the loo and set myself up on the couch and finished writing this song I'd just started – which was 'Pictures of Matchstick Men'. The song itself was chiefly inspired by Jimi Hendrix's version of 'Hey Joe', which had just been a hit. I wanted a similar sort of mood but I also wanted it to be wacky and a bit more out there, so originally I sang it in this rather strained falsetto. It wasn't until we went in to record it that John Schroeder suggested I sing it in my natural voice. I thought that would be too ordinary but we tried it and – hey presto, we had our first hit!

After 'Matchstick Men' took off for us, reaching the Top 10 in February 1968, it's fair to say that life was never the same again. We were so pleased with ourselves we used to go around singing: '*Hi ho, hi ho / We are the Status Quo / With a number one we'll have some fun / Hi ho, hi ho . . .*' Hearing 'Matchstick Men' on the radio all the time was so exciting, but I'd had that buzz before with some of our earlier singles. Seeing it go into the charts was what really sealed the deal for me. Frankly, my overriding feeling was one of relief. After months of hassle from Jean and the family to do the right thing, I had secretly decided I was going to jack it all in and become an ice-cream man if the record failed. I had passed my driving test in December 1967, which meant I could now take out my own van, and though I didn't like the idea I was ready to do it. After all, we'd had four goes at making it and failed every time. What chance was there that we would suddenly get it right now? Then 'Matchstick Men' came out at the start of 1968 and, thankfully, all thoughts of becoming an ice-cream man went out the window for ever. It was a close run thing though. Too fucking close . . .

We were touring as the backing band to the singer Madeline Bell (later of Blue Mink fame) when we first heard that 'Matchstick Men' had gone in the chart. It was something Pat had booked for us long before we knew the record was going to take off, and although we could have bailed out and gone and done our own shows we decided to see it through. Madeline had just released her first album, *Bells a Poppin*, and she was such a thoroughly lovely person that we didn't want to leave her in the lurch. We enjoyed the shows too. She used to perform a few numbers from the album mixed in with a few of the soul and R&B standards we were now playing at our own shows, finishing up each night with us doing a duet on 'It Takes Two, Baby'.

At the end of the number we used to kiss – not a real snog, just a stage kiss because it went with the song. We just did it spontaneously one time and the audience liked it so much we kept it in. Then we were playing the Princess Domino Theatre in Manchester one night and as we came to the part where Madeline and I kissed some wag from the audience piped up: 'Fuckin' hell, lads! Didja see that? Fuckin' nigger kissed him!' I'd know how to respond to that kind of disgraceful comment now – I'd have the bloke ejected from the building. Back then I was so shaken I didn't know how to deal with it at all. I was used to racist taunts from my own childhood, but until then I'd just assumed that once you became a musician you left all that behind. Unfortunately, I was wrong.

Musically, the success of 'Matchstick Men' sent us on a whole new path. Because it was looked on as this very sort of psychedelic, hippy-dippy type of song, we were now looked on by the people who had bought it as a full-on psychedelic group, which of course we weren't at all. I didn't even know how to spell 'psychedelic' back then. There was certainly no LSD-taking going on in the band at the time. Apart from that one tour with the Dixie Cups, there were no drugs around at all other than beer and cigarettes, and even then it was mainly cigarettes. Apart from John Coghlan, who had always liked a beer, the rest of us rarely even drank.

But then you only have to see that famous old black-and-white clip of us playing the song on *Top of the Pops* to see why people initially thought of us that way. From the way we were dressed – done up to the nines in Carnaby Street clobber – we could have been Syd Barrett's Pink Floyd or any number of other young 'flower-power' groups that had come floating along in the past few months. The same as when punk or Britpop later came along, it was a brand new, thriving scene and all the main bands involved in it wore the same kit. Up until then we had been suited-up mods. We used to get most of our gear from places like Take Six in Oxford Street. Now everything had changed, and Pat and John were keen for us to update our whole look.

There was a hip young booker called Tim Boyle, at Arthur Howe's agency, who represented us then, and it was Tim who basically told Pat what clothes we should start wearing. Once 'Matchstick Men' started to take off and we got offered our first TV appearances, he told Pat to take us out to Carnaby Street, to a boutique, as they were known back then, called Carnaby Cavern. It was probably the most fashionable clothes store in the world at the time and all the bands went there. It was always the same guy you went to see, too. His name was Colin, and he had this shock of red hair and wore even more way-out gear than his customers. His other claim to fame was that he was one of the regular dancers in the audience at *Top of the Pops*. You'd always see Colin freaking out down the front.

As a result, to us and all his other customers, Colin was the epitome of cool. He rigged everybody out in those days. However, there could be pros and cons to this. On the plus side you got to wear some of the newest, most fashionable threads in the world. On the downside, you'd go to a photo session and put on a bright yellow shirt you'd bought from Colin at the Cavern the day before, and the photographer would go, 'No, you can't wear that, Jimi Hendrix was in here last week wearing the same thing.' You'd sigh and put another one on and he'd go, 'No, I did that with Andy Fairweather Low yesterday.'

Everybody was wearing everybody else's clothes. Just to be different, me and Rick took to having our trousers made at this place in Soho called Bona Clouts. We used to get them specially made with twenty-two-inch flares and skin-tight crutches. They were so tight they literally squeaked when we walked, strutting around with our hair all backcombed and lacquered. We looked so gay we used to stand around holding hands, just to wind people up.

If the success of 'Matchstick Men' took the group's profile to another level, financially it didn't, on its own, have half as big an impact as we might have expected. We didn't find out until it was far too late to do anything about it, but the contract we'd signed with Pye was entirely typical of the terribly one-sided deals groups like us did with record companies back in the sixties. As I recall, we were on half a per cent of the retail price of the record – which for a single at the time was about 7s 6d, or 35p in today's decimalized currency. Which meant we received approximately 0.17 pence per copy sold. Or in laymen's terms: peanuts. Less than peanuts, in fact. The crumbs off somebody else's plate of peanuts! I once worked out that if we sold a million singles we'd have been lucky to have seen a couple of grand from the profits.

We got a bigger chunk of the songwriting royalties, but even then Valley Music ended up with the lion's share in a 60–40 deal weighted their way. And that was just at home in the UK. Any further sales made abroad would yield even smaller dividends, with either Valley or Pye leasing out the track to innumerable independent labels around the world that then did their own heavily slanted deals in their own favour. Plus there were all those little phrases in the contracts that we didn't understand back then, like what the difference was between deductions made from your cut 'on receipt' and/ or 'at source'. It was all dead clever, designed to totally baffle the bands, which of course it did.

In terms of 'Matchstick Men', I was the only member of the band who really saw any money from it. Even though our share of the profits was ridiculously small, my first royalty cheque after it was a hit was for £1,000 – a serious amount of dough back then. I remember showing the cheque to Rick and him nearly keeling over! None of us had ever seen that amount of money before, and in truth it kind of put the rest of the band out of joint for a little while, with the result that Alan and Rick immediately started writing some songs of their own. That grand was weighing heavy on everybody's minds, it seemed, and if you look at the first few Quo albums you suddenly see quite a few songs credited to the others and maybe just a couple with my name on them. But then we were meant to be a democracy. Something that could lead down some blind alleys sometimes. Like the time Alan and Rick came back from seeing Pink Floyd and announced that we should be going more in that direction. I'm not saying it was a bad idea full-stop – Pink Floyd certainly ended up doing extremely well out of it – just that it wasn't really us. Thankfully, they soon got over it and we got back to the business of trying to turn Quo into something much more authentic and closer to home.

Although I used some of the money to put a deposit on a place of our own for me and Jean and Simon, I put the rest of it straight back into the band, buying new gear and settling a few bills. Over the years that investment has obviously paid off many times over. At the time, though, it was a gamble. How was I to know if we would ever have another hit record? That £1,000 could have been two big cheques in one – my first and my last. Thankfully, it wasn't, but with Jean breathing down my neck it still felt like a gamble.

Ironically, however, despite becoming a major hit in several other countries around the world – including Sweden, Germany, Holland, Brazil, Argentina, Canada, Australia and South Africa – the place where 'Matchstick Men' struck biggest was the place I earned the least amount of money from it: America. 'Matchstick Men' got to Number 8 in America in the summer of 1968 but the people who released it over there, a weird subsidiary label called Cadet Concept, managed to do some sort of deal whereby we ended up with virtually nothing. Which was a drag because 'Matchstick Men' remains the biggest hit we've ever had over there.

Never mind. There was more to think about back then than mere money. Having a hit record, we discovered, brought all sorts of other benefits, and even though I didn't quite regard myself as a 'proper' pop star yet (a proper pop star being someone who everyone recognizes when they walk down the street; something that would not happen to me for several more years) I was determined to enjoy myself while I could.

You didn't have to be a budding young pop star in London in the late sixties to take advantage of the new sexually charged climate. Even though I loved my wife and baby, I was eighteen and on the telly and so, yes, there were times when I woke up the day after the night before in some strange bird's bed. I was always sorry straight away, though. I used to lie there staring at the ceiling thinking: Oh no, what did I go and do that for? Even later on, in the seventies, when the whole groupie thing took off for us in a big way, I was never any good at that stuff. The pulling part was always great fun, making a big play of whisking some gorgeous-looking girl off to my room in front of everybody. But once I found myself alone with her, nine times out of ten I used to end up standing in the bathroom, trying to have a piss and thinking: what have I done now? I'd come out determined to get rid of her only to find her in bed already and her clothes all folded up nicely on the chair. So then I would feel obliged, just to be polite . . .

Ultimately, I suppose the main thing I noticed about our new-found success was how little it appeared to actually change anything of real importance. Until then, I had always assumed that once you'd been on *Top of the Pops* everything in the garden would be rosy: that Mum and Dad would be fine, my marriage would be fine, everything would just be better all round. But no. All that had happened was that we'd sold some records – at last. Life in every other area of our lives, however, went on much as before. I was perplexed. I had waited for this moment for years. Why didn't I feel any different now it had finally come?

Meantime, there was now a new and previously unknown pressure on my shoulders: to try to come up with a follow-up to the hit. We were booked on to a twenty-eight-date package tour headlined by Gene Pitney – big stuff – and we needed another single out to capitalize on the fact. That was when it really hit me what a tightrope we were now walking. One slip, I realized, and we could be gone. I really felt the weight on my shoulders. I remember saying something along those lines to John Coghlan one day, and he just looked at me and went, 'Tough fucking shit.' I was flabbergasted. Whether it was because he was jealous or not, I don't know, but it wasn't exactly the show of support I was looking for.

The Gene Pitney tour went incredibly well, but unfortunately the song I eventually came up with for our next single – a self-consciously moody little number called 'Black Veils of Melancholy' – was a complete and utter dud and never even got into the Top 30. I had committed the fatal error of trying to write the same song again and the punishment that followed was swift and all-encompassing.

I realize now that we had all been guilty of very much trying to create a 'follow-up' to 'Matchstick Men'. But then it's always been the thing to do. You liked it last time, you'll like it this time. It usually works too. Pop history is full of examples: from 'Please, Please Me' and 'She Loves You' by the Beatles to 'Maggie May' and 'You Wear It Well' by Rod Stewart, up to anything you'd care to name these days from Britney Spears or the Darkness. But it's a harder trick to pull off than it looks. Particularly if your first hit was a big one like 'Matchstick Men' was for us. It's like the public love it so much they don't want to know anything else, but if you give them something too close they don't want that either. They literally want exactly the same thing again – but different. And you end up damned if you do and buggered if you don't.

The first time we played 'Black Veils' to John Schroeder, he went, 'Yes! This is the one!' It wasn't until the record was almost finished that we realized we had made more than just a follow-up – we had made 'Matchstick Men Part 2'! The critics on the pop press were not slow to point it out either. There were even DJs who played the two records back-to-back, taking the piss. Justifiably so, in retrospect, but at the time it felt like rubbing salt in the wound. It was a mistake, no doubt. But an honestly made mistake from a bunch of teenagers still feeling their way.

Fortunately, I was spared the onerous task of trying to come up with another hit for our next single when Ronnie Scott suggested a tune he had written himself with former fifties pop star Marty Wilde, a jaunty little flower-power number called 'Ice in the Sun'. It was purely a commercial proposition and, sure enough, when it was released at the end of June 1968 it became our second Top 10 hit. Although it also reached the charts in a couple of other countries in Europe, it wasn't a huge hit for us around the world the way 'Matchstick Men' had been. But it put us back on the telly and radio, and we had proved that we weren't one-hit-wonders. The relief was immense.

In September that year we also put out our first album, *Picturesque Matchstickable Messages from the Status Quo*, a catchy little title (so catchy people still struggle to say it today) that may or may not have had something to do with the album's failure to really set the charts alight. It was a bittersweet experience, to say the least. On the one hand we were ecstatic to actually have an album of our own out at last. On the other hand, it represented something of a nadir for the band. The whole trippy-dippy flower-power scene was starting to lose momentum and we seemed to be going down the plughole with it. When what should have been our next single – another track from the album called 'Technicolor Dreams' (written by Anthony King, another Valley Music songwriter) – was suddenly scrapped at the last minute in November, we began to worry.

John Schroeder wasn't quite ready to throw the towel in yet, though, and so early in 1969 we released a brand new non-album track that Rick and I had written called 'Make Me

Stay a Bit Longer'. Released as a single in January, just as we were about to embark on a tour of Germany supporting the Small Faces, despite rave reviews predicting another big hit it flopped miserably. The next single in April, a song John Schroeder actually wrote that Rick sang the lead vocal on called 'Are You Growing Tired of My Love', was a minor hit, just about scraping into the Top 50 here and in Holland. But suddenly things were looking bleak. Within the space of a year, we'd gone from 'new sensations' to 'has-beens'. It was not a good feeling, but we still somehow clung to the belief that we were good enough to claw ourselves back again. We were a good band simply in need of the right song, that's all, we felt sure.

With gigs at home in Britain now becoming increasingly thin on the ground, we spent most of the summer concentrating on writing and recording what we hoped would be our big breakthrough album, which we eventually called *Spare Parts*. Featuring twelve tracks, eight of which were songs we had come up with ourselves, it was released in September 1969 at the same time as our next single: a beefed-up version of the old Everly Brothers hit 'The Price of Love'. When they both failed to even get into the Top 100, the record company started to panic and hastily threw together a 'greatest hits' called *Status Quo-tations*, combining the best-known material from both our albums, which they bunged out in time for Christmas. When that too disappeared without a squeak it seemed like the end of the world. Which in a strange way it was. It was also the beginning of a whole new world for us; one we could not have foreseen that bleak Christmas of 1969.

By then it was pretty clear that everyone around us was now losing interest. The same people who went from telling us which clothes shops to go to, to which songs we should open and close the show with, suddenly had no advice to offer us at all. Even John and Pat seemed to be looking to get involved in other projects now. You could see why. From their point of view, we had had our moment in the charts; they had tried to help us sustain it, but it just hadn't worked. It was time to move on. For all of us.

Meanwhile, me and Rick had started to get friendly with a guy named Colin Johnson, then working as a booker for the NEMS agency, who had got us some gigs here and there. We knew he had experience and contacts and so when things started to go pear-shaped at the start of 1970, we decided to approach Colin and ask him if he could help. Specifically, we asked him to manage us.

We didn't want to lose Pat Barlow. We loved him like a father, but the truth is, in terms of the music business, Pat was like us, totally green. And though he had done brilliantly to get us as far as he had, now we were faced with the first real crisis of our careers he had no idea what to do. We'd had the two Top 10 hits but that had been *last* year and now it was obvious that things were falling apart. We needed help, serious help from someone with experience. So we fixed up a meeting with Colin Johnson where we just poured our hearts out to him.

Colin was a wonderful guy, another very caring sort of father-figure. He always made me and Ricky laugh, which always went down well, too. When he agreed to take us on we were delighted. We weren't so thrilled, however, when we sat down to write Pat the letter telling him his services were no longer required. I remember us sitting there agonizing over it. But we knew the well had run dry for us as far as that whole 'Matchstick Men' period went, and Pat was part of that, so though it broke our hearts to have to do it, we wrote the

Above. Francis's grandparents Christina and Alberto Rossi.

Above, right. Francis as a baby, aged around six months, in 1949.

Right. With his grandmother Alice Traynor and Aunt Agnes.

Childhood pictures (some cut up by Francis's mother after her divorce).
Above, aged about five: with Santa Claus and two pictures with his mum.
Below, left to right: in the back garden; happy to have a new gun;
in St Peter's Square, Rome; aged about nine with his mother.

Above. The Spectres at Butlin's in Minehead, in the summer of 1965.
Left to right: Alan Lancaster, John Coghlan, Francis and Roy Lynes.

Below. On holiday in Cornwall. *Left*. Francis and Jean with
Bob Young's wife Sue and their son Simon in 1969.
Right. Francis with Bob Young, Jean and Simon in 1970.

Francis tuning up in 1974.

Francis with Simon and Nicholas in the garden of the house in Purley, November 1976.

Elizabeth with baby Bernadette in 1983.

Francis and Eileen slip away to get married at Croydon Register Office, June 1991.

Eileen at home with Fynn and Patrick.

Above, left. Francis with Fynn in Jersey, 1993.

Above, right. Francis at the piano getting musical advice from Patrick.

Right. Francis with Bernadette, aged twelve, in the studio at home, 1995.

Above. Taken in 1994, back row from left to right: Simon, Kiera Tallulah, Francis, Eileen, Nicholas, Keiran; front row: Fynn and Patrick.

Left. Francis and Eileen's younger children in 2002, left to right: Fursey, Fynn, Patrick, Kiera Tallulah.

letter, tried to explain our reasons why, then said goodbye and wished him well. We posted it the same day.

We were still very young and it never crossed our minds that we might have had our moment. We could see what was happening around us but we always had such belief in the band it didn't really discourage us. No matter what people said against us, we just seemed convinced that things would eventually start happening for us again. Not because we were better then the rest, just that we would *make* them happen somehow, through the sheer force of our belief.

Anyway, that's how it seems now, looking back. At the time, I always kind of kept my head down. I still tend to do that now when we're working – you get into the bubble on tour and you don't get out again until it's over – but back in the early days it was the only way I could get through it, particularly in times of trouble. I would keep my head down and never fantasize about any particular scenario, other than that it would all be all right on the night. Alan Lancaster was always big on post-mortems, trying to over-analyse everything. I'd say, 'Look, just don't, OK? You'll ruin it. Sometimes things do just happen because they were meant to.'

After so many failed attempts to emulate the success of 'Matchstick Men' and 'Ice in the Sun', getting a new manager involved felt like wiping the slate clean and starting again. We weren't sure yet exactly which direction we wanted to take the band in, we just knew that we'd been through so many changes by then, both musically and fashion-wise, that we had simply wearied of the whole image-building thing. We'd started out as teenagers in Beatle-jackets, then metamorphosed into Carnaby Street dandies. Now, as the seventies dawned, that look had also become passé. It was like everybody had got sick of it at the same time. Instead, everyone was now growing their hair long and wearing jeans and T-shirts. Suddenly it wasn't about having the right clothes or the right haircut, it was about letting it all hang out. With no one left to tell us what to do, we decided to go the same way. It felt more natural, more us, and it was cheaper too. We didn't have the money for any fashionable boutiques any more.

That's when the whole idea of going back to basics first took a grip – both musically and image-wise. The idea was to have no image. Musically, what prompted the change was when we noticed how we were starting to enjoy the soundchecks at gigs – where we would muck about and play all sorts of different things – more than the actual gigs themselves. Alan had brought in this bluesy shuffle called 'Junior's Wailing' (written by a London band called Steamhammer) that he suggested we do, and that kind of set the template for the new blues-rock sound we started to explore. I admit I wasn't sure at first, then one night at a club in Germany, Rick and I heard 'Roadhouse Blues' by the Doors and that's when we thought, yeah, we'll have some of that.

By then we had also started playing with blues groups like the early Peter Green line-up of Fleetwood Mac, and Chicken Shack, and what they were doing made what we were doing sound namby-pamby. I used to be so envious of people like the Small Faces singer Stevie Marriott, who would namedrop all these obscure black singers I'd never heard of. I used to think, wow, he really knows his music, I know nothing!

Drugs played their part, too, I have to say. Not just for us but for all the bands back then – certainly the ones that were beginning to see themselves as more 'album-oriented' anyway. After touring with groups like the Small Faces and the

Moody Blues, we had become converted pot-heads and that in itself gave us a whole new perspective on where we were as a band, as opposed to where we wanted to be.

The first time I got seriously interested in smoking pot was on tour in Germany with the Small Faces when Stevie Marriott offered us a joint, already rolled. I was with Rick, we were sharing a room, and so we took it back to the hotel with us and set fire to it. I remember lying on my bed afterwards and hearing music coming from under my pillow. Every time I sat up to take a look, though, it was gone. Then as soon as I lay down again it was back. So I knew something was going on. I got up and got dressed and spent the next two hours walking around enjoying myself, listening to music coming from under pillows . . .

The first real step forward towards becoming the band we are now came unexpectedly one night when we simply decided to go on stage in our normal street wear. We were appearing at the Castle pub in Tooting, South London, supporting Mott the Hoople, and we just couldn't be bothered to put all the clobber on and go through the same old routine again. So we went on as we were, in jeans and T-shirts, and started belting out some of the blues-shuffles that we had been noodling around with at soundcheck. I kept waiting for someone to come on and tell us to stop messing around and get back to the proper stuff. That actually happened once on the Gene Pitney tour when the promoter told us off for not turning up looking 'smart and presentable'. But this time nobody came and we ended up going down a storm!

After that I don't think any of us – with the possible exception of Rick – went to the hairdresser's again for about ten years. As soon as I saw it was working I said right, that's it, I never want to be part of whatever the prevailing fashion is again. From now on we do it like this and that's the way we stay, until *we* feel different. Not when we're told to. Fortunately, everyone agreed and from then on there was no looking back.

And anyway, we were sick of looking like Christmas trees. All that stuff might look good on the telly or in pictures in a magazine but in real life it's actually quite restrictive. Dressing more like our real selves changed the way we felt about the music, too. It loosened things up and really focused our minds on the idea that whatever we did now, sink or swim, for the first time ever it was really just down to us.

It was quite a scary thought . . .

TWO

In 1965 we got our big break as the Highlights when we were booked for the summer season at Butlin's in Minehead. We were very pleased and excited because playing at somewhere like Butlin's was considered a prestige gig for an act like ours. It paid pretty well, too, though how much exactly I never knew because the twins' father, Sid, took care of all that. We were always on the same wage: £15 a set. Good dough back then; a week's wages for some people. We were booked in at the Gaiety Theatre, playing before a couple of thousand people a night. Unlike at Sunshine, we didn't have to be Redcoats or do anything except perform; that was our sole role. The big time at last, we thought.

Because we weren't considered to be official camp staff, we had to live offsite in private digs, but we spent nearly all of our time at the camp. Without anything to do in the day this time it really was like being permanently on holiday, and I looked forward to having a terrific time. What I couldn't have foreseen was how that summer season at Butlin's would quite literally change my life for ever.

It all began when I was rehearsing with the girls at the theatre one day, a week or so before the camp officially opened for the season, and I heard this terrific din coming from somewhere. I realized it was a rock'n'roll band – and that it sounded really good. So after we'd finished up for the day I just sort of wandered off in the direction of this noise. I found myself in what they called the Rock'n'Roll Ballroom – and there they were, the Spectres, hammering out 'Roll Over Beethoven'. I was utterly transfixed.

I saw that they were still only kids like me but it was obvious they were a proper rock'n'roll band, just from the way they stood there and played together. They were full of attitude and looked like a real gang. I waited until they took a break then wandered over. I just had to say hello and tell them how good they were, because they were really very good.

We shook hands and I explained that I was appearing in the show down the road. Francis was the first one I actually made eye contact with and spoke to. He was friendly immediately, as was Alan, which was a relief. Doing gigs with the Highlights, sometimes there were rock'n'roll bands on the bill too and we always used to groan when that happened because we knew they would mince us. It used to make me feel inferior because we weren't as loud or as exciting, frankly. They would get screamed at by girls; we would get enthusiastic applause from mums and dads. And of course the twins would go out with these guys in the rock groups sometimes. That really twisted the knife for me.

So I was always a bit in awe of rock bands in general, but this lot were all so friendly I soon lost my reservations and we became quite close. Francis and I got on just like that, forging a great friendship almost from the off. It was the start of something for me; the secret thought that maybe one day I could do something like that too. Even though we had just landed the biggest gig of our career, meeting Francis and the boys was the first time I allowed myself to think seriously beyond the Highlights. This rock'n'roll stuff – that was more like it, I decided.

The Beatles had come along by then, too, and of course that just made you want to do it even more. The first time I really took notice of them was when they released 'She Loves You', when I was fourteen. I remember bopping along to that on the radio back at 101 Queen Elizabeth Way. I thought, wow, this is different. Then suddenly *everything* was different. The music, the look, the way people spoke to each other, eventually even how they thought about things too.

First, though, it was important to have the look, especially if you were a teenager, and I had bought my first pair of 'Beatles' boots while I was working at Sunshine. By the time I'd got to Butlin's, however, I had to face the fact that I wasn't really a fully-fledged rocker yet. How could I be, in an act like the Highlights? I had learned how to play quite a few rock and pop songs, though. I was always picking up little tricks from the other guitarists I came across on the road. But it wasn't until I met the Spectres that I really decided the time had come for me to go for it. From that moment on, even though we carried on throughout the rest of the season, I realize now that for me the Highlights were on borrowed time.

We were halfway down the bill in the camp's big nightly Variety show, and as well as doing our regular set we also took part in the more general production, including a comedy sketch called *The Babes in Robin Hood's Wood*, in which I played Friar Tuck. I was only sixteen and so skinny my mum used to say I was like 'a needle with two eyes', so they had to pad me out each night. It was a huge palaver and at the end of it I only had one line: 'Yes, Robin, but we must look after the Babes first.'

After the show each night I would go over to the Rock'n Roll Ballroom to see my new mates in the Spectres. They would start at eight and play for about ninety minutes, then have a half-hour break and go on again until midnight. In those days people didn't really pay much attention to the group, they just got up and danced, or if they didn't do that they sat down and hand-jived. It was that sort of scene. I used to get there in time for the intermission and hang out with them in the dressing-room. After they'd finished for the night we'd go out on the pull for birds but it was usually so late that by then all the good ones were taken. Usually, anyway . . .

When Francis got thrown out of his digs after being discovered in bed with a girl – strictly against the rules at most 'respectable' lodging-houses in those days – he found himself without a place to stay for a couple of weeks. I felt sorry for him so I said, 'Look, I'm not going to let you roam around on your own, I'll come with you.' If he was going to have to kip on the beach or whatever, I'd kip with him, I decided, just to make him feel better.

He didn't say too much – as I was discovering, Francis has never been one to readily show his emotions – but I think he was secretly relieved. As it was summer it wasn't too cold at night, and at first we would sleep under the deckchairs on the beach. We would pile a few up on the sand until we had a rudimentary hut then huddle underneath and try to sleep. It was like being back in the Carpet Club. Or we would sleep in baths in the communal bathrooms that some of the cheaper chalets used. You had to be very quiet because if the camp security guards caught you they would throw you out. Other times we would wait until the camp chefs, who were always up really early, got out of their beds, and we'd jump straight in. They would still be warm from the previous body and stinking of chip oil and cigarettes. It was pretty revolting, but at the time those warm smelly beds were a godsend to us and we were soon blissfully asleep.

It was a bit rough some nights when we couldn't find anywhere at all or we kept being woken up and moved on. But we were young, so it was all a big adventure to us. It didn't matter whether we were hot or cold, whether we slept or not, we didn't give a fuck. And, in many ways, that was the start of the much bigger adventure we would have that's still going on to this day, forty-odd – sometimes very odd – years later. By the end of the season I thought of Francis as my best friend. We used to call each other 'man', and I'd never known anyone I could do that with before. Like, 'Hey, man, what ya doin?' It felt so grown-up and cool.

I don't know who Francis saw as his best friend in the band back then. I began to see that he and Alan had a sort of love-hate relationship where they would get on well most times but then occasionally not at all. I remember them even having a fight backstage one time – actual fisticuffs. They'd just come off for the intermission and within seconds they were at each other's throats. I was shocked! I'd never seen anything like that before. It was pretty rock'n'roll, I suppose, but I was meant to be mates with both of them and it bothered me.

It so happened that Alan then got friendly with the twins. He was mad for Gloria, and when I started staying out at night with Francis he actually moved in with the twins at my place! It didn't really bother me, though, because I was fairly sure it was Gloria he was after. Things went back to normal when Francis finally found some new digs and I went back to mine, forcing Alan out again. Alan and I always got on well in those days, though. He even used to let me wear some of his stage suits.

As for the others, Roy Lynes the keyboardist was a few years older than us and used to do his own thing. I don't think any of us ever really got close to Roy because he was just different. He was more like a mad inventor than a musician; always souping-up his keyboards or his car and getting them to do things they shouldn't. I remember he had one of those three-wheel Goggomobiles. They were no bigger than a motorbike, with a top speed of about 60 m.p.h., and they were notorious for having terrible over-steer. He couldn't get it started one day so he was pushing it down the street in gear and it suddenly kicked in and ran off with him still hanging off the back of it! It was the sort of thing that could only happen to Roy.

John Coghlan, the drummer, was not an easy fellow to get to know, either. John was always a very dark and moody sort of character even then. You couldn't help but like him because, by and large, he was fairly quiet and easy-going. But you never really knew who he was or what was going on behind those dark eyes. Even after I'd been in the band for ten years I still never quite knew what I was going to get from John on a day-to-day basis. He was never really one of the boys; he would usually go off and have a drink with other people. And John did like a drink . . .

Spending that summer at Butlin's, getting to know the band, the whole thing was an education for me; an induction into the rock'n'roll side of life. The thought of saying goodbye to these guys once the season was over and going back to a life on the cabaret circuit began to make me wince. I'd got used to hanging out with real rock'n'rollers; I didn't want to go back to being a poofy cabaret performer in a lamé jacket and bow-tie. I even began to secretly wish the band would take me with them, like running away to the circus. At the same time I wouldn't have dreamed of suggesting anything like that to them. They were already an established group; it wasn't for me to go having any big ideas about what they should or shouldn't do next. All I knew was that I wanted to leave the Highlights behind and get a real rock'n'roll group together somehow.

Sure enough, the Highlights split a few months afterwards. I was desperately frustrated, and the twins and I were now arguing about anything and everything. It got pretty bad, as it always does when your heart is no longer in it. The idea of getting up on stage and performing in front of people was still a magical thing for me, but I was too busy dreaming of life on the other side of the fence to enjoy the act any more. The appeal of being in the Highlights had gone and now I wanted to get to the next level, as I saw it.

We just about managed to survive one final season together at Skegness in the summer of 1966, then after one particularly bad bust-up in which I was stabbed in the head with stilettos and left bleeding and curled up in a ball in the corner of the dressing-room – take my tip, don't ever pick a fight with twins, male or female, because you're going to come off worse – I walked out and never went back. My parents came in the car to collect me and that was that. I must say, though, that it was a pretty bleak journey home that day. I knew it was the end of a chapter in my life but I didn't know yet what the next one was going to be. Ricky Harrison was dead. Long live ... who? I didn't know, just that it should be someone more like Francis and the boys in the Spectres.

After Butlin's, I had stayed in touch with the lads. I used to go over to Alan's house sometimes, or Francis's, and I would go to some of their shows at places like the Café des Artistes. If anything they were even better than I remembered them at Butlin's. Particularly Francis. He just had something about him. I didn't know the word for it then but I do now: presence. On stage, he just had something that meant you couldn't take your eyes off him.

I couldn't believe it, though, when they actually got to make a record. This must have been towards the end of 1966. It was a cover version of the old Shirley Bassey hit 'I (Who Have Nothing)', and I remember feeling physically sick with excitement when they showed it to me. A proper record with the name of my friends, the Spectres, on it! It was the nearest thing to having a record with your own name on it and I was immensely pleased and proud for them – and at the same time more than a little jealous. It really did make me feel ill, because now I wanted to be doing something like that even more. Over the next few months they released a few singles. None of them were hits but it was still incredible to me how well they seemed to be doing now. To be *on* a record that was *out in the shops* – that was like the holy grail to me back then, and I was overjoyed and filled with envy in equal measure.

Meanwhile, back on planet Earth, in order to bring some money in, I got a job working for Price's Bread, driving the van, delivering bread and cakes to various places around Surrey. There were very few 'proper' jobs that I was qualified to do and so driving the van seemed like the ideal stopgap. I had an old mate named John Booth, who also played guitar, and I thought maybe I could start something up with him. But it never really panned out. You had to be up at five each morning to get to the bakery to load up the van, and I was always so tired by the time I got home every day that I just couldn't be bothered. I spent a long time just moping around the house feeling very frustrated about what I wanted to do. Or rather, I knew what I wanted to do, I just couldn't find the right door to go through to do it. For the first time in my life I was a little bit lost.

I began to hate the bread round. I didn't mind the people you met: the stern-faced shopkeepers and their red-cheeked old wifeys. I quite enjoyed the social aspect of it. I used to knock on the doors and cry 'Baker!' and they would all come running. I had no idea of the logistics of being a successful bread delivery man, though. Apart from all the jam tarts I ate myself, I used to load up every day with anything I could lay my hands on: bread, eggs, tarts, biscuits ... I used to come home at the end of the week with half the van still full, and any produce you had left over you had to pay the company back for out of your own money, so I usually ended up with sod all in my weekly pay packet. But did I care? No, I did not. I was surviving, that's all that mattered to me. Eventually, though, it got so bad that I couldn't get any more old unsold bread into the back of the van. So I jacked it in and went back to moping around the house. I think I left still owing them money.

I worked for a while at a petrol station but that didn't last either. The next proper job I got was as a clerk at a water sewage firm, in Purford, near West Byfleet, close to where I lived. By now I'd got my first little car – my mum had bought me a grey Standard 8 for thirty quid – and I was so thrilled you couldn't get me out of it.

I had passed my driving test when I was seventeen, while I was touring with the Highlights. We were in New Brighton, just across the Mersey from Liverpool. I had four lessons and took the test – and passed! The whole thing cost less than a fiver. But I'd never really had cause to use my licence until then because Sid did all the driving. Once the Highlights was gone, however, so were the cars. When my mum bought me that Standard 8 it meant more to me than any of Sid's fancier cars because it was my own. Sid was a good guy but he wasn't my mum and this wasn't his car any more, it was *mine*. The first one I could truly look at and call my own. It was a great moment.

I used to drive myself to work every morning, where I found myself sitting in this drafty little hut all day on the edge of the sewage farm, bored out of my mind. I had to wear a suit and tie and sit behind a desk doing God knows what, I never really knew. I found it all quite perplexing. But I encouraged myself with the thought that the guys in the Spectres also did a variety of day-jobs when circumstances prevailed. Alan used to do a bit of window-cleaning, for example, and Francis was known for mowing lawns and working part-time in an optician's shop. They all had something going on so I didn't feel too left out.

The positive aspect to all this was that things were so bad it really pushed me into thinking seriously for the first time about my future. On the one hand, I couldn't stand the thought of sitting in this hut for the rest of my life pushing bits of paper around. On the other hand, I realized I hadn't picked up my guitar in earnest for months. I also realized that I could no longer pull it off as the cheeky kid who got up and surprised everyone by singing in pubs. I wasn't a cute twelve-year-old boy any more. It was 1967, I was eighteen, nearly a man, and I was starting to get seriously itchy feet. The Highlights had gone, I hadn't formed my own group, and now here I was – in this hut. I decided I simply had to do something.

Thankfully, my parents were so fantastic they really helped me through it. My mum bought me the car and my dad told me to take my time and really think about what it was I wanted to do. But I already knew what I wanted to do. It was the era of the Beatles, the Kinks and the Stones and I loved them all. I used to buy the records and sit and watch them on TV in shows like *Juke Box Jury* and *Thank Your Lucky Stars*. I used to sit there watching the Small Faces or whoever thinking, why aren't I doing that? How do I make something like that happen for me?

Then one day, in July 1967, something did happen. I was at home when the phone rang; it was Pat Barlow, the manager of the Spectres. We chatted for a bit and then he came out with it. He said he and the record company had decided to shake things up a bit in the group. They had already had three or four singles out by then, none of which had been hits, and had already changed their name once – from the Spectres to the Traffic Jam. But that hadn't worked either and now they wanted to change things round again, he said. He had been discussing it with the producer, John Schroeder, and they had decided the group also needed an extra voice in it. Then he asked me the million-dollar question: would I like to be that voice?

Can you even begin to imagine how I felt at that moment? This was something I had never expected to hear. I might have secretly dreamed of being in the group but I had long since accepted in my heart of hearts that it was never going to happen. Then suddenly it did! I was totally shocked and amazed. To be honest, I didn't really think they needed anybody else. To me, they were already great as they were.

Not that I was about to point that out to Pat. Instead, I just said yes. If he had offered me a job making the tea for them I'd have said yes. I was so excited I couldn't sleep at all that night. Then the next morning I was out of that house and up the road like a rat up a drainpipe. I jumped in the car and drove up to Lambeth Walk as fast as I could, to where they used to rehearse in the basement of this gas showroom that Pat owned.

Standing there with my guitar on, playing in the group for the first time, my first thought in among all the euphoria was that my hands were starting to ache. I was only used to playing for fifteen minutes at a time with the twins. Now I was faced with the prospect of playing for over an hour, sometimes two or three times a night. I wondered at first if I would be able to cope, but I soon got used to it as my wrists strengthened and my fingertips blistered then toughened up again.

My other big worry was the thought of trying to memorize all the songs that they did. To this day I'm always nervous during the first few shows of a new tour because I'm afraid I'm not going to be able to remember how any of the new numbers go. With the Highlights I played the same four or five songs every night for the entire three years we were together. So playing with The Status Quo, as we had now decided to call ourselves, was surprisingly challenging for me. I wondered that first day at rehearsals what the others would think of this bumbling fool . . .

But learn the songs I did, and soon enough came the great day of my first gig as one of the band. Our first official engagement as The Status Quo was at a pub in Eltham, South London, called the Welcome Inn. I went on in a green-and-yellow striped blazer borrowed from Francis because I didn't have any cool stage clothes of my own to wear yet. I was so excited the whole thing just went by in a flash and I can now only recall certain small details of that night. What I do remember of it, though, is that it felt incredible. I didn't do any lead vocals yet, or any announcing. Francis and Alan already had all that covered. I just banged away on guitar and slotted in on the three-part vocal harmonies. We'd only had about four or five rehearsals together and I was terribly nervous beforehand. As soon as we went on and started playing, though, I felt surprisingly relaxed and started to get into it. Most of all, I remember noticing how many young girls there were in the audience, which was always very much part of the dream: not just to be up there playing this kind of music in this kind of group, but to have lots of girls watching you too. That was the ultimate, as far as I was concerned: being a pop star and getting screamed at by girls – what could possibly be better than that?

Things were suddenly moving fast. We had only done a couple of gigs when we went in to make our first record together, which was the real reason I'd been brought in, to bring that extra voice to their sound in the studio. The only time I had ever been in a recording studio before, however, had been when I was twelve and my dad had wangled me what they called a 'recording test' at Decca Records. I sang 'Travelling Light' – in the style of the Cliff Richard version, which my dad and I both loved. But I was obviously crap because the producer turned to my father and said, 'We like the lad but bring him back when he can breathe properly.' That completely stumped me and for weeks afterwards I would walk around trying to breathe 'properly' until I started panting like a dog. It wasn't until years later I realized it was just something to say to get rid of me nicely.

Going into the studio now as part of a rock'n'roll group was totally different. I wasn't particularly nervous because I had all my pals around me and they had all done this before, so it felt quite comfortable. And of course it was great to drop it into the conversation when I was with my mates down the pub. 'What you doing tomorrow?' 'Oh, I'm in the studio recording...' In truth, however, much as I tried to disguise it, I did feel a bit like the new kid in class compared to the others because for me this was a total learning experience. This was to be our first single as The Status Quo, my first really important gig with the band, and I desperately wanted to do well.

The song we initially recorded for the A-side was one of those straightforward, reasonably catchy, off-the-peg Tin Pan Alley numbers written by Kenny Young titled 'Gentleman Joe's Sidewalk Café'. For the B-side, however, Francis had come up with a new number of his own called 'Pictures of Matchstick Men'. The producer, John Schroeder, was the one who suggested making it the A-side but the first time we heard it played back in the studio we all knew it was a hit. It was just a brilliant song: the words, the chording, the intro – all brilliant. The moment that chiming little guitar intro kicked-in, you knew it was a winner. It even made Alan Florence, the engineer, put his newspaper down and listen; something he never did normally when we were recording. All of a sudden the atmosphere in the room just completely changed. It was just a magic tune. We only played it through about three times before they had the take they wanted, and every time we played it the tingles went up my arms.

'Pictures of Matchstick Men' was released as a single on 5 January 1968. Although it sold slowly at first, it began picking up radio plays almost immediately. Word was Pat had paid to have it played on Radio Caroline, which I now believe was the norm back then. Soon all the other stations started picking up on it too and within weeks it had crept into the lower reaches of the Top 30. Two weeks later it was Top 10, eventually climbing as high as Number 7!

We were out on tour, acting as backing group to singer Madeline Bell, when we got the news. Hardly the most glamorous surroundings, but it was a paying gig Pat Barlow had picked up for us that we had been glad to get straight after Christmas when we were all skint. When 'Matchstick Men' went into the charts, though, suddenly we were having to jump in the van and shoot off for all these other engagements of our own: live sessions for Radio One shows and – holy of holies – *Top of the Pops*, then the biggest pop show on TV. Once all that started happening ours fees started going up too and we were pressured to walk out on Madeline and start cashing in on our own success. But she was such a lovely, talented person (who would go on to greater success herself in the seventies with Blue Mink), we said no, we'll see this through first.

In terms of some of the history-making events that we have been fortunate enough to have been a part of throughout our careers, you'd have to put Live Aid at the top of the list, without question. But for me the big personal milestones had already occurred long before we got to that great occasion. One of the biggest was standing there with my mum listening to myself with the group on the radio for the first time. These days I have trouble remembering what happened last week, but I will never ever forget that day. It was a Saturday morning and they were broadcasting excerpts from a live session we'd recorded for Radio One's *Saturday Morning Beat Club*, presented by a very plummy-voiced Brian

Matthews. I was in the lounge at home, listening to it on the stereogram – a then very modern record-player-cum-stereo radio all set in polished wood with a heavy lid. When we came on I literally went weak at the knees. My mum was in the other room and I remember calling to her. 'Mum, Mum! Come quick! Your son's on the radio!' We hadn't done any telly yet and it was mind-boggling. To be on the radio – it instantly legitimized everything, both to me and my parents. It meant I was really going somewhere at last. I hoped so, anyway.

To begin with, I had kept my job at the sewage works. I remember going in when 'Matchstick Men' was first starting to get played on the radio, and saying to the boss of the firm: 'Just to let you know, I may not be able to stay in the job for much longer as I'm also in a group, and there's a chance our new record is going to get in the charts. If that happens I'll have to leave.' He didn't take a blind bit of notice, just waved me away, like, yeah, yeah, yeah. And told me to get back to work. Sure enough, I was still there when 'Matchstick Men' suddenly leapt to Number 11 in the charts. It still gives me an inner glow to recall the moment I was able to go in and tell this guy that I was leaving. He seemed surprised and asked why. I said, 'Well, I did warn you that I was in a group and that we had a record out. Well, now it's become a hit and I've got to leave.' I didn't add 'so there' but he got the message.

Pat had called us all up for a meeting a few days before, where he told us: 'All right, lads, that's it, you can all give up your day jobs. From now on you're going to be full-time professionals.' We literally jumped in the air for joy! That was another huge milestone in our lives. Being told to give up your boring day job because you are now going to be a proper full-time pop star! It was all I had dreamed about for years. Now it was all happening so quickly – from doing my first gig with them in the pub to making our first record and having our first hit – my feet didn't touch the ground for months afterwards.

The pinnacle of that period for me was doing *Top of the Pops* for the first time. Like everybody else in Britain of my generation I watched it avidly as a fan, so the thought of actually being on there at last with my own group – it was unimaginable, dream-laden stuff. Yet we ended up on there a few times in the late sixties, first for 'Matchstick Men' and then for our only other hit from that time, 'Ice in the Sun'. In those days the show regularly featured groups like the Marmalade, Amen Corner, the Herd, Love Affair, and they all had one thing in common: they were bigger than us. Any doubts we might have had on that score were swiftly dispelled every time we left the BBC studios together, and they would immediately get chased down the street by hundreds of crazed fans. We would stand there watching this, unmolested and embarrassed, wondering where all our frenzied fans were? Lots of girls used to come to the gigs but we had never actually been mobbed, Beatles-style. We even stooped to *trying* to get mobbed. We'd come out sometimes a little bit earlier than the other groups and walk very slowly past the fans, waiting for them to take the bait, as it were. But it never happened. We had a few admirers and some autograph hunters, but it was years before anyone would actually start chasing us down the street.

It really pissed us off, actually. In the very earliest days of success, when you're still just a fan yourself, silly little things like that matter. For instance, after gigs sometimes we would get back to find some girls had written Francis's name – or

'Mike' as he still was then – in lipstick on the side of the van. They would draw his name inside a big red lipstick heart and put kisses all over it; they would put their own names in there too sometimes, and even leave a phone number. The rest of us were all jealous, because no girls ever wrote our names on the side of the van and we knew they only did it for Francis because he was the singer and girls always go for the singer first. I grew so sick of it that in the end I surreptitiously wrote my own name on the van in a couple of places. It's a sad thing to have to admit it but yes, it's true, I did do that, your honour. I got really good at it too. I became like a master forger, making sure the handwriting didn't all look the same. I even had my own lipstick and felt pen . . .

As the writer of the song, Francis was also the first member of the band ever to receive a gold record. I was tremendously pleased for him, but at the same time I couldn't help but feel a tad envious too. Then he got his first royalty cheque for the song and I nearly fainted – it was for £1,000! He showed it to me at rehearsals one day and I couldn't believe it. He might as well have been showing me a cheque for a million, that's how much £1,000 seemed to me back then. And all for one song! I was staggered and again, I confess, more than a little green around the gills. You could buy a flash car and put a deposit down on a smart pad with that kind of money. I decided to try to start writing some hit songs of my own. I think Alan must have had the same idea because he suddenly started coming up with all sorts of new material too.

We now know, of course, that Francis never received anything like what he should have done for 'Pictures of Matchstick Men'. It became a hit all over the world, including America, where it went Top 10. It remains, in fact, one of the biggest hits the band has ever had. But Francis lost out. Different deals were done with different companies around the world for the song and he ended up with a fraction of what he should have got. But we didn't know anything about contracts yet. We just did what we were told. All we cared about was that we were on the radio and the telly and that people were coming to the shows. We hadn't learned yet that it was a good idea to actually read the bits of paper they put in front of you before you signed them. We were all just floating along in one boat and it was a very happy-go-lucky existence. The money wasn't really a factor yet; it was the success of the group and the excitement and new experiences that it brought us that mattered most. In retrospect you might say that, in those terms, things have never really moved on from that idea. Certainly not for me. All I have ever really wanted was for the band to be good and to be successful. The rest was just the small print and still is, as far as I'm concerned.

Nevertheless, some money did start to come in that we could all get a share of after 'Matchstick Men' was a hit. We'd started headlining our own shows now and our fees went up considerably. I remember coming home one night from a show we'd just done at the Links Pavilion in Cromer, where we'd played to about 400 people. When Pat gave me a bundle of notes at the end of the night as my share of the booty I didn't even bother to count it until I got home. When I did I discovered I'd been given £300! This was in 1969 – big, big money at a time when the working man's weekly wage was probably a tenth of that. And just for one night's work! I may not have had any gold records yet or any big songwriting royalty cheques, but life in the band still seemed very sweet. It was about three in the morning but I went upstairs to Mum and Dad's bedroom and woke them up. I said, 'Have a look at this!' and showered the bed in pound notes. I think they thought they were still dreaming . . .

Once I had a few bob in my pocket, I knew how to spend it, too. As a kid I'd always joked to Mum and Dad that I'd have a Jag by the time I was twenty-one. In those days, if you had a Jag you'd made it. Never mind a Rolls Royce, this was the Swinging Sixties and for me Jags were where it was at. In the end I had one by the time I was nineteen. A mark II, 3.8 litre, six cylinder maroon Jag. Number plate: BPB 723B. I paid about £800 for it.

I loved driving it. I must have looked totally wrong in it – long hair, suede tasselled jacket, guitar in the backseat – but I didn't care about that. I was too busy racing round being the pop star with the flash motor. When I first got it, I couldn't pull up to the side of anybody at the lights without my tongue creeping into my cheek. I'd look at them and go, 'Hello, mate. Nice Zodiac. How about the Jag, though? Looks nice, dunnit?' Then shoot off the nanosecond the lights turned green, leaving them trailing in the dust. Or I'd be down the pub with my mates giving it large, as we say down our way. 'Oh yeah, we're in the studio tonight, then hanging out with the Herd at *Top of the Pops* tomorrow night, and the night after that I'm going for a drive in my new Jag . . .' It's amazing I still had any mates left.

The only blot on the horizon was that having found success, we now had to work hard to try to keep it. After we had said goodbye to Madeline, we were booked on to a six-week 'package' tour headlined by Gene Pitney and featuring us and a bunch of other acts on the bill like Don Partridge and Amen Corner. It was marvellous, because even though we were far down the bill we were still getting the experience of playing at these big theatres in front of packed houses, sometimes as many as 3,000 people a night. We would only be on for twenty minutes but we were working with some of the biggest acts in the pop business and we learned so much just by standing in the wings watching them up close.

To coincide with the tour we had been thrown into the studio for a day to come up with a suitable follow-up to 'Matchstick Men'. It was hardly ideal, but Francis had been one step ahead as usual and had already come up with what we all thought would be the ideal follow-up: a similar sort of ditty called 'Black Veils of Melancholy'. It wasn't a bad little number apart from the fact that it was more or less an exact copy of 'Matchstick Men'. The only thing it was missing was that little bit of real magic that the original had and it died miserably, barely creeping into the Top 40.

Not that that deterred us. From day one, I don't think I have ever felt that the band was ever truly down and out, no matter what we were going through. We were young and the belief in the band was intense. For me it simply boiled down to the fact that I'd always known how good the band was; right from those early days as a fan when I first saw them play, up to when I became a part of it and we really established our own sound and identity in the seventies. And I still feel that way now. To me, it's the greatest little rock band in the world and always has been. So as far as I was concerned, it was simply a matter of getting on with the next thing. Nevertheless, we were aware too, more than ever now, how short-lived the life of a pop star could be. I remember Francis and I having a conversation around this time in which we both agreed that if we could keep the whole thing ticking along for another four or five years, and we could walk away with maybe as much as fifty grand each, that that would do us fine. We could all retire to some tropical island for the rest of our lives. Little did we know . . .

These days, the thing people probably remember best about us back then is what we looked like. As the old black-and-white clips from *Top of the Pops* reveal, at the time the group sported what you might call the post-Sergeant Pepper look. The suit-and-tie image of the beat group era had more or less gone, and because of the Beatles we were all now into this flower-power, Carnaby Street thing. Truth to tell, none of it came from us. We now had these big tours lined up, plus television work and photo sessions and so on, and we were told what to wear and how to look and what to say and when to say it. It wasn't like they held a gun to our heads; we liked the clothes. But none of it was actually our idea. We were just taken to the right shops in Carnaby Street, shown what the other groups were wearing and told to buy the same sort of clobber. If you look at the pictures now we all look like different little versions of Austin Powers.

The whole thing left us somewhat bemused, to say the least. We were so busy being told what to do and trying to fit in that the music was the last thing anybody thought about. Apart from 'Matchstick Men' we didn't have any other so-called psychedelic songs. It was all a bit schizophrenic. Because we were on the package tours we didn't even know who 'our' audience were. Didn't even know what they looked like, just that hundreds of thousands of them had gone out and bought the single. But this was how our bread was being buttered, and being professional now we turned up, put the flash Carnaby Street gear on, and performed. Buy a frilly shirt? All right then. Get a silly haircut? No problem . . .

It was all very regimented. One night on the Gene Pitney tour I had a peek through the curtains just before we went on and the promoter, a typically tough customer back then named Ron King, caught me and said, 'If I *ever* see you do that again you'll be off this tour and I'll see to it personally that you never work again!' Bloody hell! Did I feel told off! It was like being at school again. Another time, when Francis's hair had grown quite long even for those days, Pat came in one day and shouted, 'Ross!' (which is what we all called him then) and as Francis went over Pat grabbed him by the head and cut off a big chunk of his hair with a pair of sewing scissors! He did it so quickly he cut it about halfway up the back of his head and Francis ended up looking like Max Wall! He wasn't too happy about it, but Pat was the manager so that was that. Unbelievable, really, but that's what it was like for us back then. You didn't like it but what could you do?

It was the first time I noticed the difference between the way people treated us now that we'd had a bit of success, and the way things had been before we'd had the big hit. Until then we'd pretty much done our own thing. Now there were all sorts of bigwigs hanging around telling us what to do. Not because they were looking out for us but because they smelled money and they wanted to protect their investment. Not knowing any better, we went along with it. Just like all those manufactured boy-bands do now.

Once we had finished the Pitney tour we were well known enough to headline our own ballroom shows. Even though our second single had flopped we were still The Status Quo – as seen on TV! – and there would be fifty or sixty girls down the front every night, jumping up and down and squealing. So we had our fun with it but even then it was fairly clear to us that this sort of thing never lasted for long. In our case it felt like five minutes, though in reality it was probably about eighteen months.

The worst bit about fame is that you're expected to know how to speak and act around other famous people, and I'm terrible at that. Even now I go all tongue-tied and turn into a fan again. I remember meeting the Yardbirds backstage once at a gig we opened for them, and being totally in awe but at the same time completely thrilled to be there rubbing shoulders with these players that I held in such high regard. I never knew what to say at the time but I always did the next day. 'What did you do last night?' 'Oh, I was chatting to the Yardbirds'. Of course, that childish naïvety wore off rather quickly, but strands of it are still there now whenever I'm called upon to speak to someone that I would consider to be really famous, like Prince Charles. I'm not ashamed of it, though. I'm quite proud of it, actually, because to me that's like the last bit of me from when I was a kid that's still alive, and I cherish it.

It extends right down to my own band. Even now, after all these years, I still get a little thrill every time I walk into the dressing-room for the first time at one of our shows. It just dongs me sometimes like a big clanger on the head – I'm in Status Quo! You can ask Francis. I still walk up to him sometimes in the dressing-room and go, 'Isn't this great?' He just looks at me and goes, 'Oh, no, not again . . .'

Getting back to the sixties, however, somehow we had managed to sail through the failure of 'Black Veils' fairly unscathed. We still had plenty of live work off the back of 'Matchstick Men' and, thankfully, the next single, 'Ice in the Sun', was another hit for us. It wasn't in the same league in terms of outright commercial success as 'Matchstick Men', but it got into the Top 10 in the UK and a few other countries in Europe.

This time we got the song from our publishers, who told

us they had this perfect song for us that Marty Wilde had written. Marty had been a pop star himself back in the late fifties and had already written hits for other people, and when they played us the demo of the song we liked it immediately. I think Francis may even have been secretly relieved that he didn't have to try and come up with 'Matchstick Men Part 3'.

We agreed to go in and record it as the next single with Marty Wilde producing, and it was Marty who came up with the idea of running a guitar plectrum up and down the strings of a piano to make this zinging sound, which, along with the guitar riff, became the most catchy thing about the record: this chiming little motif. It was a good lesson for us because the song just came to life as soon as we added this one bit of fairy dust to it. These days it would all be done on computers, but back then one of us actually had to climb inside this big old grand piano they had in the studio and physically run a plectrum up and down the strings. It was a good little song anyway but that was the magic ingredient that turned it into a hit, of that I have no doubt.

So there we were again, back on the telly and radio again and back in the charts. In reality, however, it didn't change things much for us one way or the other. We were still playing ballrooms with mainly girls down the front. It was around then that it started to dawn on us that in order to get on to the next rung of the ladder we would have to try something different. Having a couple of pop hits was fantastic, but we also knew how precarious it was being a singles band after the failure of 'Black Veils'. We had learned the hard way that you were only as popular as your last hit. When our next single, one of the first songs Francis and I actually wrote together, called 'Make Me Stay a Bit Longer', was a terrible flop, we were back where we started again.

We had also released an album by then: the ludicrously titled *Picturesque Matchstickable Messages from the Status Quo*. Released in September 1968 and containing all three Quo singles up until that point plus B-sides and a smattering of other tracks, it was basically a cash-in job. But it was the first chance we'd had to think seriously about our music. It was also where I got to sing properly for the group for the first time, contributing the lead vocals to a handful of tracks; mainly cover versions like 'Green Tambourine' but also another new song I had written with Francis called 'When My Mind Is Not Live'. Don't ask me what it was 'about' – as I recall, Francis came up with the lyrics and I came up with the melody – it just felt great to get my name on a songwriting credit for the first time. Alan got his name on a song, too: 'Sunny Cellophane Skies', which he wrote and sang himself.

Now, in the summer of 1969, we wanted to take things a step further and record a proper album, as we saw it. The era was changing too. Jimmy Page had left the Yardbirds behind to form Led Zeppelin; Steve Marriott was about to leave the Small Faces and join Peter Frampton from the Herd in a similar, much more 'serious' album-oriented band called Humble Pie. Albums were now where it was at – if you wanted to be taken seriously. And we decided we did. We had played with a lot of these bands, we had seen what was going on, and we desperately didn't want to get left behind. The result: *Spare Parts*, an album comprising mostly original compositions that quickly sank without trace. Book-ended by a brace of further flop singles, suddenly things were starting to look very shaky for us indeed.

And that's when everybody began to bale out. Or at least, that's how it seemed. As soon as the discussion turned towards how we wanted to push more in an album-oriented direction, the various powers that be – both management and record company – began to get even more nervous. By then, I realize now, they had already decided we were a lame duck. We had had two big hits but now times had moved on. They made it fairly clear that we could do what we liked, but they themselves were already starting to consider their options.

It was kind of a shock to see the rats deserting the sinking ship like that but at the same time it did help us. From now on everything we did would be done the way we wanted it. That's what we decided anyway. If only life were that simple . . .

THREE

The seventies was, in many ways, the most exciting decade of my life. It was also, in other ways, a time I would not necessarily wish to live through again. Fame and success brought their own rewards; they also brought confusion and despair. A lot of it self-inflicted. Not that we understood that then. We were simply on a roll. One of those unrepeatable creative curves you find yourselves on as a band sometimes, if you're very lucky, where everything you touch just turns to gold. Or almost everything . . .

Musically, the band had already begun the metamorphosis from the 'Matchstick Men' era into what we became in the seventies while Pat Barlow was still working with us. The first single in our new guise was 'Down the Dustpipe', in March 1970. Produced once again by John Schroeder but written this time by an Australian singer-songwriter – and yet another Valley Music client – named Carl Groszmann. Though it was not one of our own songs, 'Dustpipe' was the first Quo record to feature our soon-to-be-trademark boogie shuffle. It already had that blues element to it anyway but we just took it that little bit further, and it quickly became one of the most popular numbers in our new live set.

Radio One largely ignored it but by then we were playing live practically every night and it became a word-of-mouth hit among the club-goers. Eventually it even showed up in the charts, reaching Number 12 for one week in May 1970. Even though it didn't crack the Top 10 the way 'Matchstick Men' and 'Ice in the Sun' had two years previously, it took so long to get to where it did and then fall back down again it was kicking around the charts for months – all the encouragement we needed to keep going in our new direction.

'Down the Dustpipe' also featured, on harmonica, someone who was to play an even bigger part in my story – a gentleman by the name of Bob Young. We had first met Bob at the Hammersmith Odeon, in London, on the Gene Pitney tour back in '68. Alan was having problems with his bass at the soundcheck when out of nowhere this guy just strolled on stage, gently took the guitar from him and fixed it. Just like that. He was working for Amen Corner at the time, who were also on the bill, but we were so impressed we badgered Pat to find out who he was and see if he could entice him into working for us. About a week later Pat walked in and said, 'I've got good news,' and Bob walked in behind him.

Our road manager at the time was a scouse guy named John Fanning, who had once worked with the Beatles. But when he left not long after to work with Sounds Incorporated, we promoted Bob Young to tour manager. Before us he had worked with quite a few different bands like Amen Corner and the Herd. He was on the verge of going to work for Jethro Tull, who had offered him £10 a week, when Pat intervened at the last minute and offered him an extra fiver on top to come and work for us instead. Being good at adding up, Bob gratefully accepted.

Bob knew about more things, though, than just how to

butter his bread. He was a few years older than me, Alan and Rick, and much more experienced in life on the road, and we used to have such a laugh together. Sometimes Rick and I would travel with him in the equipment van rather than drive with the others in the band car, which at that point was a big American Pontiac Parisienne. It was just nice to get a break from the others sometimes. We would roll a few joints and chill out together...

That was when we discovered that Bob was more than just a great tour manager, he was a pretty good musician, too. Prior to becoming a full-time roadie he had been in a group called the Attack, which was about to have a hit with a track called 'Hi Ho Silver Lining' – until the better-known Jeff Beck beat them to it with his version. Before that, Bob had run his own blues-and-folk club in Basingstoke, where he sang and played guitar, and wrote lyrics and poetry.

In the beginning, Bob tended to gravitate more towards Roy Lynes. He was more his age and they started coming up with their own little songs together, just for fun. Then Alan Lancaster started taking an interest in what they were up to and things got more serious, with the result that between them they came up with three of the songs we recorded for the *Spare Parts* album. Because Bob also played harmonica, once we started changing into more of a blues and boogie band we encouraged him to join us on stage for a couple of numbers each night, too.

Given that backdrop, it was inevitable, I suppose, that sooner or later I would also become interested in trying to write with Bob. We had started one or two things out on the road, like the original slowed-down country-flavoured version of 'Caroline'; the lyrics scrawled on a paper serviette in the dining-room of a hotel in Perranporth, Cornwall, in the summer of 1970. But the first time we got serious was when Bob came round to my place one day and we sat together in the kitchen with the guitars. Practically the first thing we came up with was 'In My Chair', which became a minor Top 30 hit for us later that year, and another mainstay of the new show. From there it was plain sailing all the way and we started coming up with some great stuff together. As a result, Bob soon became more to me than just a great tour manager; he became a close personal friend and artistic collaborator. We would work together on the road, write together off the road, then go on holiday together with our wives and kids.

People ask why I wrote more with Bob than with Rick or the others, and the honest answer is: because I seemed to come up with better stuff with Bob than I did when I wrote with anyone else. There is just something I find very comfortable about working with Bob. Maybe it's because he's *not* in the band that he comes at it from a very pure, open-minded angle. He's not afraid to go with the flow and try things. Alan could never write like that. Rick could, but he has his own thing going, which is coming from a very rock'n'roll angle. Whereas me and Bob would mess around with anything: blues, country, pop . . . Grabbing bits and pieces from all sorts of places and throwing them together like a stew.

Also, Bob was just a good guy to be around; solid as a rock. Unlike so many people in the music business, who think that selling records and making money somehow makes them more important than everybody else – when in reality, we're all still the same bloody idiots we ever were – when fame and success came along for us, Bob never changed one bit. Not one tiny bit. He didn't suddenly want to stop being the road manager and join the band; he didn't want his picture taken with us or to be interviewed by the press. He just kept his head down and got on with his job. We used to call him Bob Young: Friend of the People. Because Bob knew and got on with everybody, and everybody knew and got on with Bob.

Back in 1970, however, the main item on the agenda was to get the band back into the spotlight again. We had found a new agent; someone much more in sympathy with what we were trying to do and more willing to get us spots on all the right tours. His name was Neil Warnock and, though I'm pleased to say he is still our agent today, he couldn't have had a worse introduction to the band. Pat had booked us into the upstairs room at Burton's the tailor's – one of those odd gigs Pat would unearth for us sometimes. There was this really steep staircase leading from the street to the club, and as Neil was going up them he bumped into the guy that had booked the gig coming the other way. Neil asked him how it was going and the guy just scowled: 'That's the worst fucking band I've ever heard!' Thankfully, Neil has never been the kind to be deterred by the opinions of others, and he obviously saw something in us that night that our friend the promoter hadn't. As a result, Neil was to become one of our staunchest allies, and outside the band is now the person I have known longest in the business. The fact that he only told me that story recently shows you just what a gentleman he is.

For the next year or so we played every pub, club, US airbase and rundown scout hut that would let us through the doors. Pye, who no longer knew what to do with us but decided to take one last punt off the back of the semi-success of the 'Dustpipe' single, even let us release another couple of albums – *Ma Kelly's Greasy Spoon* (a title suggested by Bob), which came out in September 1970, and *Dog of Two Head*, the following year. For the record, *Dog of Two Head* was a title suggested by a roadie of ours named Paul Lodge – aka Slug. Slug had nicknamed the equipment van the Dog of Two Head – no 's' on the end. Don't ask me why, that was just the way Slug said it. We had probably just smoked a joint and thought it would be hilarious to call the album that, too. Ha, yeah . . .

Despite picking up some encouraging reviews in the music press, neither album did well enough to get into the Top 40; once again cracks in the façade began to appear. Roy Lynes bailed out. He had a new girlfriend he missed back in London, and he felt that his keyboards were contributing less and less to the new sound we were developing, so he quite simply jumped ship when he got off the train one day – I think we had stopped off in Stoke, on our way to a gig up north – and never got back on again.

We soldiered on as a four-piece for a while and managed to have another minor hit single in November 1970 when 'In My Chair' clawed its way to Number 21. We didn't know whether to feel pleased or not. On the one hand, it proved we hadn't slipped completely off the radar. On the other hand, we appeared to be going backwards again. Worse still, we were all skint. It wasn't so bad for Rick and John because they were still living at home with their parents. But I had a family to feed and a mortgage to pay and Jean was forced to find a full-time job in order to help make ends meet, as did Alan Lancaster's wife, Patricia. It was around then that the words 'shit' and 'creek' began to assume a certain prominence in my mind. Which is when we decided to go and see Colin Johnson.

There was a guy called Nigel Thomas, who already managed Leon Russell and Joe Cocker's former backing group the Grease Band, who had expressed an interest in taking us on. But that only lasted one gig: our first, fateful appearance at the Albert Hall, headlined by – you guessed it – Leon Russell and the Grease Band. We were low on the bill, halfway through our set, right in the middle of a deeply sensitive ballad written by Alan called 'Is It Really Me', when someone from the audience – possibly a critic – stood up and shouted: 'Fuck off! You're rubbish!' We brought the number hurriedly to a close and duly obliged. It was like an omen – a very bad omen – and the allure of working with Nigel quickly wore off.

Right from the word go, we felt much more at home with Colin Johnson. Colin had quit NEMS by then and was running his own agency, Exclusive Artists, which looked after a number of top name acts like Amen Corner, Manfred Mann, Middle of the Road and Edison Lighthouse. Between us we were going to conquer the world. Or at the very least conquer the charts again. Which was the same thing to us back then.

The most important decision Colin made early on was to get us out of our contract with Pye. They were an old-fashioned, mainstream record company that liked working with acts that had hit singles. We wouldn't have minded having a few more hits as well – our final single for the label, in June 1971, a number Bob and I had written on tour in Ireland called 'Tune to the Music', had been another titanic flop – but we now saw ourselves as primarily an album-oriented band. Colin decided, therefore, that we needed a much more up-to-date, album-oriented label to help us get that message across.

After four dud albums and countless flop singles, I don't think he had to fight Pye very hard to get us out of our deal with them. They still insisted on getting a small cut from the first handful of records we made without them, but that was standard practice. (What wasn't standard was the slavishly minute royalty rate we had been on with them!) Where Colin really scored, however, was in the label he took us to next: a new, more 'progressive' subsidiary of the giant Philips record company, called Vertigo, which we eventually signed to in the summer of 1972.

Vertigo already had such acts as Black Sabbath, Uriah Heep and Gentle Giant, so it felt different from Pye straight away. These people appeared to actually get it. Brian Sheppard was the A&R (artists and repertoire) guy at Vertigo who actually signed us. A former roadie with the group Magna Carta, Brian was someone else who was to become a tremendous driving force behind the scenes for us over the next ten years.

At the same time as negotiating our new deal, Colin had formed his own management company, Acorn Artists. He then merged Acorn with Gaff Masters, run by Rod Stewart's powerful managers, Billy Gaff and Robert Masters. Operating out of Wardour Street, and now renamed simply Gaff Management, Colin had hooked up with an old pal of his named David Oddie, who was a director of the newly merged company, and so his position – and therefore ours – was extremely strong there.

Having spent the summer playing at outdoor festivals – including a well-reviewed appearance halfway down the bill at that year's Reading Festival – we recorded our first album for Vertigo in London during September and October 1972. Afraid of what an outside producer might try to make us do to our new but by now well-honed sound, Colin talked us into the idea of trying to produce ourselves, recording more or less live in the studio with the aid of an enthusiastic young engineer, Damon Lyon-Shaw. Brave or stupid, I don't know, but it appeared to work, and none of us had any doubts as we completed it that this would be our best album yet.

The first track the new record company jumped on was a song I had worked up from a poem Bob had written called 'Paper Plane'. (The '*three grand Deutche car*' in one of the verses refers to the new Mercedes 600 the band was now travelling in.) Vertigo liked 'Paper Plane' so much we agreed to let them make it the first single – then looked on astonished as over the next few weeks it soared its way into the Top 10! It was January 1973, and suddenly, for the first time in nearly five years, we were on Radio One and *Top of the Pops* again with a big hit single. It was hard to escape a certain feeling of déjà vu. The subsequent album, *Piledriver*, also went Top 5, the first Quo album ever to do so, spending a total of thirty-seven weeks in the UK charts that year. We had finally turned the corner. It wasn't until we'd done it that I realized how deeply I had doubted we'd be able to. But we had and now here we were, back in the charts again and bigger than ever. It was unreal.

By now we had dropped the 'The' from our name – too sixties, we decided; you didn't hear of The Deep Purple or The Led Zeppelin – and become simply Status Quo. Ultimately, I don't think it really matters what you call a group. Was there ever a sillier name than the Beatles? We even had a very brief period in 1971 as S. Quo – because T. Rex had just become all the rage and we thought it might work for us too. It didn't and that's when we settled on just plain Status Quo.

Despite our newfound success, we desperately wanted to be taken seriously as an album-oriented band. In the early seventies, a real album-oriented band only released one single per album. Therefore, that's what we did too, and no immediate follow-up to 'Paper Plane' was scheduled. This was in the days of two vinyl albums a year, with each album rarely containing more than ten tracks and often as few as seven or eight (less if you were Yes), and it was seen as a 'sell-out' to release more than one track per album as a single. Cobblers, really, as Elton John proved. But somehow it became the unwritten rule and for a long time we all did it: us, Queen, Rod Stewart, the Stones ... Led Zeppelin declined to release any singles at all from their albums!

Because of that it was over six months before the next Quo single appeared, and when it did I worried that it would be like starting again. But the next single was 'Caroline' and once again we looked on in relieved disbelief as it flew like a dart straight for the bull's-eye of the Top 10! Far removed from the much slower, strait-laced country tune Bob and I had originally conceived, by 1973 the band had breathed new life into it and turned it into a real rocker. As a result, 'Caroline' is now regarded as one of the most popular songs we've ever recorded. We still open the show with it to this day.

Best of all, this time the album that it presaged, *Hello!*, actually went to Number 1. What a moment that is, to be told your new album has gone to Number 1! That was the first time I felt deep down inside that we really had cracked it now. Sure enough, the next five years saw us go from strength to strength. Suddenly it was like we could do no wrong, and between 'Caroline' in 1973, and 'Rockin' All Over the World' in 1977, we released ten singles, all of which went Top 5, including our first Number 1, 'Down Down', in January 1975 (replacing 'Lonely This Christmas' by Mud). In the same period, we also released six studio albums and one live album, all of which had also gone Top 5, with three of them getting to Number 1. It was the kind of success story we had always dreamed of but had never really believed would actually come true. Now, against the odds, it all appeared to be happening.

Because of our image as a no-frills rock band, all our hits back then were perceived the same way: unpretentious rock'n'roll for the long-haired, denim-clad masses. Fair comment, and I'm more than happy to stand by that. Personally, however, I always saw records like 'Down Down' or 'Whatever You Want' as essentially pop songs done in the rock mode. Catchy tunes done four-to-the-bar. I certainly never made any distinctions in my own mind when I was writing with Bob over whether they were pop or rock or country or whatever. They were just the songs we were coming up with that day.

Of course the music papers were always fond of pointing out that there didn't appear to be much 'meaning' to our lyrics, and at the time I would have agreed with them. Putting 'meaning' into the lyrics was never top of my agenda when it came to writing a song. The tune was everything, and the words would be written to fit in with it, not the other way around. It wasn't until some years later I realized, in fact, that all our lyrics are about something. I look at them now and think, this one was about my wife and that one was about that time with the band ... They were all written about people I knew or things that had happened to me, however obliquely it might have appeared. For instance, in 'Down Down', the bit that goes: '*I want all the world to see / To see you're laughing, that you're laughing at me / I can take it all from you / Again, again, again ...*' I realize now that that line was a dual-purpose message from me to both my wife and the press at the time.

Initially, though, it was the *sound* of the words I was interested in and how they complimented the melody. With 'Down Down', we'd written the chord sequence, the melody was there, but I couldn't come up with anything lyrically for the chorus that sounded right. I wanted something like 'Deborah' by T. Rex, which has a very staccato chorus where Bolan deliberately stutters the first 'deb' syllable. We tried all sorts of ways of doing it until finally I just sang the word 'down' repeatedly, which fitted perfectly.

I said to Bob: 'But it doesn't make any sense with what's gone before.' Bob just shrugged and said: 'No, I suppose not.' It just sounded good, so we used it. I've now lost count of the times people have written to me, or sidled up to me at some party, to tell me they know what 'Down Down' really means. I always assure them that it has nothing to do with 'going down' – in any sense – but of course they never believe me. And that's the secret of Pink Floyd – people put their own meanings into things, especially music, whether it's classical or pop.

It's funny how it works. When I listen now to 'Paper Plane', for instance, it sounds horrendously out of tune to me. But it doesn't matter. As punk rock later proved, when it comes to making a hit, being in or out of tune is almost beside the point. It's whether the sound you're making has that X factor that turns people on and makes them want to listen to it again and again. Was the theme to TV's *Doctor Who* in tune? I don't know and I don't care. I just know that when I was a teenager it was the most wonderfully eerie piece of music I'd ever heard.

After several more 'meaningless' hits, the critics then took to accusing us of having a magic formula which allowed us to simply recycle the same old stuff over and over, giving birth to the heads-down-three-chord-mindless-boogie jibes that still haunt us to this day. The answer to which is – I wish we had! Because if we had we definitely wouldn't have changed it just to suit some critic. But all that kind of talk is rubbish. You can't just go to the cupboard and grab a hit; we've had enough flops along the way to know that better than anybody.

Besides, Bob and I didn't want to be boxed in. We were aware that we now had a Quo signature sound and we were proud of it. We had reached that exalted stage where the minute one of our records came on the radio you knew immediately who it was; the same as with all the best bands, from the Stones to U2. But that didn't mean we wanted to keep repeating ourselves. Bob and I knew we were always looking for the next hit but we tried not to make it too conscious an effort on our part. We always knew when we'd found one but we would wait for the rest of the group to jump on it first. It would usually be obvious, especially in the days of just one single per album; that made things very simple. Once things moved on, however, and we were now releasing two or three singles per album, instead of saying, well, that's obviously the one, it was now, well, that one could be good, too, or maybe that one would be better first. Too much choice made things harder, in that sense.

Apart from our sound, the other defining characteristic from those days that has stayed with us over the years was our so-called new look. Which is ironic, as what we were actually trying to do was get away from having any sort of image at all. The first time I became aware of how we were now perceived was when I was interviewed by one of the teeny mags just after 'Paper Plane' was a hit. The girl said, 'I love the new image,' and I was genuinely taken aback. The point was, we didn't have an image any more. We just wore jeans and T-shirts like everybody else.

Then it started coming up in all our interviews and so I decided to play along. They would ask how we came up with our 'new image' and I would act all coy, like 'Ah, well, that's a long story . . .' Like we had been through some altered state of consciousness and come out the other side. Or something. The music press lapped it up, and that's when the whole 'denim army' image really began to build. It was great, because if you've got to have an image, what better or easier one to have than ours? It's completely fashion-proof. Even today, it doesn't matter where we perform in the world, or on what sort of occasion, by now everybody knows what we're going to look like when we walk out there.

There are other advantages, too. I remember meeting Gary Glitter in Harrods once, just as he and Quo were having their first big hits. He came over and said: 'God, I wish I was you.' I asked why and he said: 'I'd save a fortune on clothes!'

The downside to all this sudden success was that we never stopped working. It makes me wince when I look back now at some of the date-sheets from those days. One moment we would be headlining our own forty-date British tour, the next we would be out on a three-week package tour of Australia and New Zealand with Slade. We were always either touring or recording. Mostly touring. With such a tight sched-ule, we didn't spend too long mucking about in the studio; we just went in and bashed it out, threw on a few overdubs, then went straight into rehearsals for the next tour. There were breaks here and there but I can't say I remember too much about them. It was never for more than a few weeks at a time, and just as you were starting to recover you would find yourself out on the road again.

You could say it paid off in terms of building the large fan-base we still have around the world today. Or you could say, simply, that we were being milked for all we were worth. Both points of view would be correct. We knew we were being flogged to death, but we didn't mind that. We wanted to milk it while it lasted, too. Even after several hits in a row, I never forgot what it was like to be a struggling band, and we all still looked on the success we had as incredibly finite. We genuinely believed we were working against the clock and had to make the most of it before our time was up, so we never said no to anything. Australia, Japan, Europe, Britain, America, and then again – and again and again. Why not? We were a big rock band now and that's what big rock bands did, right?

The seventies was also a big groupie period for us. That was one of the other things big rock bands did. It's important, though, to understand what I mean by the term 'groupie'. For example, I don't mean the sort of wide-eyed female fans we might have chatted up in the sixties. We still got those coming to the shows but we never saw them as groupies, *per se*. Your real common-or-garden groupie was not a particular fan of any one band. They were happy to sleep with us all. Like it was their job, which I suppose us and a lot of the other big bands back then saw it as, too. The good ones could be fun to have around for a few days. Good sex, good dope, and no big tearful goodbyes at the end. And they did things for you like wash your clothes and make sure you ate once in a while.

But the good ones were few and far between – and the best ones of all were in America, where we only toured infrequently – and most of the groupies we encountered regularly back then were just silly giggling girls you knew had already given blowjobs to half the crew in order to get into the dressing-room. As a result, I was never a great participator in that whole scene. I had my moments – on the basis of you don't know what it's like until you try it. But knowing they had already slept with half the other bands on the circuit took the novelty out of it, too. There was no sense of having to chase them, and therefore no real sense of reward once you got them up to your room, just a strange inevitability, like you were both merely going through the motions.

It got to the stage, in fact, where we all became totally blasé about groupies. By the mid-seventies we had girls literally jumping out of doorways and throwing themselves at our feet. But by then we were more likely to step over them and keep walking. One night in Germany someone set up a cine-projector in one of the hotel rooms and we were all in there watching porn films. This was in the days before twenty-four-hour TV, laptops and PlayStations, and you had to make your own entertainment out on the road. I remember we had a German groupie in there with us too, slithering around desperately trying to get our attention.

'Shag, Englishman?' she asked each one of us in turn. 'Jiggy-jiggy?' We were far more interested in what was happening on-screen, however; all sat there with our strides round our ankles having what we called a good 'polish'. Communal wanking was nothing to us back then. We had known each other since we were teenagers, sleeping and farting in the backs of vans and cheap guesthouses for years. There was very little left to hide. You could tell this German girl was shocked, though. 'Die Engländer sind *crazy*!' she announced with barely concealed contempt.

The upside of constantly being busy was that the money

really started to roll in. We weren't millionaires yet, but by 1973, with a couple of hit albums to our name, for a typical headline date in Britain we would get paid about £1,500. After deductions for things like hall hire, staffing, ticket printing, advertising, agency commissions etc., we might clear about a grand in cash. Over the next few years that figure would multiply considerably but even then, playing five and six nights a week, it soon added up. And of course you made more if it was a big place like the Empire Pool (now the Wembley Arena) in London, or some of the big arenas we were now playing in Germany and elsewhere in Europe. Best of all, it helped you sell truckloads of records – and T-shirts and tour programmes and denim patches and all sorts of other stuff with our logo on it. It all helped to sweeten the pot.

As a result, we were all reasonably well off by the mid-seventies, though I was the one making the lion's share by dint of the fact that it was me and Bob, in the main, who were coming up with the hits. While the band was happy to bask in the knock-on success they afforded our albums – on which some of their songs also appeared, thereby earning them substantial royalties too – it wasn't difficult to detect a certain level of envy among the others, particularly Alan. Sometimes, just to keep them happy, we even added their names to the credits on some of the songs Bob and I had written. Colin Johnson talked us into doing it. Otherwise, he said, it just rubbed their noses in it when the royalty cheques came in. We said, 'Yes, but *we* wrote the songs. We were the ones that took the time to sit there and try to come up with something – not them.' But we acquiesced in the end because Colin was right, it was the simplest way to keep the peace. It was either that or start recording songs the others had written that might not be as good but were done just to throw them a bone. 'Stuff that,' I said, 'We should only record the best stuff, whoever writes it. We'll go with the four-way credit.'

Unlike America, where the pursuit of money for its own sake is regarded as the height of sophistication, in Britain you're not supposed to love money; it's considered vulgar. But I'm not ashamed to admit that I love the stuff. Of course I do. Money gives you things you could never have had otherwise; not just possessions but opportunities, experiences, knowledge. Back in the seventies, though, I still laboured under the notion that you had to play those things down. I may have had more money than the rest of the band, but that didn't mean I had to draw their attention to it. Secretly, however, I loved the sound of the envelopes carrying the royalty cheques plopping on to the doormat. First it was for amounts like ten grand, then it was for thirty, then fifty, eighty, a hundred, a hundred and fifty . . .

Let's face it, who wouldn't like that, if they're being honest? And yes, I do think that suddenly having money changes you, to a degree, and not always for the better, judging by some of the hard cases I've known over the years. But it wasn't just us. Everyone around us seemed to change, too. Or rather, they didn't change; it was the way they looked at you now; the way they smiled all the time and tiptoed around you. They assumed that because we now had money everything else in our world must also be right. And of course it isn't. Just as with most people, things go wrong sometimes. Things go wrong quite a lot, in fact. You just happen to be richer than the other guy the same thing happened to. Or poorer. There's always somebody with more money than you: more houses, more cars, more wives, more everything. You have to know where to stop. Or at least, I do. And what I quickly realized was that I got into this to make money and have some fun. I didn't get into it to become the richest man in the world. I don't want or need to be the richest man in the world. I just want to be comfortable.

Because of that, the drive for success I had back then was never merely money-motivated. Revenge also played its part. Revenge on all those friends and relatives who had told me bluntly time and again how I had 'no chance with that rubbish' – meaning the band. Revenge on all the people in the biz that had written us off in the barren years between 'Matchstick Men' and 'Paper Plane'. Revenge on all the critics who laughed and took the piss. The more people put us down, the more determined I became to prove them all wrong. I used to read this stuff in the music papers and think, 'Oh, I see. So you think I'm a prick? Right, well, watch this,' and go off with Bob and write another Top 10 hit.

I always felt that we were struggling against the whole media machine in Britain; struggling to get airplay, fighting for recognition. Alan used to joke and say we were at the top of the tree in our own field, but you would never have known it from the way we were portrayed in the music press. I learned to laugh about it. The first time I read that I was too old to do this any more I was twenty-seven! It was good, too, in that it provoked some powerful responses – and a lot of hit records.

Most bands when they first become successful find themselves falling into the same old traps. Suddenly it's limos everywhere instead of the back of the van; the hotels go from B&Bs to five-star suites; expectation levels on all fronts are driven to fever pitch. That's when you need expert advice. Because you may be at the top of your tree musically, but that doesn't qualify you to know what to do with the money once it starts arriving in large quantities. Especially if you happen to be out of your tree at the time, which we usually were now. Nothing heavy yet, just speed and pot – mainly, pot.

Smiling on the surface I may have been, but after our false start in the sixties, I was painfully aware just how quickly things could change. There are always plenty of bumps in the road – ask Rod Stewart, David Bowie, Elton John and the rest. The trick is getting over them. Most artists don't make it. We did and that put us into a very small minority. But we hadn't made that leap yet back in the seventies, we were still riding the crest of a commercial wave. How long it would last, no one knew, least of all me. And so in a moment of brief clear-headedness I decided to set some of my newfound wealth aside, against that rainy day when our new album didn't go straight to Number 1.

I took the plunge and put all the spare cash I had into buying a new house. We had already moved out of Jean's mum's place by then, living first in a back room at my parents' house in Bromley, then, after the success of 'Matchstick Men', in a rented flat in Lordship Lane. Bob Young and his missus had a flat in the same building, directly below us. It was above the local Co-Op supermarket, the part of the building where they housed the morgue (cut-price funerals being a big part of the Co-Op's business back then). Not the jolliest spot, you might have thought, but we had our fun.

By the time things started taking off for us in the seventies, I'd been able to put a small deposit down on a mortgage for a three-bedroom place in Forest Hill; next door, coincidentally, to where one of my aunts lived. We got it for £10,000; more than I could really afford, but Jean had given birth, in January 1972, to another beautiful baby boy, who we named

Nicholas, and we really needed somewhere bigger. Now, three years on, I was able to go a step further and buy us an even more substantial property: a beautiful house situated on its own private estate in Purley, one of the loveliest, most cosmopolitan parts of Surrey. The same house, in fact, that I still live in today.

It was towards the end of 1974, the first year I started to see serious money. We had just had our second Number 1 album in a row with *Quo* and I was able to buy the new house outright. It was a beauty, too: eleven bedrooms; outdoor swimming-pool; all set in beautiful, spacious gardens. The asking price was £80,000 – which wouldn't even buy you a one-room bedsit in Purley now. But I eventually got them down to £50,000 by playing a waiting game. My offer was in cash and I knew that would be hard to resist for long. So it proved, and Jean and I moved in at the start of 1975.

Sitting in my enormous new garden, overlooking my new, heated swimming-pool, I discovered that counting money and measuring success were not necessarily the same things. My dreams had already come true when we were able to afford the three-bed semi in Forest Hill. Now I had to rethink the whole thing. Suddenly I was free of that web of mortgages, insurance, loans, etc., that most young married couples find themselves trapped in, but I was not exactly sure where that left me. Unlike Rick, who seemed happy to plough it into buying another new car, I didn't feel the need for *things* so much as my own private space.

As a result, I remain very comfortable where I am and have never seriously thought of moving. Of course it's gone up in value astronomically in the last thirty years, and I'm told it's now worth nearly £5 million. But I don't see five million quid when I'm sitting there at night watching TV with the missus and the kids; I just see my home. For some people in my position, that would not be enough. They would have bought and sold ten houses in that time and have a place worth £50 million by now. You see them on MTV in that show *Cribs*, where American stars you've never heard of show you around their houses with their specially built closets with 500 pairs of trainers in them. You think: why would you need 500 pairs of trainers? I've been wearing the same pair for years ...

Until I bought the house in Purley, my only luxury was my car: a brand new BMW. I have always loved BMWs. The first one I ever bought had a maximum continuous road speed of 110 m.p.h. – positively supersonic for those days! But so safe and reliable. I thought, this is the one for me. Later on in the seventies, I also had a Porsche and a Range Rover. I liked the Range Rover, it was a real novelty at first, but let's face it, you really don't need one to drive in London. As for the Porsche, that was very nice for a while, too, until the early eighties when Porsches suddenly became groovy. If there's one thing I can't stand it's being thought of as someone who gives a shit about being groovy, so I flogged it and went completely the other way, buying a smart new Golf Mark One; a very sensible choice of car. Then I thought, to hell with it, and went back to my faithful old BMW. Like Quo, they're totally fashion-proof.

I still drive one now. It's got nothing to do with them being flash or expensive, it's to do with them being super-comfortable, super-fast and super-reliable. When I was a kid, if you went two hours down the motorway at 60 m.p.h. you'd have to stop for an hour to let the engine cool down. Even in the early seventies, when we first started using rental cars on tours, they were notorious for breaking down if you drove them at 70 m.p.h. for more than three days running. It became my pet hate: I've broken down in so many cars I never want to break down again. Hence my trusty BMW, which promises never to do that to me.

But if I was reasonably sensible with my money, fame was a far more corrosive influence, and when we first became successful again I admit that I did turn into Jack the Lad for a while. I was already Jack the Lad on stage, but success seemed to exaggerate that side of my personality so that I now became that guy offstage, too. One of those mouthy young men with money you avoid in hotels and restaurants. A horrible thing to have to own up to here, but that's about the size of it. Besides, I couldn't let the world see how vulnerable I really was; how unsure I was at first of all the sudden changes now going on in my life. Because of the blokeish veneer of the band that Alan always insisted on anyway, it became like my protection; my hard outer shell concealing the soft, sensitive little tosspot inside.

Something like that anyway. Whatever it was, it's a pity, because I have met so many people since that have said how frightened they were of approaching me back then. I'm always dismayed to hear it because of course that wasn't the real me. But we had developed this gang aura and it rubbed off on all of us, especially when we were together, which was most of time. The only one of us who was really hard like that, though, was Alan. You didn't fuck with Alan; not if you knew what was good for you. Some people find that kind of uncompromising attitude appealing. I never have. I've been in plenty of fights, but that doesn't mean I liked it or ever wanted to do it again. Alan was different; he did.

Once I'd bought the house in Purley, I soon retreated from the seedy London scene. The whole thing just bored me. Plus, I was a married man – a rare, almost extinct species back then – and that came into it, too. Instead, for the next few years, whenever we weren't touring, I would become a virtual recluse, never leaving the house unless I absolutely had to. It became my sanctuary from all the madness of life in the band. It still is.

Once I'd calmed down again, one of the really odd things I discovered about money was how quickly you got used to having it. They say that when people who haven't been born into money suddenly become rich they have one of two reactions: either they want to go out and spend it on the flashest, most expensive stuff around, in order to demonstrate to the world that they really have made it; or they don't want to spend a penny, terrified that if they're not careful with their money they might go back to being poor again. Being a Gemini – the sign of the twins, which means I tend to see both sides of the argument, or that I'm a two-faced bastard, depending on your point of view – I suffered from both reactions. I wanted to spend it all *and* keep it! Meanwhile, Jean developed a taste for going to Harrods, so although we didn't flaunt it we soon built up quite a collection of expensive furniture and knick-knacks at the house. I was into it; I saw it as feathering the nest, and I do like my nests.

That said, we have never been as rich as some people assume we must be, for the simple reason that Quo never cracked the American market. Despite the success over there of 'Matchstick Men', we were a very different band in the seventies and though we always drew a good crowd to our shows, nothing else we ever did on record really seemed to catch on. Maybe if we had made it big in America I would have gone completely barmy, who knows? Because that would have meant very serious money indeed. You only have to watch an episode of *The Osbournes* to see what that kind of success did to Ozzy, so maybe I was lucky.

We went and toured the US a few times in the mid-seventies, after things took off for us everywhere else, and we have started going there again in the past few years. These days, however, we only go when we're invited and we're paid well. Back then we were trying to break into the charts and so a fortune was always spent on fruitless promotion, with the result that we always came back from America with less money than we'd started with.

It became apparent that if we really wanted to crack America we would have to devote all our time and energy to it, and I didn't fancy that. I looked at Slade, who had gone to the States for a couple of years, yet got nowhere. By the time they came home again everyone had forgotten about them and it was almost like starting again. When Quo was faced with the same choice my attitude was: to hell with that, we've got more than enough success on our plates everywhere else in the world, let's worry about America some other time. It seemed insane to me to think otherwise. I really did think: five years max, if we're lucky, and that will be our lot. Why waste that time losing money trying to chase our tails in America?

Nevertheless, there has been the occasional wistful moment over the years, I now confess, when I've regretted that decision not to pursue American stardom more ardently; brief moments of rueful reflection on what might have been. Like when I read recently that Bruce Springsteen grossed over $60 million for just ten shows on his last American tour! I doubt we've grossed that much from ticket-sales in the past ten years. But if I have any lingering regrets on the subject, they are swiftly dispelled once I remember what happened to groups like Slade, T. Rex, Mott the Hoople, Cockney Rebel, Roxy Music, Thin Lizzy, and dozens of other big rock acts from that era, none of whom were ever able to export to America the same level of success they enjoyed back home in Britain.

Meanwhile, the impact we were now having on the domestic scene was unmistakable. Not just with our growing number of fans but with other bands, too. I remember coming back from a tour in 1974 and tuning in to the weekly chart show on Radio One, to find out what had been going on while we'd been away. I turned on the radio and there was Mud with a Quo sound-alike song, Suzi Quatro with a Quo sound-alike song, and the Sweet with a Quo sound-alike song! Suddenly they were all doing exactly the same sort of rock-shuffle thing we'd been perfecting – and all having hits with it!

I wasn't sure if I liked it or disliked it, but it made the whole sound very mainstream, which opened up the audience even more for us, so all you could do was shrug. We felt there was a big difference between what groups like Suzi Quatro and Mud had to offer and what we as Status Quo now stood for, and that the audience knew what that was. They were singles bands doing what they were told to, just as we had once been. Now we were an established album band that played and wrote its own stuff – an area none of those bands had a foothold in. Compared to them, we were, to borrow a phrase, the real thing.

So were Slade, actually, who we toured with on a number of occasions in those years and became friends with. Slade were one of the best live bands I've ever seen, yet they became trapped on the same hit-making treadmill as Mud and Sweet. I remember talking to their singer, Noddy Holder, about it, telling him I thought they should concentrate more on albums, because Slade should have been capable of making some truly classic albums. But they were on a different path to us, with every single they put out going straight to Number 1. At one point they were banging them out at a rate of five or six a year.

I said to Noddy: 'You're gonna kill yourself. You're gonna run out of steam at some point and then what do you do?' He just smiled wearily. He knew the singles market was fickle, but by then it was simply too late to apply the brakes. Slade bassist and Noddy's songwriting partner Jim Lea was there, too, and I remember him dismissing the idea out of hand. Then I bumped into them both some years later and Noddy nudged Jimmy and said: 'Well, tell him he was right.' By then they'd started to lose their touch in the singles market and had nothing to fall back on. Once the hits were gone, they were gone, too. A shame because, boy, Slade was some band.

For Status Quo, the peak of that period was probably the *Rockin' All Over the World* single and album, released within a few weeks of each other towards the end of 1977. In March that year, we had released a double live album – imaginatively titled *Status Quo Live!* – recorded in Scotland a few months before at the Glasgow Apollo. What was seen initially as a convenient stopgap in effect rounded up the early part of our career on Vertigo, as though clearing the way for something new. Even the single we recorded to promote it – a rocked-up version of Hank Snow's 1952 country hit 'Wild Side of Life' – seemed to be pointing in a fresh direction for us. Produced for us by Deep Purple bassist Roger Glover, it was the first time we'd used an outside producer since John Schroeder – not for any particular reason, Roger was just a mate who happened to show an interest. He had begun producing after leaving Purple and so we thought it might be interesting to see what he could do with our sound. Another big hit for us, it was also the first inadvertent step, perhaps, to where we ended up going in the eighties, which was much more into the mainstream again. It still sounded like Quo but we were starting to loosen the reins a little and by the time the *Rockin' All Over the World* album finally came out it was seen by both us and our longstanding fans as something of a departure.

This turned out to be a double-edged sword. We had another big hit on our hands with the 'Rockin' All Over the World' single, which sold half a million copies in the UK within the first few weeks of release and reached the Top 10 in dozens of other countries. As an album, *Rockin' All Over the World* was an equally big hit, and the eight-month world tour that accompanied it was our largest and most successful yet. Paradoxically, however, it was also the album that provoked the most complaints we've ever had – not merely from the critics this time, but from actual fans. In a nutshell, they accused us of 'going soft'. But we weren't thinking 'hard' or 'soft' when we were making the album, we were simply thinking 'good' or 'bad'. Up until then, that had always been enough.

The main gripe seemed to be with the production, which was ironic as, to me, the production on *Rockin' All Over the World* is immaculate – or as immaculate as you could get using seventies' technology. For certain fans, though, that was the problem: it was *too* immaculate. So far, we had produced all our albums on Vertigo ourselves and only knew one way to make them – flat out, as live. Now, after our positive experience with Roger Glover, we decided we needed someone who could do more than that. We found him in a guy named Pip Williams, who Colin Johnson recommended.

I liked Pip straight away. He wasn't groovy-looking, he just knew what he was doing and I respected that. He was a talented multi-instrumentalist, composer and arranger in his own right who had once been in an outfit called Big John's Rock'n'roll Circus, fronted by vocalist 'Big' John Goodison, who Pip wrote a great many songs with, including a couple that had ended up on some of the early Quo albums. We thought he would be a good choice in terms of knowing what we were essentially all about, but at the same time having enough talent to try and add a bit more depth and colour to what we did. It was the era of big expensive hi-fi systems and of course we all had them in our homes now: thousands of pounds worth of gear that made Pink Floyd sound like they really were going to the moon. We desperately wanted our own records to sound great on them, too. Thanks to Pip, *Rockin' All Over the World* was the first time we ever got close to that.

Despite being one of our most famous hits, I have to admit that I wasn't that taken with the song 'Rockin' All Over the World' originally, other than the title, which I thought was great. Rick had discovered it on some obscure John Fogerty album, and when he played it to us I thought it was all right, nothing special. But it was towards the end of the recording sessions and we still needed another track, and so we decided to give it a go. It was actually the last thing we recorded for the album.

What can I say? I was wrong. And even though we didn't write it, I hope John Fogerty will forgive me when I say we really did make 'Rockin' All Over the World' our own. So much so it's now arguably the best-known Quo song of all. Like Queen's 'We Will Rock You', it's become an all-purpose anthem for every major sports event going. Someone told me, for instance, that 'Rockin' All Over the World' was the first record they played through the stadium PA after the final whistle blew when England beat Australia in the Rugby World Cup final in 2003. Apparently someone on BBC's Radio Five Live station joked that the victorious England rugby team would be joining Status Quo on their forthcoming British tour, in order to show off the World Cup to as many people around the country as possible. I had to chuckle. I thought, if only they knew how much I disliked sports . . .

The other thing I always remember when I think of 'Rockin' All Over the World' is the video we recorded for it. It was the very early days of video so there was nothing flash going on, no wind in the hair and running down corridors, nor any gorgeous babes in miniskirts writhing around (more's the pity). Just us standing there belting out the number. All perfectly normal except for one thing – a life-size marionette of Alan Lancaster on bass!

He never forgave us for that but we had no option. Alan had recently separated from his wife and begun a new relationship with someone he'd met in Australia on our last tour there. Consequently, he now found himself living in Australia full-time. It isn't exactly handy having your bass player thousands of miles away but we just had to get on with it. When we rang to ask him to come back to shoot the 'Rockin' All Over the World' video, though, he simply refused to leave. Admittedly, it was a fairly last-minute thing the record company had suggested once they got wind of just how big a hit it was going to be, but that should have acted as an even greater spur for Alan to come back as quick as he could. Typically, though, the more we pleaded, the more he dug in – to the point of forbidding us to shoot the video without him! By then, however, the single was already on the radio every day and we couldn't wait any longer. It was now or never. We chose now. Then fretted over what Alan was going to do to us once he found out . . .

It was Colin's bright idea to come up with a life-size puppet of Alan. It was Colin who actually operated it, too, from the roof of the studio. It was weird, actually. It worked so well we kept forgetting while we were bopping around that we actually had a puppet on stage with us, as opposed to the real thing. During breaks the puppet was left slumped at a table and when we'd get back it would look just like Alan sitting there. Even funnier, though, was the fact that not many people noticed it was a puppet when they first saw the video. To be fair, the cameras were mostly on me and Rick, and it was only after the press picked up on it that people started looking out for it in the video. Alan was convinced we were taking the piss, but we really weren't. We would all have preferred it if he had been there for the video, but he chose not to be and so we did the next best thing. Ironically, that clip became one of our most often shown on TV around the world as we set off on a five-month, 100-date tour of Britain and Europe, followed by an equally lengthy trek around the Far East, New Zealand and Australia. Alan would always get up and walk out whenever it came on the telly.

But if 'Rockin' All Over the World' signalled our giddy seventies peak, the next few months would see the start of a steep decline in my personal fortunes that would take me to hell and back over the next ten years – beginning with the break-up of my marriage to Jean.

I had spent a few weeks at home here and there during

the Rockin' All Over the World tour. After it finally ended in Australia in the summer of 1978, there was another short break and then we were straight back in the studio to record the next album. Apart from short breaks, by the time I got home again that Christmas I had effectively been away from Jean and the kids for over a year. Jean was eight months pregnant and very unhappy, and I didn't know what to do about it except maybe go away again. And I'd had enough of being away. I badly needed to be at home; to have a rest, regroup, get my act together. Fat chance.

The next few months were pretty dire, and Jean and I eventually came to our senses and agreed to separate – that is to say, she walked out on me – in 1979, just a few months after the birth of our third son, Kieran, in January. Our marriage appeared to have run aground for all the usual rock'n'roll reasons. We were away so much of the time that all the family relationships in the band seemed to suffer, with the result that all four of us would go through painful divorces over the next few years. But I believe now that there were deeper, underlying reasons why my own marriage broke down. Jean and I had been sixteen when we met; eighteen when we married. Now, ten years and three children later, we had grown up and turned into different people. We no longer related in the same way, to the point where I was almost willing her to end it.

Why? Guilt, mainly, I suppose. When we'd first met, I'd had all these preconceived ideas about what making it in life meant. My definition of success was being married, owning a modest semi-detached house and having 2.2 children. Exactly as my own parents had done. The trouble was, I'd never stopped to ask whether that was what Jean wanted too. Then suddenly I'd achieved my little dream and it was like, Oh ...

now what do we do? That's when the marriage started to seriously go downhill. Because now neither of us knew what we really wanted out of it. Until eventually Jean came to her own conclusions and walked out, taking the children with her. I came home one day and she announced that she had bought her own house, and that she and the kids would be going to live there. I suppose I was fortunate. Most people just get a note.

I was on her side, though. I wanted her to leave too. Truth to tell, it was a relief. But I didn't know how to admit that to myself yet. Despite not going to church regularly for years, I was still, at root, a Catholic, and a failed marriage is about as dismal a prospect as it gets, from that perspective. I felt I deserved to be punished. Not just for the infidelities, both physical and mental, but because I had dragged Jean into my little dream without bothering to check if that was all right by her. I just went ahead and did it, putting pressure on her to marry me practically from the day we met.

It wasn't the first time Jean had walked out on me, but so far she had always come back once the thunder had subsided. This time though, we both knew it was final. I felt it keenly within. Watching her walk down the drive and put the children into the car nearly made me crack. I had never felt so ripped apart inside before. On another level, once they had gone and I was left alone with my thoughts, I tried to be philosophical about it. I knew I would miss the children but I consoled myself with the thought that they were moving to a house only two minutes' drive away. Jean was keen for us to stay friends, she'd said, and so there would be no hassle over access or anything ghastly like that.

Sure enough, the new arrangement worked quite well. Being away on tour so much, I was already used to the idea of being periodically separated from my family, so I quickly adjusted, and so did they. We tried to make it an adventure for the kids – having two homes to go to! They didn't entirely go for it, but they were smart kids and I think we all saw it as the only way forward, no matter how painful. We all knew it was for the best and that we just had to get on with it.

By then my mother had also separated from my father, and I had invited her to move in with me. Originally I was supposed to be employing her as a live-in housekeeper, but of course she quickly became more than that: a real force to be reckoned with. Having her there helped enormously, in terms of maintaining some sense of normality in my life, and especially, of course, for when the children came over. To my dismay, however, I discovered that my mother had become a religious zealot. She had always been a devout Catholic but this was something else. She had been living in America for the past couple of years with her sister, who was a total religious fanatic, and when she came back my mother had gone the same way. Not only that, but she had now become vehemently anti-Italian. Suddenly, Italians were the scum of the earth. It was around then that she confided in me how she had never actually slept with my father and that I had been born – 'like baby Jesus' – by immaculate conception. I didn't actually mind that idea so much as the fact that it made having a child the normal way sound dirty, and I did start to wonder if she wasn't a little mad. By that point, however, I was starting to feel a little mad myself and in no position to judge.

I was also about to become a tax exile. Such was the lamentable state of affairs in Britain in the late seventies, *vis-à-vis* what was laughingly called the Wealth Tax, that becoming tax exiles – that is to say, spending a year out of the country in order to avoid paying the exorbitant rate of tax Her Majesty's Inland Revenue was then demanding off people like us (as much as 90 per cent, at one point!) – was the only way to keep hold of most of our hard-earned cash. I have no objection to a proportion of my earnings going towards paying taxes, the same as everybody else who enjoys the benefits of living in this country, but I do object to being asked to hand over all of it, or near as damn it. It was positively communistic; it made the whole concept of working hard pointless. Bollocks to that, we said. As did almost every other major British rock star, at that point.

I decided to go to Ireland. Some of the early sessions for *Rockin' All Over the World* had taken place in Dublin and I'd really enjoyed it there. Also, I didn't like having to say goodbye to my kids all over again and Ireland was close enough for them to come over for regular holidays. I was still allowed into the country for sixty days, too, so it wasn't such a trauma.

It was strange at first, though, not having either Jean or the band around. Alan was already living more or less permanently in Australia anyway, while Rick was now basing himself out in Germany, where his wife's family lived, and John had set up home on the Isle of Man. For reasons I will get to a little later, Bob Young and I had also started to fall out by then, which served to make me feel even more isolated. Then I found myself hanging out with a guy called Bernard Frost and the pieces slowly started to fall into place again. Bernie was someone I had been introduced to some years before by John Coghlan. He was working as a truck driver when we met but, as I discovered, he was also a good singer who had a certain flare for songwriting, too. With my relationship with Bob now more distant in every sense, Bernie was handily poised to fill the gap and we would become regular songwriting partners for the next few years.

For a while we lived at Dromoland Castle, a very plush hotel in County Clare. It was the autumn and out of season and there was absolutely nothing to do except get stoned and write songs. The only exciting thing that happened was when Burt Lancaster came to stay one weekend, accompanied by two women. Egged on by me, Bernie went over to ask for his autograph, but when he came back and looked at what he'd got he realized Burt hadn't signed it at all, just printed the words BURT LANCASTER in capital letters. Grumpy bastard. I learnt something there, though, and whenever I've been asked to give an autograph since I've always tried to do it with a smile on my face. Otherwise, why bother, Burt?

Dromoland Castle was like the wilderness to a city boy like me. Twelve hundred acres of beautiful, green nothing; just the animals and the woodland and the hills and the streams – and us. Bernie and I used to take the acoustic guitars out into the fields and serenade the cows. I discovered that if you go near a herd of cows they will usually disperse. But if you stand there singing and playing and keeping them entertained you'll soon have about forty or fifty of them gathered round you, going 'Mmmmm . . .'

As a result, by the time the band reconvened at Dublin's Windmill Studios, in January 1980, Bernie and I already had a bunch of great new songs waiting to be recorded and it was a very relaxed, creative time for me. We were staying in the Jury Hotel and on the ground floor there was a little bar called the Coffee Dock. It was open virtually around the clock and every musician in Dublin used to hang out there. Whatever time of day or night it was, Bernie and I would always order 'breakfast', which would be beans on toast with mushrooms and fried onions – and a pint of Guinness. We'd sit there eating and drinking and working on lyrics together. Then we'd go to the studio and put them straight down on tape.

Things were looking up for me in other respects, too. For it was while I was living in Ireland that I got involved with a wonderful Irish girl named Elizabeth Gernon. I'd met Elizabeth at a show we'd done at Dublin Stadium the previous summer, not long after Jean had left me. Elizabeth was working for her brother-in-law, Pat Egan, a lovely fella who was one of the promoters. Her job was to look after the band and make sure everything backstage went smoothly. She did a fantastic job, too. There had been some last-minute cock-up which threatened to wreck the show. Liz got hold of the guys who had been the cause of the problem and screamed at them until they were bawling like babies. Then she kicked their arses and told them to get back out there and fix it – pronto! Men are always much more scared of women than they are of other men, and it was comical seeing these large, hairy roadies scurrying off quickly to do what they were told. I thought she was magnificent.

I whispered to the rest of the lads, 'She's great, we should try and get her to work for us.' They agreed, but nobody really made a move and so in the end I just asked her straight out: 'How would you like to come and work for us?' She looked at me and smiled, and said: 'No, thank you.' Wow, I thought, class! Most people in the biz would have jumped at the chance to work for a major act like Quo. I was intrigued.

Liz wouldn't take a full-time job but when I first arrived in Dublin, in 1979, she offered to help me get settled. She was great, sorting hotels out for me and arranging transport, that sort of thing. We also went out for dinner a couple of times and that's when it started. By the time I was ready to leave Ireland, Liz was not only working for me almost full-time, she was sharing my bed. Before I knew it I had fallen for her; my first serious affair since Jean. The combination of that and my new songwriting partnership with Bernie made it a very fresh and exciting time for me. It wasn't until I began seeing Liz that I realized how lonely I had been until then; how much I preferred being in a long-term, steady relationship. Even though we never actually set up home together, I had someone there for me again now, and it felt good. Very good.

Unfortunately, however, it was also in Dublin that I started to get seriously into cocaine. Once that happened, everything else – including Liz and the band – would have to come second, and stay that way for a long time to come.

Maybe for ever . . .

THREE

It was almost five years exactly between the success of 'Matchstick Men' and the arrival in the Top 10 of 'Paper Plane', in January 1973. A long time in pop terms, and a lot of water under the bridge, in terms of all the failed singles and flop albums we'd had in between. There were moments, I now admit, when even I started to wonder whether we would ever manage to claw our way back to the top again. But I never seriously lost faith in the band: Quo was still the best thing that had ever happened to me, whether we made it again or not.

The main thing was we had now taken control of the band again. By 1972, when we finally left Pye and signed with Vertigo, we not only had a new sound, we had a new record deal, a new manager in Colin Johnson, even a new keyboard player, Andy Bown, formerly of the Herd, who came in after Roy Lynes left.

'Paper Plane' had been written by Francis with our tour manager Bob Young, a wonderful guy with many hidden talents who also played harmonica on stage with us on a couple of numbers each night. Francis and Bob really had a good thing going as a songwriting team, and 'Paper Plane' became just the first of many hits they would pen for us. I didn't mind in the least. I have never been what you would call a prolific songwriter anyway. I just enjoy contributing here and there. Plus, Bob was just one of those guys we all got on really well with. I also did a bit of writing with him further down the line, when we worked together on Quo's 1979 hit, 'Living on an Island'. But it was always made pretty clear that Bob was Francis's partner.

We had a new image by now, too. Or rather, we were told we had a new image. We had no idea. We thought we'd left all that behind when we dumped the Carnaby Street gear. Apparently not, and our 'new look' – dirty jeans, faded T-shirts, and in Francis's case, an old waistcoat – was soon being dissected in all the music papers as though it was something we had gone into the laboratory and invented. You couldn't buy jeans that looked five years old in those days, you had to buy them brand new when they were still stiff and bright blue, and then wear them in for five years first. You had to pay your dues. We didn't have time for that. We had some old things of our own but we got most of our gear by stopping people in the street and asking to buy their old denims off them. The older and more beat-up-looking the better. They thought we were mad; we thought we were geniuses.

Once we had the gear, it definitely changed the way we performed, too. We stopped being showroom dummies from the Carnaby Street Cavern and developed a whole new, much more full-on attitude. To me, we looked like one of those horrible gangs of guys that turns up uninvited to your party and takes over the place. A bit menacing but at the same time very ordinary and down-to-earth. Very likeable, once you got to know them. By the time 'Paper Plane' was a hit, we looked as one, and though it wasn't intentional, it was a powerful image for a rock band to have.

That was when we developed that whole heads-down, legs-apart stance. We got it from simply copying the audience. It was the hippy era, and sitting down cross-legged on the floor at gigs was the norm. We used to pride ourselves on how quickly we could get everybody off the floor and on their feet, grooving around. In order to try to make some kind of connection, though, we found ourselves stooping ever lower on stage until we were virtually doing the splits, our heads almost touching our knees . . .

Same thing with headbanging. With so much long hair in the audience, it became the thing to stand there with your head bowed, as if in a trance, shaking your hair around. We saw this and started imitating it, then the rest of the audience started doing it back to us, and suddenly the whole head-banging phenomenon was born. Once we started racking up the hits and we began playing bigger and bigger places, the sight of thousands of hairy heads, all shaking in unison, became one of the trademarks of our show. Suddenly, wherever we played in the world, there they would be: the Quo army headbangers!

Apart from the new-found success of Quo, the other big development in my life in the early seventies was that I met the woman who was to become my first wife. Before I get into that, though, I should explain how, until then, I had been having a not-so-secret affair with an older married woman. That makes it sound seedy, but it was never that. This involved someone very special indeed, who not only helped heal the sexual wounds inflicted by my traumatically unrequited love for Jean Harrison, but introduced me to a world I had never known existed before.

Her name was Mary. It wasn't really, but for the sake of propriety that's what I will call her here. Mary was twenty-eight when I met her; I was eighteen. Her husband was a successful businessman and I think he had his bits on the side too: it was all very civilized. They belonged to that smart Surrey golf club set. It was all lawyers and doctors and entrepreneurs. Given that background, Mary was very much a woman of the world to me. It was funny because the film *The Graduate* came out when we were first together and I couldn't help but feel a bit like Dustin Hoffman's character, Benjamin.

Mary was definitely my Mrs Robinson. She wasn't middle-aged yet, but she might as well have been because to me she was 'older' in every sense, and the things she taught me couldn't be learned from any book. None I had read anyway. It wasn't just sex, it was everything. Mary not only restored my sexuality, she gave me an education. She was the first person to take me to Harrods, the first to invite me to proper dinner parties and involve me in social circles I would never have been accepted into otherwise.

Best of all, she was intelligent and great fun and always full of adventure. It was inspiring. Once we went and bought one of the new Polaroid cameras that had just come out: the ones that developed the pictures for you. She said, 'Come on, let's get the stockings and suspenders and the basque! We'll do a photo session...' I thought all my Christmases had come at once! It was my first foray into anything kinky and I loved it. She let me take all sorts of pictures of her, the sexier the better. Apart from anything else, it was such a laugh! We just had a fantastic time together whatever we did.

There was never any question of her leaving her husband or anything morbid like that. Mary loved me and I loved her but it was fun we were after; nothing more involved than that. We had to be reasonably discreet, though. Sometimes it was more like a *Carry On* film than anything with Anne Bancroft in it. We'd be in bed together at her house when we'd hear the crunch of her husband's car tyres on the gravel outside. Luckily, it was a long drive and I'd have just enough time to jump out of bed, get dressed and be sitting downstairs reading the paper when he walked in. Mary used to pass me off as her sort of odd-job boy, and he was so used to seeing me round the house he wouldn't bat an eye, just ask where she was. I would say she wasn't feeling well and had gone upstairs to lie down.

We were lovers, but even better than that, we were friends. We came from different backgrounds, but we liked the same things. She had a Jag which she let me drive sometimes when we went out together. Then when I wanted a Jag of my own – the aforementioned maroon monster – it was Mary who lent me the extra dough I needed to pay for it. I got it from one of the biggest car dealerships in Surrey. Mary knew one of the owners, and she had called him on the phone to ask him to give her friend a good price, and to make sure the car was in tip-top condition. It worked like a secret handshake, and by the time I drove it away they had been through it with a fine-tooth comb. In fact, it was in the workshop for so long I thought I'd never get my hands on it. I used to visit the mechanic there every day, leaning over his shoulder, asking him what he was doing now. I expect he liked that.

My relationship with Mary had endured throughout the ups and downs of Quo's on-off career in the late sixties. Now, in the early seventies, just as the band was about to be reborn, our affair ended suddenly.

The first crack in the relationship appeared when I started seeing another girl I'd fallen for, more my own age, named

Patty Beeden. This was in 1970. She was an eighteen-year-old blonde bombshell with her own Morris 111, and I was totally bowled over by her. We used to live around the corner from each other as kids, in fact, her mum and dad knew mine, but somehow we had never met. Then one day I was parked outside the shops in Woking in my new Mini Cooper S – which had now replaced the Jag – giving it the full pop star bit, when I suddenly saw this absolutely gorgeous bird get out of her car and start walking down the street towards me.

I loved Mary in my own way, but she had made it clear she was not planning on leaving her husband, and that meant my options were still open, if I wanted them to be. Until I clapped eyes on Patty, I never really had. I fancied her like mad, though, and no sooner had I introduced myself than we were going out on a date. I'll never forget it – I took her to a pub called the Bleak House! I was very nervous because I liked her. I always got nervous around girls I really liked. But we got on well together. Despite her glamorous model looks, I discovered that Patty was a very down-to-earth person, and we started having a little scene together. She started coming to some of the gigs, too, and I was always very proud to have her on my arm. She looked like a rock star's girlfriend was supposed to look – long blonde hair, miniskirt, thigh-high yellow boots – and I suppose I thought that made me look more like a rock star, too.

It all went wrong, though, when I decided to be honest with Patty and tell her about Mary. I did the same with Mary and told her about Patty. Unsurprisingly, neither of them took the news kindly. Mary was not the possessive type usually but she just hated it, I think, that I was seeing someone so much younger than her. Patty got the hump, too, and that's when I went back to Mary full-time.

It stayed that way for a few months, until fate took a hand in things and I met the woman I was eventually to marry. Her name was Marietta Boöker and, quite simply, she was the most beautiful girl I had ever seen. Until then, I think maybe Patty was secretly hoping that my affair with Mary would fizzle out and we'd get back together again. But then I met Marietta and the next thing I heard Patty had emigrated to Australia! I didn't know it then but that wasn't the last time I would hear from her, though it would be several years before we saw each other again.

In the meantime, I had become completely besotted with Marietta. We had met while Quo was on a two-week tour of Germany in November 1970. The band had just performed at a club in Göttingen, and after the gig Francis and I grabbed a couple of local girls hanging around backstage and persuaded them to take us to a nightclub. I hadn't decided which one I fancied, then I suddenly saw this blonde girl dancing on the floor and completely forgot about the girls we'd come with. I simply could not take my eyes off her. She was extremely beautiful: a wonderful figure, very elegant and slim, with gorgeous blonde hair, long, long legs and an unbelievably serene smile – moving around on the dance floor in a way that had me utterly hypnotized.

I turned to Francis and the first words out of my mouth were: 'I'm gonna marry her.' Admittedly, I was drunk, and that's the sort of thing drunken musicians are wont to say late at night when espying a female of a certain allure. But this time I actually meant it. I knew I did, even through the haze.

Later, when she walked past the table where we were sitting, I couldn't help myself; I stood up and touched her arm. She stopped walking and turned to look at me. 'Hello,' I said. She was German but everybody understands 'hello'. In perfect English, she replied, 'Oh, hello. Are you from England?' So cool! I smiled and asked her if she would like to join us for a drink, and to my delight she said she would, and we ended up getting quite drunk together. And that's how it began between me and Marietta.

She was a couple of years younger than me, studying languages at university, and she was brimming with confidence. I was very impressed. I loved the way she glided across the room like a swan; the way she tilted her head prettily when she talked. At the end of the night, when the club closed, she invited us all back to her place. Now I was really impressed, because by then the whole band and management were there, too, so it was quite a crowd that gathered back at her gaff that night. By the time we all staggered back to our hotel the following morning, I'd fallen completely under her spell. Look away at this point if you're squeamish, but it really was a case of love at first sight. From the moment we met, I knew there was no one else I wanted to be with – including my precious Mary.

It was confusing. I didn't feel any less for Mary; I just felt more for Marietta. Having to leave her behind in Germany was almost unbearable. But I bought her a little gift at the duty-free shop at the airport and sent it to her when I got back to London. After that she started writing to me and I began phoning her, running up huge bills out on the road. I missed her so much I invited her over to stay with me in England. I was still seeing Mary at this point because I didn't know if I would ever see Marietta again. But then she said she would come to England and that's when I knew I had to tell Mary about her.

I could have bullshitted and kept both of them dangling,

I suppose, but Mary had been so good to me, it was only fair she should know the truth. It was with a heavy heart, though, that I set out for her house that day. When I arrived she could tell by my face that something was up. I came straight to the point: we would have to stop seeing each other like this because I had met someone else. I even showed her a picture Marietta had sent me.

After the business with Patty, I think Mary must have known that sooner or later I would meet someone else. Instead of kicking up a fuss, this time she just sighed and said, 'Well, I can see why you have fallen for her – she's stunning!' She looked at the picture again and said, 'A woman like that, I don't mind. You've got to do it. Good luck.' What a great woman Mary was! What a great human being! I knew she wasn't happy about it, but she took it in her stride and we agreed to stay friends, which I'm pleased to say we did, and still are to this day.

Marietta got the boat over the channel to England. I went to meet her at the dock. It was only a ferry, but to my mind it looked like one of those huge white ocean liners you see pulling into port in those romantic old black-and-white movies, with everybody standing on the side waving their hankies and cheering. Suddenly, there she was! I couldn't believe it. She looked even more beautiful than I remembered! I held her tightly in my arms, hardly able to believe she was really here at last, until she begged me to stop because I was squeezing all the breath out of her. Then I got her to the car and drove us back to meet my parents. They were equally enchanted by her, as I knew they would be. She was so beautiful and had such good manners, how could they not be?

I slept on the sofa and Marietta had my room. Once I was

sure Mum and Dad were asleep, I would creep quietly up the stairs each night to join her, then creep quietly back down again and on to the sofa in time for when Mum got up to make breakfast. Of course they knew what was going on, but as long as they didn't have to have it thrust under their noses, so to speak, they were very cool about it all.

I told Marietta I was madly in love with her and that I wanted to marry her and she just laughed at me. But I kept on saying it until she stopped laughing and started to believe me. She said she loved me too and would think over my proposal. When the time came for her to go back to Germany I missed her horribly, but we stayed in touch, as usual, via letter and phone. Her letters used to melt me and I longed to see her again.

I got my wish when Marietta was able to talk her parents into returning the hospitality my family had shown her in England by inviting me over for a visit to Germany. It was coming up to Christmas, and when she wrote inviting me to stay with her family over the holidays, she didn't have to ask twice. The band wasn't working over Christmas, so I packed some things and a couple of weeks later caught a flight to Hanover.

Her father, Willie, came with her to the airport to meet me. Her mum, Elizabeth, and her sister, Astrid, who I later met at the house, were immediately welcoming and friendly. Willie was a different kettle of fish. Marietta had warned me that her father could be a bit cold and distant but not to take any notice. I had told her not to worry and that I could handle it. Then I met him.

Willie Boöker was a hard-looking, bull-nosed German businessman, replete with the hat and feather. He wasn't wearing lederhosen and carrying a Luger, but you get the picture. He had this bottom lip that protruded disapprovingly at everything, and he took one look at me and his face just fell. I was clearly the personification of all his worst nightmares rolled into one. My hair was down to my waist at that point, and I was dressed in my usual patched-up, second-hand denims. I tried shaking his hand and offering a warm hello, but he just looked me up and down and grunted. We got to the car. It was about an hour's drive to the village where they lived and you could have cut the air with a knife. Marietta sat in the back seat with me and did her best to keep the conversation going. But her dad just sat there and drove, not uttering a word.

Speaking now as a father myself, I can see where the old man was coming from. Willie owned his own large furniture-making business. He and his wife were upper-middle-class Germans who had worked hard to give Marietta a fabulous upbringing; sophisticated, educated, well-off. Now I had come along, this long-haired layabout so-called musician with not much to show for it yet, who had somehow stolen his poor, clearly misguided daughter's heart. Worse still, I was English! Could it have got any worse for the poor bloke?

Even I could see the difference between us. Marietta was really quite suave, very well-to-do, and I loved that about a woman – like Mary, she was class. She actually used to smoke a cigarette through a long holder, like Marlene Dietrich. It used to turn me on, especially when she spoke to me in her heavily accented English. If Mary had seemed sophisticated, Marietta was positively exotic.

Needless to say, however, my visit did not turn out to be a resounding success. The house was a huge place on a hill overlooking this tiny, picturesque village. It was a typical German household – lots and lots of food, very comfortable.

I loved being with Marietta again, and her mum and sister were wonderful and always very kind. But her father scared the hell out of me. Marietta tried to sway him by talking about the group but he was decidedly unimpressed. Willie liked waltzes and German orchestras.

The trip did have its lighter moments, though. I had bought a suit to wear specially on Christmas Eve – which is the day they really celebrate in Germany. It was a blue crushed-velvet number I had got from Marks & Spencer's for £12. Even though I was all skin and bones in those days, it was still an incredibly tight fit. But I had a shower (it was bizarre, I thought, how the whole family seemed to have a shower every day), brushed my hair into semi-respectability and squeezed into the suit.

When I got downstairs the scene was set for a traditional German Christmas. One large room had been set aside for the occasion, in which Willie had put together his own nativity scene. There was a large artificial hillside erected in the middle of the room, with charming miniature trees and waterfalls, along with the stable and donkeys, and, tucked in his manger, little baby Jesus. Willie had built all this by himself, going out collecting real moss and holly from the woods. I had never seen anything like it, and despite my misgivings about the old man I was completely entranced.

You weren't allowed anywhere near the room while he was still putting it all together. The first time you got to see it was when you were taken in there on Christmas Eve. At seven o'clock on the dot, the old man called the rest of the family in, including me and Astrid's husband. Willie lit candles, put a tape of some Christmas carols on, and then we exchanged presents. It was all very nice but quite formal.

I'd only arrived the day before. Apart from Marietta, I

hardly knew anyone yet. So I was very nervous and definitely on my best behaviour. I reassured myself with the thought that, even though I couldn't understand a word anybody was saying, at least I was looking the part in my nice new blue suit. I was cool. Or at least I was until I dropped something and bent over to pick it up – and the back of my trousers split from crotch to arse! God, the embarrassment! I thought: I'm in a room full of people I don't know, in the middle of her father's beautifully crafted nativity scene, and I've completely disgraced myself! He never said so, but I'm fairly certain that's when Willie made up his mind that there was no way he was going to allow his daughter to throw herself away on the likes of me.

Apart from the sheer embarrassment of the situation, it was the only suit I had. What did I do now? The only other trousers I had with me were my patched-up jeans and I knew I couldn't wear those in Willie's nativity room. Thankfully, Marietta saw the funny side and took me upstairs and quickly sewed them back up for me – the German efficiency machine went into action! There wasn't much it could do for my red face, though.

I went back to London a few days later and immediately started working with the band again. But I missed Marietta more than ever and it wasn't long before I was begging her to come back to England. A couple of months later, during a break from college, she did come back and we continued where we'd left off, with me on the couch and her in the bed, waiting for me . . .

By now, Willie had realized I was a problem that wasn't going to go away. He had begged Marietta not to go back to London. He couldn't stand the thought of his immaculately brought-up daughter being swept off her feet by a scruffy urchin like me. When she refused to listen, he decided to take drastic action. He told her he was prepared to offer me a substantial amount of money to vanish from her life for ever. He would give her the money to give to me when she got to London. It was a few grand, I think. Big wonga back then.

Again she refused, bless her. But it hurt, knowing that her father, who she had always looked up to, would stoop so low. When she got to London and told me all this, naturally I was furious. I had already asked her to marry me again in Germany, and she'd promised to raise the subject with her mother and father after I'd gone. Willie had hit the roof, though, and absolutely forbidden it. We talked about it back in London and realized her father was never going to allow us to be together. It was the first real crisis of our relationship and neither of us knew what to do for the best.

On impulse, I said, 'What if I make a phone call to the local registry office in Woking, and we just go down there tomorrow and get married? How would that be?'

Amazingly, Marietta thought that would be a great idea. I suppose we both saw it as romantic and exciting. So I phoned up and made the arrangements. Then I told my parents, who agreed to act as witnesses. They were thrilled, because they adored Marietta. All my family and friends did. When we told them how Willie was trying to split us up – because I wasn't good enough for her – they understandably took offence and decided to stand by us, no matter what.

So a couple of days later we went and got married – just like that. I wore the same blue crushed-velvet suit that Marietta had sewn back together for me at Christmas. Well, it was either that or the jeans. Other than doing my hair, I didn't really put much more thought into it. But then I've never been one for thinking too far ahead. If you want to do it, just do it; that's always been my philosophy. I never worried about whether anybody else thought it was a good idea – if it felt right to me, that made it good in my book and I just went and did it.

We got married in the morning. Apart from my parents, the only other person there was my cousin Sue. My dad had to lend me the three quid I needed for the marriage certificate. I hadn't realized we'd have to pay for anything and hadn't brought any money with me. Afterwards, Sue went back to work and me and Marietta and my mum and dad drove to this lovely pub called the Row Barge. It was a beautiful sunny day and we sat out on the lawn with our lagers and wines.

There was no honeymoon. We couldn't really afford one, and I had to go away for a few days with the band again shortly afterwards. We just set up home in the spare bedroom at my parents' house. It was all very cosy and we were all quite happy there together. The only problem was when *Dad's Army* came on the telly. It was a comedy show based on the elderly English home guard in the Second World War, and my parents were worried that Marietta would take offence if she caught them watching it. Marietta didn't care. She used to find the show funny, too. But my parents still remembered the war and didn't realize their children had a completely different take on things. It was the same with all those war films you got on the telly back then: if Marietta came into the room and my dad was watching one of them, he would go red and quickly switch channels.

The only fly in the ointment was when it came to telling Marietta's family what we had done – in particular, Willie. I remember her phoning him when we got back from the pub that day. The conversation was in German, of course, so I don't know what she said exactly, but I could tell by the way her face turned white what the response was. As we expected, her mum was fine about it but her dad went absolutely berserk. He was so furious he said he would never speak to her again, and she was terribly upset afterwards.

After a few days he had calmed down, and he phoned back and said: 'Look, if you're married now, there's nothing I can do about it. But I'm not having it that my daughter was married in a registry office in England without any of her friends and family there. I want you to come back to Germany and have a proper wedding, arranged by me.'

I had no say in the matter. I could see how much it meant to Marietta and her family, so I reluctantly agreed to go along with it. I didn't know what reception to expect from Willie once we returned to Germany as man and wife, but hats off to him, he was great about it. The machine really went into action this time and we ended up having the greatest wedding anybody could dream of! I had literally never seen anything like it before. Thirty of my family and closest friends from England were flown in, some of whom had never even been abroad before, let alone been on an aeroplane. There were about eighty more guests from the German side, and between us we all had the most marvellous party!

Nobody else in the band came – German weddings not exactly being their scene – but Bob Young and his wife, Sue, were there, which was nice. As was my best mate Peter Gibb. Gibby and I had been friends since our days on the same snooker team at the Woking Working Men's Club. We had always had the same tastes in flash cars and birds, and we were both now getting to the stage where we were able to indulge our passions properly. I was doing well in Quo and he was climbing the ladder as a copywriter for the Saatchi & Saatchi advertising agency.

Again, I wore the blue suit. (That was two marriages and one Christmas I'd got out of it: you can't say I didn't get my money's worth.) The tradition was that when anyone from the village got married everyone turned out to celebrate. It all began the day before the wedding, when I had to go out on to the balcony of the house and address the entire village; to welcome them to the start of the celebrations and invite them down to the local watering hole for a drink. It was a tiny village so there were only a couple of hundred people there, but I was terribly nervous. I was used to playing to crowds ten times that size, but the speech had to be made in German. At first I baulked at the idea. 'I can't do that!' But Marietta sat me down and explained how it was the tradition, and that I *had* to do it.

She wrote it out for me phonetically and I learned it parrot-fashion. I had to have a couple of shots of Schnapps before I went out there, but somehow I made it through. It wasn't a very long speech. What I actually said was: '*Vielen Dank! Ich lade euch alle herzlich ein zu Groll!*' A polite version of 'Thank you all for coming, right, let's go and have a drink!' It must have come across like Arthur Mullard addressing the Queen, but they all clapped and cheered, and then I came down and led the way to the local tavern. After that, nothing else mattered. We were speaking the international language of alcohol.

The next day the wedding took place in the big local church. There was none of this stuff about the groom not seeing the bride until she comes down the aisle – we actually walked down the hill to the church together arm-in-arm, followed by the whole village carrying lanterns and bells. It was magical, like something out of a fairy story.

The vicar didn't speak a word of English and I was hoping all I'd have to say was the occasional 'Yah.' But no, it was trickier than that and I had to have Marietta translate for me first, then give the vicar my answers back in German. That provoked a few sniggers from the congregation but we didn't care, it was all part of the fun. Everything was done with such great spirit that day. As we walked out of the church again, the children of the village all held ribbons and ropes across the door: another tradition. You had to throw them some money, for luck. I gave them a handful of coins and they let us through . . .

That night there was a big party in our honour in this lovely place by a lake. It was a most fantastic evening. There were fireworks and a band playing traditional German wedding songs. Not my cup of tea usually, but it was all so gleeful everyone was up dancing and enjoying themselves all night.

The next day I helped Marietta pack up all the things she wanted to take with her initially, and we returned to London. We had agreed that she should continue her studies, so she applied and got a place at one of the London University colleges. But things didn't work out and a few months later she got a job teaching German in a school in Hersham. Again, it didn't last long. She was an extremely attractive young woman, not much older than some of the boys she was teaching, and she got nothing but hassle. It didn't exactly help that she insisted on going to work in the same short skirts and plunging necklines she wore when she went out with me. It was the fashion, but it acted like a red rag to a bull on the kids in her class. The boys couldn't stop drooling – there was a lot of dropping of pencils going on – and the girls thought she was a bitch. In the end she just quit.

The trouble was, with the band starting to get more work again I was away a lot and Marietta had nothing to do. She began to feel restless and lonely, missing her friends and family back in Germany. I felt for her but what could I do? When I got back that first time she had completely decked out our room. She'd put curtains up and arranged cushions and bits of furniture, and turned it into a proper little nest for us. By the time Quo's first album for Vertigo, *Piledriver*, went Top 5 at the start of 1973, however, she must have wondered what she'd let herself in for. The band was now getting global recognition and suddenly we were off to America, Australia, Japan ... plus at least two major tours of Britain and Europe each year. I was hardly home at all any more. Meanwhile, Marietta was never anywhere else. Far from her own family and friends, in different ways it made both of us feel very isolated, and our home life, such as it was, suddenly became complicated.

The good side was that we were now able to afford to buy our own house. We looked around and found a nice two-bedroom bungalow just outside Woking, going for around £20,000. I had most of the money and Marietta had some money her father had given her as a wedding present, so we put it all into buying the place outright. It was at the end of a cul-de-sac, the last house you came to as you drove in. The only drawback was that it was right next to the London to Portsmouth railway line. We didn't care, though. It was our first real home together and we couldn't have been more delighted. It was a cute-looking place, too, with its own name: Wych End.

Although we had put everything we had into the new bungalow, the money from Quo was really starting to roll in now and I felt pretty confident that we had done the right thing. The way I saw it, even if the band ended tomorrow, we were still doing all right for a married couple in their twenties. We owned our own house and we both had a car. Things were sweet.

Everything changed – as things so often do in these circumstances – when Marietta fell pregnant with our first child, Richard. It was just after we'd moved to Wych End. In fact, we could pinpoint the moment she conceived exactly: the room, the day, the time, everything. I know it's a cliché, but I really was over the moon to have a son of my own. He was blond, of course, and utterly gorgeous-looking. He'll hate me for saying that, but it's true; he was so pretty he looked more like a girl than a boy. I'm not sure how I liked being called Dad because I still felt like a kid myself, and I missed great chunks of his early years, of course, because I was away practically all of the time with the band. But Richard being there transformed us into a real family at last and it felt surprisingly good. I had never really given the subject much thought before; it was enough for me that I was with Marietta. Then Richard came along and it changed things. I felt older – but better.

By the time Richard was starting to run around, however, Wych End suddenly felt small and uncomfortable. We had discussed having more kids by then, and that's when we decided to start looking for a bigger place. We searched around for a few weeks and eventually discovered the most fantastic house in West Byfleet: Highland Court. It stood on half an acre of land, at the end of another cul-de-sac, a beautiful, tree-lined road where every house had its own distinctive look and character. Highland Court was obviously the pick of the bunch, though; just a bit bigger and a bit more special than the rest. It was going for £38,000 – almost double what we'd paid for Wych End and more than I could really afford to splash out in one go. But I just looked at it and dreamed of what it would be like to live somewhere like that. To call it your own . . .

Impulsive as ever, I decided to make an offer for it there and then. Full asking price, as long as they promised to take it off the market that day. They did. All I had to do now was find the cash. Again, I had most of what I needed – it was 1975, the year 'Down Down' gave us our first Number 1 single – but I was just short the last six or seven grand. I thought about going to the bank, but that would have meant a mortgage. I didn't fancy that. On the other hand, I simply had to have this house. Fortunately, Willie stepped in at the last minute and offered to lend us the extra money, on the basis that I would pay him back when I could, which I was able to do quite soon after.

Compared to the huge place Francis had recently purchased in Purley, Highland Court was fairly modest. But as far as I was concerned, it was a palace: four bedrooms, three bathrooms, one en suite. If I thought I'd arrived when I got the Jag, now I really felt like I'd made it. There was a huge back garden and a long, swooping drive into a courtyard at the front with a fountain in the middle. I used to love coming home, wafting through the electronic gates in the car, up the drive, past the fountain and into my fabulous new rock star abode . . .

What really underlined the significance of the move in my own mind, I think, was that it was only around the corner from Mary, and much the same sort of house she lived in. In order to fit in, I even started emulating some of Mary's ways. Every Christmas, for example, she would have all her friends and neighbours over to the house for a big celebration. I used to love those parties, so when I got my own similar-sized place I thought I would take on this mantle too and start having all my friends and neighbours over to the house at Christmas.

By then I had introduced Marietta to Mary. I still regarded her as a friend and didn't want to hide that from Marietta. Because she knew we'd had an affair in the past, though, Marietta understandably had reservations about her. Nevertheless, I always made sure to invite both her and her husband over to these parties. I have to admit there was a small element in that of simply wanting to show off to Mary. She had taught me so much about life and I suppose I simply wanted to show her that I had learned those lessons well; that I had absorbed all the good parts of our relationship and that even though we were no longer lovers I still regarded her as a great inspiration. Because of Mary I knew things which fed into my relationship with Marietta too. 'You want a new dress? We'll go to Jean Muir...' I had never heard of Jean Muir until I met Mary. She, I thought, was the one person in the world who would really appreciate what I was trying to do with my life now.

It wasn't just Mary, though. Having the house full of people at Christmas was my way of showing the whole world how well I'd done. The group was well-known by then – not to the point it is now, but the neighbours had seen us on the telly enough times and so I was like the local colour: that pop star bloke who's moved into the area. I used to invite them all round at Christmas and ply them with champagne while they had a look at all the gold records on the walls and the swimming-pool being built out the back. They loved it and so did I, and Marietta and I ended up becoming quite close friends with a lot of them.

It was also around then that I started building up my car collection. Given her origins, Marietta always had to have a Mercedes, of course. Top of the range, natch. Meanwhile I'd got a new Porsche and a vintage Daimler Sovereign. The maroon Jag and the Mini Cooper were long gone. My dad had smashed the Jag up. I'd lent it to him once when I was on tour. His car had broken down and he needed something to get to work in. Maybe he'd had a drink, or maybe going from the power of an Anglia to a 3.8 Jag was something he hadn't got right yet, maybe both, I don't know. But driving home one night he took a roundabout, totally misjudged it, and sent the car smashing into a wall. Luckily he only broke his arm, but my beautiful maroon machine was a total write-off.

I was absolutely gutted. It felt like a death in the family; my pride and joy suddenly, cruelly taken from me! I got home and there was my dad sitting there feeling sorry for himself. He'd taken an entire wall out with the car, and as well as the broken arm he had a black eye and was covered in cuts and bruises. I sat down next to him but he didn't know what to say other than repeating the word 'Sorry' over and over again. He couldn't get enough weight behind the word, though, because he knew how much I loved that car, and we both ended up sitting there crying.

The next day I went to see the car. It had been left in a field and when I saw it I felt like crying again. It was all smashed up and covered in mud; so sad to look at. It had been such a handsome car; one of those cars that sits up and looks at you. Now it was battered and ugly – and dead. I should have let it be taken to the scrap heap, but instead

I got the garage to try to repair it, which they duly set about doing. It cost a fortune, but it was never the same again and I ended up selling it for next to nothing. It's funny, I must have owned at least 100 cars since then, but that's still the one I remember most fondly today. My first true car love.

After the Jag, I had bought myself the aforementioned Mini Cooper S, which were also fashionable back then, and had it souped-up by Lotus. I had racing seats put in, the body shell sprayed champagne, the steering wheel extended down between my knees, new wheels put on, mesh over the head-lamps, new racing coil, half-race gearbox ... all sorts of stuff. By the time I'd finished it was a flying machine! It would do around 130 m.p.h., no problem. It was the greatest thing in my life. This was in my burn-up days, and this car would leave everything else on the road choking in its fumes.

And then one day I was burned up at the traffic lights by a Porsche. I couldn't believe it! I'd never even seen a Porsche before, but this thing just left me for dead. Then Mary's husband came home one day with one – this green bug-eyed monster – and I thought: that's the car that beat my Mini! I was smitten immediately and knew I had to have one for myself – followed by twelve years of driving nothing else. Until I had one of several bad experiences in one when I fell asleep at the wheel and nearly killed myself. In desperation, my mum pleaded with me: 'Rick, promise me you won't buy another Porsche.' And I never have. But we'll come back to that ...

As Quo's success continued unabated throughout the seventies – *Blue for You* in March 1976 was our fifth hit album in a row and our third to go to Number 1 – and bigger and bigger cheques arrived in the post, I was starting to feel quite flush with myself. But because the two worlds I inhabited –

the one with Marietta and the one with the band – were so far apart, it made for quite a schizophrenic life. At home, I was still knocking about in the same Surrey social circles that Mary had first introduced me to and that Marietta and I now cultivated. But while I enjoyed that, there was another part of me that felt the opposite: that I didn't belong anywhere near that scene. I was a rough-and-ready rock'n'roller. All I needed was my guitar, my car, and Marietta in the seat next to me. Which still happened, of course, just that now we would be driving to Harrods to spend a fortune on a new chandelier . . .

In the end, it all boiled down to who I was with. Even my speaking voice would change. If I was with the band, it was all-cor-blimey guvnor. If I was with Marietta and our posh new friends it would be much more considered and better enunciated. I would switch effortlessly between the two personas: one minute, this hard-drinking rocker razzing it up on the road; the next, this fairly hard-drinking society-type that went to dinner parties and chewed with his mouth closed.

Meanwhile we took the bare shell of Highland Court and really built it up. We had the outside of the house painted white and installed these Spanish-type canopied blinds over the windows, with green-and-white stripes for that Riviera look. Then I had a playhouse built for Richard in the back garden. It was made of wood and had a crooked chimney on the roof. Just as I had as a kid, when making my own makeshift huts in the back garden of the café, he thought it was the greatest thing ever. His friends would stay over and they would sleep outside together in their own little house.

All the trees in the drive were sprinkled with electric fairy lights, as were the gates and doorway. At night, the lights reflected off the house and made it glitter like gold. There was one beautiful evergreen in the drive, and when Christmas came around one year I thought how cool it would be to get some festive lights up there too. But it must have been over eighty feet tall and I didn't fancy trying to climb up it myself. Then I mentioned it to some of the builders one day – we always seemed to have builders around at Highland Court – and this one lad said, no problem, he'd climb the tree for me. I promised him a bottle of Scotch on top of his wages if he could do it and off he went. I bought all these different-coloured bulbs, hundreds of them, and he strung them up over the tree, top to bottom. The first time we turned them on I couldn't stop grinning. I must have spent most of that night just looking out of the window at this thing. By today's standards it sounds a little unsubtle, to say the least, but by seventies standards it was the dog's bollocks! I used to drive through the gates at night and feel like I was entering a mini-Disneyland . . .

The next thing was, I thought, well, I'm a rock star, I've got to have my own swimming-pool. It was off to talk to the builders again.

'I want a swimming-pool. Can you do it?'

'Well, you'd have to get a JCB in there.'

'Can we get a JCB in there?'

'We can.'

'Fucking right then, let's do it . . .'

Next thing, there's a JCB out the back of the house digging a bloody great hole in the ground. When it was finished we literally stuck the end of the garden hose in and turned on the tap. About a week later it was full and I had my swimming-pool! Thirty-five feet by eighteen. Three feet deep at the shallow end, graduating to eight feet at the deep end. Heated water; diving board; slide; paved all round. It was blue and absolutely beautiful. The whole thing cost eight grand to install and a small fortune to keep running because I liked to keep it hot all the time, especially in the winter. I loved the idea of going skinny-dipping when there was snow on the ground. Sheer luxury. The water would be so hot there would be steam coming off it. I used to say you could virtually see the fivers evaporating before your eyes . . .

Apart from splashing the cash on big houses and fast cars, I didn't really go in for the so-called celebrity lifestyle, not at that stage anyway. Those clubs up in town that all the bands went to, like the Speakeasy, just weren't on my radar. They were all up in the West End and I was not a West End boy. And I'd kind of done that already, when John Coghlan and I would go out together sometimes in the early days. We used to meet in the Ship in Wardour Street, have a few drinks, then go down the Marquee Club and hang out. The guy who ran the Marquee back then, Jack Barry, also used to have this private, members-only club upstairs called the Shaz. It was one of those places where you always remembered going up the stairs but could never recall coming back down them again.

I did about a year of that malarkey. By the time we started having serious success in the seventies, I still liked to have my fun but it was all done much closer to home now. I just preferred the atmosphere there. I was round the corner from my mum and dad and at the same time close to Marietta and my friends; I knew my way around. It was also a good place to go when you didn't want to be that bloke in that group for five minutes. In the summer, whenever I wasn't working, I just sat around the pool feeling comfy; and in the winter I had my shag-pile carpet and a big colour telly to keep me happy, along with this brand new gadget attached to it called

Above. The Status Quo in 1967. From left to right: Roy Lynes, Francis, Rick, John Coghlan, Alan Lancaster.

Below. After the success of 'Matchstick Men', Carnaby Street beckoned. A publicity shot from 1968 showcases the new look.

Above, left. Playing live in 1968, at a US Air Force base.

Above, right. Rehearsing, around 1969.

Below. On *Top of the Pops* in 1969, playing their single 'Are You Growing Tired of My Love'.

Above. 1970 – with a new decade came a new image as this photograph of Quo's *Top of the Pops* appearance for 'In My Chair' shows.

Right. By 1972 the transformation was complete. A shot taken after a gig, and post-joint.

Above. Rick and Francis with members of Slade and Lindisfarne's Alan Hull, on their first Australian tour in 1973.

Below. Quo being presented with gold discs in 1974.

Above. On stage in 1975 – the bent-leg stance was the band's way of getting closer to the audience.

Right. Birth of the blues? Publicity shot for the *Blue For You* album.

Left. The last show of
the End of the Road tour.
Clockwise, from top left:
Andrew Bown, Alan Lancaster,
Francis, Rick and Pete Kirsher.

Below. The new line-up
in 1986. Left to right: Jeff Rich,
John 'Rhino' Edwards, Francis,
Rick and Andrew Bown.

Above. Straight after the final gig at the Rock 'Til You Drop event, backstage at Wembley Arena, 21 September 1991.

Below. At Butlin's Minehead, where it all began, to celebrate the band's twenty-fifth anniversary with Chris Tarrant and Alan Freeman, 10 October 1990.

Above. At the Prince's Trust gig, 1994, meeting Prince Charles, and with Brian May backstage.

Centre. On stage at Norwich 1997, Rick's first appearance after his heart surgery.

Left. Status Quo backstage in Hamburg, June 2004.

a video player. (The first thing I ever taped was *Barbarella*, with Jane Fonda at her most scrumptious.) So I had no need for flash London clubs. I was fine where I was, thanks, at home with my family and my cars.

The only conscious bit of celebrity 'hanging out' I did back then was when I tried to get myself introduced to Cliff Richard. Marietta had always been quite religious, but in a very private, non-evangelical way. I had no interest in religion whatsoever but I didn't mind that she did. Each to his own, that's always been my motto on things like that. Anyway, she'd started attending a Bible class in town. She had tried getting me to go with her a couple of times, but I'd always refused. Then she told me that Cliff Richard went there too sometimes, and that's when I got my coat on! I didn't pretend to Marietta that I had suddenly seen the light or anything; she knew why I wanted to go. But she went along with it, I think, because she hoped some of it might rub off on me anyway.

I had no idea if he'd be there the night we went, I just took a chance. Rather wonderfully, however, he was already there when we arrived. I'd been in the business long enough by then to have met quite a few of my musical heroes, but I had never been so starstruck before. I'd been such a huge fan of Cliff's since I was ten years old; bought all the records, seen all the movies. In the Highlights I'd even sung 'Living Doll' and 'Travelling Light'. Seeing him there in the flesh for the first time, my former idol, I was completely transfixed. I didn't go over and introduce myself; I couldn't summon up the courage. Maybe if it had been at a party and I'd had a drink in my hand, I might have done. But under these circumstances, where all I had was a Bible, I couldn't do it. It was fascinating, though, just to watch him up close. I felt like a stalker but I couldn't take my eyes off him. He obviously noticed me, too, but he just ignored me and got on with his prayers. I suppose he was used to being stared at by then. It happens to me now. You realize there's some nutter across the room that can't stop grinning at you. It rather puts you off whatever it is you're supposed to be doing. Sorry, Sir Cliff...

Other than that, I just kept rolling along. I never worried about money any more. I never had anyway. Now, though, I didn't think about it all. As long as the band was doing well, that's all I cared about. And it was. Quo was now selling more records and tickets than ever. It was just a fantastically happy time. I loved my house, I loved my wife and son, and I loved what was going on with my band. Surely it didn't get any better than that?

I was right, it didn't.

The high point came in 1977, when Quo released *Rockin' All Over the World*. One of our biggest singles and albums ever, in many ways it was a turning point for us – we were more than just a rock band now, we were right back in the mainstream again. It was a turning point for me personally, too. During the early weeks of the subsequent world tour, Marietta gave birth to a beautiful baby girl – an angel we named Heidi Marie Elizabeth. I was gutted not to be there for the birth, but there was nothing I could do. Andy Bown, who was with me when I got the phone call and saw how upset I was, went off to his room and came back an hour later with a song he'd written called 'Rock & Roll Baby Blues'. It was such a beautiful gesture. It went: '*A good friend of mine became a father today / His wife gave birth a thousand miles away / He's suffering in shock / From the rock'n'roll baby blues...*'

It was one of the nicest things anyone in the band had

ever done for me and I was genuinely touched. Not that it cheered me up for long. Because the Rockin' All Over the World tour was so successful it kept me away from home for most of Heidi's first year; something I bitterly regret now. But then it was the same for Richard. Both had been born at a time when Quo was still out there building empires, and I missed huge chunks of them growing up.

Maybe that's why I was hitting the bottle so hard now, I don't know. But it was definitely around then that I started to get seriously messed up, first on booze and later on drugs. Like my dad, I had always been a drinker. It was an occupation in which he positively encouraged me – and everyone else around him. Is it any wonder then that I have always enjoyed a gargle, too? By the time we were living in Highland Court, though, I was hitting the bottle pretty heavily. Whisky, beer and wine – the old staples.

I'd also started getting into speed. Amphetamine sulphate, mainly, but anything would do: blues, black bombers, you name it. At first I used to lick my finger and have a few dabs from a packet of white powder. It tasted disgusting, so I got into chopping it out into lines and snorting it. It used to really sting your nose, though, so in the end I used to pour half a gram into my morning tea and that would be me sorted for the next eight hours. The other reason why I got so carried away on speed and booze at that time was because I'd quit smoking dope after a nightmarish experience on tour in America in 1975, when I'd made the deeply foolish error of smoking a neat Thai-stick. I think I literally just wrapped a few makeshift cigarette papers round it and set light to it. Big mistake. It turned out to be extremely strong, far more powerful than anything I'd ever experienced before, and I completely freaked out.

Don't ask me how – the details of this story are lost in Thai-stick fumes – but things began to turn weird when I got into a conversation after the show one night with this woman who claimed she was a witch. I had just smoked this huge fat joint and I was having a bit of a laugh with her backstage when the conversation took a very strange turn. We were suddenly talking about churches and candles and she looked at me piercingly and said, 'How long can your wick last?' That stopped me in my tracks. Before I could think of an answer, she said, 'Do you know how to use the cross?' By now she was starting to do me in. The Thai-stick was starting to come on strong, too, so I had a word with Bob Young and got her removed from the dressing-room.

She wouldn't leave quietly though – she was uttering all sorts of oaths as Bob got her out of the door, and I just couldn't get it out of my now very stoned mind. By the time we got back to the hotel I had the full-scale horrors. Francis and Bob took my clothes off and got me to bed, but as soon as they left I got up to have a shower. That would sort me out, I decided, my thoughts cascading inside my skull. I lurched into the bathroom and turned on the shower taps. They sounded incredibly loud. I stepped under the water. I tried to lather myself with this oblong sliver of soap. Then I dropped the soap and the most amazing thing happened – it stood upright and winked at me! That's when I totally lost it. I stood there trembling, my eyes bulging out of my head. Then the phone started ringing. I thought, maybe it's the chaps ringing to check on me. Then I thought: what if it's the witch? I stood there frozen like a statue as this bar of soap looked up and laughed and the phone rang and rang and rang.

OK, I thought, I'll answer it. As I stumbled out of the

shower, I got it into my head that if the phone stopped before I could get to it I would be doomed! I ran, panicked, to the phone – it stopped just as I got there. I was doomed! For ever!!

I lay there on the bed, dripping wet, completely freaked out and exhausted. Then my whole body started to convulse. I'm lying there convulsing and suddenly a vision of the witch appears before me, standing at the foot of the bed with an effigy of me in her hands that she's sticking pins into. That's when I knew for sure: I was going to die. I was definitely going to die. Any second now . . .

At which point I must have blacked out, because I can't remember any more about that night. All because of this one particularly strong joint. It literally blew my mind. It also removed overnight any taste I had for smoking dope. I have never knowingly smoked a joint of any description since.

All well and good, you might expect. The trouble was, it caused a rift in the band. Myself, Francis and Alan had always been heavy dope-smokers. I had also tried LSD but it wasn't a social drug; you couldn't take it and expect to pull a bird. Whereas dope – marijuana, cannabis, we weren't fussy – tripped you out but still left you able to function, in a vague, contentedly confused sort of way. Or so I'd always thought before my encounter with that Thai-stick.

Now that I'd stopped all that, it set me apart from Alan and Francis – and put me in the same boat as John, who had never been into pot and consequently never really enjoyed the same sense of humour as the rest of us. Back at the hotel after the show, there would always be one designated room where we would go for a major post-gig smoke-a-thon. Suddenly I didn't get to go there any more. John would be down at the hotel bar and I would be standing outside the door to this room, listening to Francis, Bob and Alan laughing. I wanted to go in there and laugh too, but I knew that without the dope there probably wasn't anything really funny to laugh at. So I used to stay away, and I must say it was a very difficult time for me, having to deal with that aspect. We used to travel together to gigs in this beautiful Mercedes 600 stretch limousine. Up until then, you'd open the doors and we'd all fall out in a great puff of dope smoke. Suddenly I became the one sitting up straight in the back. I really did feel ostracized. Then speed came along and we had something in common again; a whole new way of relating. Or so we thought.

If you look at the pictures of us from the seventies and eighties, you've only got to see the bleary expressions on our faces, or notice the slight smirk on our lips, to tell what's going on. Francis and I look at those pictures now and go: 'Ah, yes, we were coked-out in that one; doped-up to our eyeballs in that one; and speeding out of our heads in that one.' It's scary actually, how easy it is to tell. As far as we were concerned, though, we were simply living the life of a 'normal' successful rock band. Queen, Elton, the Stones ... who wasn't living like that back in the seventies? No one we knew.

As far as the sex went, other than my relationships with Mary, Patty and Marietta my experience of girls had been fairly limited until then. In between the lingering trauma inflicted by my unconsummated love for Jean Harrison, there had been a few one-night stands while I was with the Highlights; mainly holiday camp romances that fizzled out as soon as they departed on the coach and the next lot of campers arrived. And when Quo first took off in the sixties there were always a lot of girls hanging around. But the first time I encountered what you would call proper groupies wasn't until the seventies. They were everywhere suddenly and yes, even though I was a happily married man, I took advantage sometimes. You're up there in the groove, all these girls are looking at you, getting off on it, and a lot of them are fair game. What young guy wouldn't take advantage of that? Plus – and I don't expect sympathy here, I'm just trying to be truthful – to most young heterosexual men, getting a blowjob off some groupie is no more meaningful than having a wank. It was hard to feel like you were cheating on your wife when you didn't even know the names of the people you were supposedly cheating with.

I realize now, of course, that a lot of the bad behaviour was just a way of papering over the cracks that had begun to appear. Despite our ever-growing success, beneath the surface there were serious tensions within the band. Alan and Francis, in particular, now seemed to have more bad days than good together. Alan had also recently gone through a divorce and was now living in Australia with his new girl-friend. Rather than ease the bad feeling between him and Francis, however, it just made things worse. Alan would fly over for meetings but it wasn't as easy then simply to hop over from the other side of the world. It's no picnic now, but back then it would take three days to recover, by which time we'd forgotten what the meeting was supposed to be about and Alan would go back to Australia all pissed off.

Hence, all the hassle over the 'Rocking All Over the World' video. We had phoned him in Australia and told him he had to come back quickly. The record company had got all excited about the single and felt it could be our biggest hit for years, so they wanted to pull out all the stops. This included making a video, which at that time was still a new medium that only the biggest artists got lavished on them.

We explained all this on the phone and Alan's response was: 'I can't drop everything and get over there just like that.' We said, 'But you have to, we're shooting the video next week!' He said: 'Well, I can't come over that quickly and don't you dare shoot it without me.' But we had no choice – which is why the 'Rocking All Over the World' video features a life-size puppet of Alan. Of course, as soon as he found out what we'd done the shit hit the fan big time. That was one time we were glad he was thousands of miles away . . .

The next album, *If You Can't Stand the Heat,* preceded by the single 'Again and Again', a song I co-wrote and sang lead on, would be equally big hits, as would the ones that immediately followed that, but 'Rockin' All Over the World' was where things seemed to climax for us in the seventies. After that, things started to change. We had decided to take the following year 'out' as tax exiles, for the simple reason that we didn't agree with handing over most of our money to the government. A percentage of it was fine, but not most of it, guv.

It was the summer of 1979. We did some shows and finished off some tracks in the studio for our next album, then spent the rest of the year conspicuously out of the country. Alan was now living permanently in Australia anyway, so it didn't really affect him, while Francis went to Ireland and John went to live on the Isle of Man. Marietta and I stayed in the tax haven of the Channel Islands for a while, renting a big place in Jersey. Then we flew to Los Angeles for a long family holiday. When it was over we went to stay at Marietta's parents' place in Germany, where we intended to see out the rest of the year. The months quickly slipped by. Quo had been on the road solidly for over ten years by then and we all sorely needed a break. In fact, my body seemed to be screaming for help. It had begun on the Rockin' All Over the World tour, when I awoke one morning in agonizing pain. I couldn't move my arms or legs – and this time it had nothing to do with booze or drugs. Indeed, this was worse than any hangover I had ever known.

I was taken to Harley Street, where a bunch of eminent private doctors told me I had a muscular virus. They gave me a couple of injections of cortisone, some sleeping pills and told me to rest. I did, and for a time it seemed to help. Now it was back, whatever it was. By the time we got to Germany I could barely lift myself out of the chair some days, my whole body felt so painful. It got so bad in the end that I agreed to go to the local hospital, where they immediately gave me a bed and told me to prepare for a long stay. After nearly two weeks' worth of tests, the doctors there diagnosed me with something called sero-negative-chronic-poly-arthritis of the spine. The cure: none. The only way to make the symptoms go away: lots of pills and potions and lots of rest. Mainly lots of rest.

With nothing but empty days stretching before me any-way, I said I'd give it a shot, and for the next few weeks I was forced to do some serious lying around, being waited on hand and foot by Marietta and her mother, in an effort to get better in time to go back to work in the new year. I joke about it now, but it was terrifying being so incapacitated. The docs in Germany conducted all kinds of tests and devised all sorts of weird and wonderful treatments: everything from having fluid drained from my knees to caking my body in mud, in order to draw out all the impurities. There were also various injections, including one from a syringe the size of a beer bottle. I can't stand injections – I nearly passed out when they walked in the room with that. I was like, 'There is no fucking way you're sticking that in me!' But they did. Thankfully, however, whatever they were doing to me, after a few weeks it appeared to have worked. I still wasn't 100 per cent, but I was better than I had been for months and the prognosis for a full recovery was good, they said. As long as I looked after myself. Oh, I intended to look after myself all right. It was now nearly Christmas – a whole new decade about to dawn – and I couldn't wait to see the boys in the band again. To prove I was back. 'Whatever You Want', a song I had written with Andy Bown, had been a big hit for us while I'd been in Germany. It's probably the song I'm now most proud of contributing to Quo and it was a drag not being able to go out there and bask in its success when it was such a big hit. Now I was in a hurry to make up for lost time. The plan was that I would join Francis in Dublin in the new year, where we would begin work on some of the new material for the next Quo album. What should have been a fairly low-key, casual arrangement, however, turned into a life-changing event – and not necessarily for the better, though we both certainly thought so at the time. For it was in Dublin that Francis and I first got seriously into cocaine.

The trip to Dublin had already turned into a nightmare when I woke late that morning and had to drive like a madman to get to the airport in time. At the time, I had a lovely Mercedes 280 SE; a beautiful machine for its time that I'd taken out to Germany with me. The plan was for the whole family to drive to Amsterdam airport, where I could get a direct flight to Dublin, while Marietta took the car and the kids back to London on the ferry. For some improbable reason my flight was booked at a stupidly early hour and suddenly there I was hammering down the Autobahn, doing 130 m.p.h. at four in the morning, with Marietta in the seat next to me and the kids in the back with my mum, who had been visiting us out in Germany.

Suddenly, my mum said she felt sick. I couldn't stop, though, or I was going to miss my plane. So I offered to slow down enough for her to stick her head out of the window and chuck up. Which she rather embarrassedly did. I didn't dare think of what it must have done to the outside of my beautiful Merc, I just put my foot down again and drove.

'Better now, mum?' I asked when it was over.

'Yush, fanksh,' she said.

I looked in the rear-view mirror: she'd lost her false teeth. They must have gone flying out the window when she'd chucked up. She began smacking her lips together dejectedly.

'Never mind, Mum,' I said, trying not to laugh. 'I'll buy you a new set.'

The last laugh appeared to be on me, however, when I got to the airport and discovered the flight had been cancelled. Marietta and the gang had already driven off by then to catch the ferry and I was left stranded. I had an enormous amount of luggage with me too – suitcases, guitars, even an amp – all ready for a long stay in Ireland. There were no mobile phones in those days to get Marietta back. I didn't know what to do.

All right, I said to myself, taking a deep breath and trying to think like a tour manager. What about another flight?

It turned out there was another flight that day, but after I'd dragged all my gear over to the check-in desk and queued for half-an-hour, I was told it was full. Now I really didn't know what to do. I wasn't very good at looking after myself in those days anyway; I'd always had Bob or Colin there to sort it out for me. And my legs and back were now aching. I decided to take drastic action and do what I always do when

I'm in trouble – throw money at it. Like, I don't care what it is or how much it costs, can you get me to Dublin today somehow or not?

The girl at the information desk said it was always possible to charter a flight – then looked me up and down, as if to say, 'But, obviously, someone like you would never be able to afford that.' The band was massive in Germany by then but not that well-known in Holland, and she obviously didn't recognize me. At which point, it became like a challenge.

I said, 'So how much would it actually cost for me to charter an aeroplane to Ireland?' She reluctantly checked it out. There were two choices: either a propeller plane, which would be cheaper but had a journey time of three to four hours. Or a private jet, which would get me there in an hour. I said, 'I'll take the jet, please.'

It cost me three grand but it was worth it just to see the look on her face. Plus, it got me where I needed to be and ended the nightmare of trundling round the airport trailing my whole life behind me in a carry-cart. As soon as I flashed the Am-Ex card, people came running from all directions. 'Don't worry about your luggage, sir, we'll take care of that. There's a private lounge for you upstairs where you can wait for your plane in comfort.' Now that was more like it! Two hours later I was airborne with a glass of champagne in my hand . . .

For my money I got a fourteen-seat Corvette Jet Star! Very yummy. The stewards all stood at the bottom of the steps saluting me as I clambered on board in my T-shirt and jeans. I spent the flight stretched out on a plush leather sofa, plonking away on the guitar and guzzling champagne. Sixty minutes later I was at Shannon airport and there was Francis waiting for me on the tarmac. I had told the captain to radio ahead and get someone to phone Francis to tell him I would be arriving in the VIP section of the airport on my own private landing strip. By now, of course, I'd drunk the plane dry and was feeling no pain whatsoever. I literally fell out the door of the Jet Star and ended up in a heap at the bottom of the steps, the crew all standing there saluting me again. Then I picked myself up and got into the rented Cortina Francis had come to pick me up in. A classy touch, I thought.

When we got to the hotel, Francis's new songwriting partner, Bernie Frost, was there waiting for us. We dropped my stuff off and went straight to the studio. Although I was completely shit-faced, for these guys it was only ten in the morning and they were ready to go to work. I was so out of it I thought I was too. The minute we got there I staggered into a whole stack of reel-to-reel tapes and sent them flying across the room! Then somebody handed me my guitar and I couldn't figure out how to put it on.

Francis, who would normally have lost patience by then and started scowling, just said, 'Don't worry, I've got something that will sort you out.' He reached into his pocket and brought out a small polythene bag full of white powder. I assumed it must be sulphate but he said, no, it was cocaine, and that it was better then speed in every way. 'Marching powder,' he called it. I gave it a go.

The only previous time I had ever touched cocaine had been on an American tour a few years before. Francis always claims it happened in Canada, but we had just done a show in Los Angeles, in fact, and we were at this party up in the Hollywood hills. When we got there it was the full clichéd seventies scene: velvet curtains, gold fixtures, big chandeliers, incense fumes, and lots of far-out people in fancy costume wandering around sipping from huge soup bowls of wine.

In the middle of the room there was a long, ornate-looking coffee table, on which sat a large silver bowl full of this sparkling white powder. Guests were invited to help themselves. Well, we had to try it, didn't we?

The very first lines we snorted were chopped out for us by the guy who was throwing the party; a nice bloke who thought he was doing us a favour. But the effect was so negligible that at first Francis and I thought he must be playing a joke on us. He looked at me and went, 'Well, that was a waste of fucking time!' We'd been told it was like speed only more 'subtle'. But we felt absolutely nothing. I thought: I won't be bothering with that again. Famous last words . . .

Whether it was because I was so drunk this time, I don't know, but when I tried it again in Dublin I noticed the effect almost immediately – bang! Wallop! Hello! I had a couple more lines and after a few minutes everything came sharply back into focus. Suddenly I wasn't drunk any more. Or rather, I was, but not that you'd know it: I was in some sort of warped control again. Not crazed like speed but intensely focused suddenly and very, very confident. 'Can I help write some lyrics? Give 'em here!' 'What about that melody, can you add anything to it?' 'You fucking betcha!' Give me a trombone and I would have been able to play it – it was that sort of feeling. All because of the coke. And that was the moment I started to fall in love with the drug; to get it; to finally see what all the fuss was about.

After that, of course, I went mental on it. We both did. For years and years . . .

FOUR

Just as every cloud is said to have a silver lining, so, I have always believed, the opposite must also be true, and good luck comes at a price. So it was that, just as Quo was achieving its greatest worldwide success in the early eighties, I somehow contrived to turn that period into a desperate downward spiral that would see me forsake first my marbles and then my band; my whole life whittled down to how much cocaine and alcohol I could shovel into my system each day.

That said, it would be too simple and convenient, too selfish, to solely blame booze and drugs for the virtual collapse of my life over the next ten years. The seeds of destruction had been sown into both my marriage and my band long before I ever got messed up on drugs. It couldn't have helped, though, that by 1984, when I took the decision to finish with Quo, I was drinking two bottles of tequila a day and snorting three grams of coke. That's the irony of booze and drugs: you start doing them because they seem to take you away from all your troubles. Next thing you know, they're the *cause* of all your troubles . . .

In terms of my own descent into drug and alcohol hell, it all went back to 1975 when I first got seriously into amphetamines – speed. I had dabbled with various uppers and downers, but mainly I had always been a dope-smoker. Weed, resin, Thai-stick, Nepalese Temple Ball, Afghani Black, Lebanese Red ... you name it, I smoked it. By the time we came to make the *Blue for You* album in the autumn of 1975, however, speed had reared its ugly head and suddenly the whole band – with the exception of John Coghlan, whose only drug was alcohol – had become speed-freaks.

Not a plant but a man-made chemical, and therefore a much more serious proposition than simple marijuana, speed was a hellish drug to get hooked on. It certainly left its mark on us. If you listen to *Blue for You* you'll notice it's cranked up to almost hysterical levels. I left Rick sitting there in the studio one night while he carried on tinkering with the riff to 'Mystery Song', one of the singles from the album. When I came back the next day he was still sitting exactly where I'd left him twelve hours before, still banging away at the guitar. I said, 'Blimey, mate, you're in early.' He said, 'What do you mean – early? I haven't gone home yet...'

Until then, apart from smoking dope, I had never really been into drugs. I never even liked beer, preferring sweet-tasting drinks like lemonade. And I never got into acid or psychedelics; it just wasn't my scene. Speed was different. It still kind of tripped you out – particularly after you'd been up for two or three days – but it didn't rob you of your edge. Quite the opposite: if anything, it made you too sharp. We'd spend all week speeding out of our skulls in the studio, coming up with some great stuff. (The album went to Number 1 and Rick co-wrote and sang one of the best tracks, 'Rain', another Top 10 single.) After a week of amphetamine-fuelled madness in the studio, though, I'd get home at the weekend utterly shattered, nerves completely frayed, jumping at my own shadow. Speed comedowns are killer like that. My whole mood would be black for days.

That's when I got into downers – heavy-duty tranquillizers like Seconal (reds) and Mandrax (mandies) – just to try to get over the speed comedowns. We used to get them on prescription from a private doctor in Harley Street. I used to love dropping a mandy and feeling my whole body go into total relaxation mode – or complete collapse, depending on how you look at it. You could walk into walls on a mandy and you wouldn't feel a thing. Why that should have been so appealing is a mystery to me now, but I used to love it back then.

You could argue that a lot of it was down to peer pressure. Attitudes towards drugs were certainly different in the seventies. There was no stigma attached to taking them. They were still a relatively new phenomenon and we really did think of them, at best, as consciousness-raising; at worst, as a bit of a giggle. I certainly saw speed and dope as a spur to creativity, and whether I like it or not the fact is that some of the best songs I've ever written were produced under the influence of a cocktail of different drugs over the years, starting with marijuana and speed and ending with cocaine and alcohol. I'm not saying you need to take drugs to write great songs, I'm just saying that there is, after all, a reason why so many of us fall for them. They get you high. You feel good, inspired. Of course you write good songs! You also write a lot of terrible fucking songs, too, and being high is definitely not the way to tell the difference; a lesson I would learn the hard way.

The first time me and Rick tried coke was at some swish party we were invited to when we toured Canada in 1975. Rick always remembers it as Los Angeles but I'm pretty sure it was at a hotel in Canada. Anyway, it was the proverbial glass-bowl-in-the-middle-of-the-room job. 'Help yourself, guys!' Neither of us had ever even seen cocaine before, let alone taken it, and we decided to give it a go. I seem to remember that the guy with all the coke was a roadie for Manfred Mann. Rick and I had a couple of lines, then went out by the pool, waiting for something to happen. We were disappointed, though. There didn't seem to be any discernible kick to it. We thought: what does everybody see in this? It's rubbish compared to speed...

It wasn't until a few years later, during my stay in Ireland as a tax exile, that I really discovered coke for the first time. Speed had stopped being a buzz and become a nuisance. Even with the downers, it simply took too long to climb down off the relentless amphetamine grind, by which time it was nine in the morning and you were completely freaked out. When somebody in Dublin suggested I try coke again, assuring me that it was like speed but without all the rough edges and terrible insomnia, I didn't take much persuading. I was already in the frame of mind where I was convinced I needed *something* or I wouldn't be able to write. So I snorted a couple of lines and this time I not only got it, I *really* got it! I got it so good I didn't want to get anything else for the next ten years...

In the end, I was almost as addicted to the act of snorting it up my nose as I was to the effect of the drug itself. I was hooked on the sensation of it trickling down my throat. The first time I experienced it I thought it was gross. Two years later it was all I lived for. I got so into snorting that if I couldn't get coke I'd buy snuff and take big pinches of that instead. Everywhere I went, I used to leave black handkerchiefs behind. When I simply couldn't shovel any more coke up my nose I'd sprinkle some into a joint. Smoking it always made me gag, but that didn't stop me wanting to do it. Or I'd toss some into a glass of tequila, like a spray of salt. By then I'd put coke into anything. I used to rub the crumbs from the mirror around my gums, then massage great swathes of it into my knob, to keep it hard. I'd have shoved it up my arse if I thought that would have worked better. I was a dog for it. A dirty dog. Scrounging around on all fours, tongue hanging out, begging for it, night and day.

It was through becoming a coke addict that I got seriously into booze for the first time. One vice fed the other: I'd get so uptight on coke I'd need a drink to calm me down again, then I'd start to get sloppy and need some coke to help me 'straighten up'. Then I'd be so wired again I'd have to have another drink. And so on and so on . . .

Tequila was my favourite tipple. I had never been a boozer until then. I didn't even like wine. Imagine – an Italian boy who doesn't drink wine! I only liked the cheap fizzy stuff, and even that made me pull a face. Then, in the autumn of 1981, we were making an album at Mountain Studios, just outside Montreux – a wonderful spot literally halfway up the Swiss mountains – and I discovered tequila. Queen actually owned Mountain, and as chance would have it they were all in town when we arrived, so we went out together for an expensive meal at this fabulous Mexican restaurant they knew.

As soon as we sat down the waiters brought out all these pitchers of Tequila Marguerita. I had never tasted it before, but I absolutely loved it from the very first sip. It was deliciously sweet but with a real kick to it and I knocked back about six glasses, one after the other. It was like a baby duck waddling out on to the pond for the first time; I just immediately took to it.

From then on, I started ordering pitchers of Marguerita wherever we went. If I couldn't get a pitcher I would order six glasses of quadruple Tequila Sunrise (tequila and orange) instead. Then I got into drinking it the traditional way, straight out of the bottle with the salt and the chunk of lime. Then I thought, I don't want the salt, it's making me dry. Then I decided I didn't want the lime either, because it was too sour. That left straight tequila. I would still have a splash of orange in it sometimes but that was just for social reasons.

For instance, if I was out with a group of friends, I'd always offer to buy the first round of drinks. Then I'd go to the bar and tell the barman to put four shots of tequila into a long glass. He'd do it, then hand me the glass, and I'd drink it straight down. I'd say, 'Four more shots in the glass, please.' He'd put four more shots in, hand me the glass and I'd drink it straight down. By now he'd learned and would be standing there waiting with his hand out. 'Four more shots, please.' I'd say. He'd dutifully pour them into the glass and I'd drink 'em straight down again. Then I'd go, 'All right, that's better. Now give me four shots in the glass and a splash of orange.' That would be the drink I'd take back with me to the table, along with everybody else's drinks. Now I was ready to socialize and I would sip that fourth drink (or sixteenth, depending on how you look at it) the same way everybody else would sip their first.

Once I got on to the coke-and-tequila merry-go-round I never wanted to get off again. It was the same on stage. I'd be half-gone before we'd even started. By about the third or fourth number the feeling would start to sag and you'd find yourself running into the wings and snorting lines off the top of a flight case, then gulping down a quick quadruple tequila. The only time I didn't drink or do drugs was when I was unconscious. It was like I wanted to find out what it was like to become that coke-snorting, booze-guzzling, rock star wanker. Stupid as it sounds, I now believe that actually had a lot to do with it. There's a reason why people do most things and it's nearly always the simplest one: because they want to. The way I saw it, without Jean and the kids around any more there was no compelling reason for me to do anything else. Even after I met Elizabeth Gernon and started to get some shape back into my life, once I got the coke bug it became my number one priority over everything – and everyone.

Meanwhile, the band played on. The *Whatever You Want* single and album had come out at the end of 1979 while I was in Ireland. Released on Rick's thirty-first birthday, although the album got to Number 3 and featured one of our most memorable tunes, and biggest hits, with the title track – co-written and sung by Rick – we had actually recorded it all nearly a year before and by the time it was in the charts it already felt old to me. With the band now scattered to the four winds of tax exiledom there was no one around to celebrate with anyway. For the first time in a long time, we were all doing our own things, further away from each other, both physically and emotionally, than we had ever been.

In those terms, being forced to leave the country definitely had its benefits. It forced us into taking a break, which we desperately needed then. The band was suffering from burn-out. Recording dates and the odd brief holiday aside, we had been on the road almost non-stop for ten years and now the cracks were beginning to show.

We were all getting on each other's nerves. Alan, in

particular, was driving me crazy with his resistance to wanting the band to grow musically. He hated it if I came in with a song that didn't fit what he saw as the Quo musical template; something that was starting to happen more often now. Meanwhile, Rick was so busy living the rock star life we no longer saw each other outside the band anyway; and John was getting drunker and more at odds with the world every day. He had always been moody but now he would go days without speaking a word, beyond the occasional grunt when his glass was empty. The only relatively normal one was Andy Bown the keyboardist. Andy was someone we had first met back in the sixties when he was in the Herd. After Roy Lynes left, at first we simply used Andy on a session basis. By now, however, he was a full-time member. But because he'd been the last to join, he wasn't so embroiled in the politics and wisely kept his distance.

Surprisingly, however, the first major rift that led to someone actually leaving occurred not between any of the original band members but between me and Bob Young. Things had got so bad between us, in fact, that by the time I'd gone to Ireland he and I were hardly even speaking any more, let alone writing songs together. After the breakdown of my marriage, it was the most painful thing I'd ever been through. It pains me even more now to know how unnecessary the whole thing was, and that we had been set up, in order to get Bob out of the picture.

It took a long time for me to figure out how it happened – more than twenty years, in fact – but I realize now that the root of the problems between me and Bob went as far back as 1976: the year Colin Johnson and David Oddie decided to break away from Gaff Management and form their own company, Quarry Productions, managing both us and Rory

Gallagher. It was at this point that some new faces appeared in the office, including one whose real name I won't mention for legal reasons. An advisor, let's say.

Nothing if not shrewd, he could see the state the band was in – permanently out to lunch and constantly bickering with each other – and he used that to take advantage of us. The last thing we cared about was reading through the various contracts and bits of paper he put in front of us. This was in the eighties, at the height of our commercial success, and there were literally millions of pounds being moved around various bank accounts, on our behalf.

Unfortunately Bob was in the way. He was one of those tour managers who knew where every penny went on a tour. But because he was one of us, he had the kind of loyalty that went beyond money. It was a two-way thing: we wouldn't move unless Bob said it was all right to do so. So Bob had to be got rid of.

Suddenly I started hearing bad things about him. Stuff like how I didn't give him enough credit for his role in writing the songs and how it was mainly him that wrote them anyway. I was astounded! It didn't sound like Bob at all. But I was so paranoid and coked-out all the time that suddenly it all fell into place in my over-exercised mind. What I didn't know was that at the same time Bob was being told about all the nasty things I had apparently been saying about him behind his back. How he had got above his station since success had come along and that it had turned him into a third-rate tour manager . . .

Overnight the air turned bad between me and Bob. By the time I'd become a tax exile, we had gone from being the best of friends to the bitterest of enemies. By the start of 1980 Bob finally quit after being told we didn't want him around any longer, and we let him do it after being told he was sick to death of us and wanted out. It was so perfectly done that neither side suspected a thing. It wasn't until Bob and I became friends again years later that the truth finally came out. The worst thing of all is that we fell for it so easily. To the point where we would not speak properly again, as friends, for over twenty years.

It wasn't just the end of our friendship, of course, it was also the end of what had been until then an incredibly fruitful songwriting partnership. If I was concerned by that fact, though, I didn't let on to anyone, least of all myself. I had met Bernie Frost by then and so I just tried not to think about it. With Bernie, I seemed to have a sort of second wind as a songwriter. One of our first songs to be released as a Quo single was 'What You're Proposing', in 1980, which reached Number 2 in November that year; kept from Number 1 for three weeks by 'Woman in Love' by Barbra Streisand.

I was chuffed because it was one of those jolly-on-the-outside songs with a much darker interior. The catalyst was a bust-up I'd had with this guy who used to come around sometimes. He made these wacky guitars and I ended up buying a few off him. I soon realized, however, that the only time he ever phoned was when he had another guitar to sell. He wasn't coming to see his old pal Francis, he was trying to drum up some dough. All right, I thought, at least I know where I stand. Then he came around again one night and sold me yet another guitar, only something strange happened this time. As he was leaving he started bending my ear about some project he was involved in that could 'use a little financial support', as he disingenuously put it. I shook my head and tried to get him out the door but he suddenly came on strong, giving me a really hard time about it.

When I finally got rid of him I was so angry I sat down with this guitar he'd just sold me and immediately began bashing out what became the opening signature riff to 'What You're Proposing'. I was really fucking angry, which is why it was so staccato and multi-layered, I really wanted to pound on something! Bernie came round the next day and we wrote the lyrics together in the kitchen in about ten minutes flat. One of the quickest things I ever did – and one of the most successful.

By the time the song was a hit, though, it was hard to get too excited about it. Rick's daughter, Heidi, had died just two months earlier, and to say that it felt peculiar – bordering on the macabre – to see him trying to put a brave face on it as we bopped around on *Top of the Pops* is an understatement. Needless to say, all our other commitments were put on hold while he tried to come to terms with what had happened, including the massive tour we had been planning around the release of the accompanying album, *Just Supposin'*.

Heidi actually died during the making of that album. I was in the studio working on the track 'Rock and Roll' when I got the call. Just as the phone started ringing, the tape ran out in the middle of this guitar solo I was doing. Everything just stopped dead in the studio. That's when they called me into the control booth and told me Rick was on the phone.

At first I found what he had to say hard to believe. I thought he must have got it wrong somehow, that it just couldn't be. I had only been playing with her the day before, watching her skip round the garden. But the longer we talked the more it began to sink in. It was true. She had died at home in an accident.

'Fucking hell, Ricky,' I said. 'Now what have we done?' She was such a lovely little girl; it was dreadful to see what her death did to Rick and his poor family. That was a bad time; very bad. Up until then Rick had always been the bloke who cheered you up just by walking into the room; he was always so happy and full of fun. Now he just went to pieces. Completely black. No vibe at all. It was awful, and it would stay that way for a long, long time to come . . .

Yet another album, *Never Too Late*, came out in March 1981, less than six months after *Just Supposin'*, yet it still went to Number 2 and we were back touring again, harder than ever. Rick said he needed to get back on the road to help him get over the loss of Heidi, so we started with a long British tour in March and carried on throughout the spring and early summer all over Europe. We stuck out a new single – a revved-up version of 'Something 'Bout You Baby (I Like)', which got to Number 9 – and as far as the outside world was concerned it was business as usual again for Status Quo. Underneath the surface, however, personal relations between the four main members were at an all-time low. In retrospect, it's easy to see how it was only a matter of time before something had to give. Or, in this case, someone.

I can't say I was surprised when John Coghlan was the first to crack. Our drug problems had increasingly alienated him, to the point where he just couldn't stand it any longer. That said, John had his own problems with his drinking. He may not have indulged in speed or cocaine, but John could drink for England. He used to have a pint glass by the side of his drums, and a roadie kept it permanently filled throughout the gig. Now he had become messy and put on weight. John had always had a problem with his weight, earning him the nickname 'Spud'. (Rick started calling him that after reading a review where it said John looked like a sack of potatoes.) Now, though, he just ballooned.

It was all very sad. He was such a lovely guy when we first met: handsome, talented, pleasant. Nearly twenty years with us had turned him into someone different. I think the break-up of his first marriage fucked him up, too. At different times, we all tried talking to him about it. You'd come down the next morning and tell the others, 'I had a good chat with Spud last night and I think everything is going to be fine from now on.' Then the next day, off it all went again: these terrible booze binges which would end in him walking across tables and brandishing knives, or locking himself away in his hotel room and refusing to come out.

These days maybe we would have sent him for rehab or counselling or whatever. But we were too busy back then with our own bad habits to come up with any bright ideas like that. Drummers tend to be a breed apart anyway, and John was always a very dark, solitary sort of character. The fact that he was such a heavy drinker only added to his sense of isolation. It just got worse and worse until finally the dam broke and this river of frustration and anger and God knows what else came flooding out. He just blew up in the studio one day and walked out.

It was in 1981, while we were in Mountain Studios making what was supposed to be our happy twentieth anniversary album, *1+9+8+2*. I had gone to the studio early to set up his drums. John hated setting up his own drums and it became something I did for him whenever we were about to start a new album. I'd recently got quite into playing the drums so it wasn't a chore. On this occasion, however, he came in, took one look at the kit and just freaked out, kicking it to pieces. It was totally unacceptable behaviour in a professional studio, but it was that rock star thing of doing it because you know you can get away with it. Just pissing down people's legs. We were all furious and told him to get out and not come back. He was on the first flight home the next day.

And that's how it ended: not with a whimper but an almighty bang. It was sad. But not that sad. We didn't want John to leave, but when he did I have to admit the relief was immense. We especially didn't rue John's departure after we got a new drummer in, because that's when we realized what we'd been missing all these years: someone stable and reliable who liked a drink but knew his limits and always turned up for work on time with a smile on his face. His name was Pete Kircher and he was an absolute diamond.

Pete had first known success in the sixties with a group called Honeybus – best remembered now for their 1968 hit 'I Can't Let Maggie Go'; also the theme tune for the *Nimble Bread* TV ad campaign at the time. I first met him in 1976, when the band he was now in – Shanghai, formed by ex-Johnny Kidd & the Pirates guitarist Mick Green – supported Quo in Germany. We became mates and I had invited him to play on some sessions I produced the following year for ex-Atomic Rooster guitarist John Du Cann. Since then Pete had been in another band called the Original Mirrors, who released a couple of albums then broke up again.

When John walked out, Pete was the first person I thought of. Andy Bown, who'd also worked with Pete, gave the idea the thumbs up, too. When I phoned him from Switzerland he said he was back doing sessions – his most recent gig had been a Nolan Sisters tour – and he didn't take too much persuading to come out and join us in Montreux. We brought him in on a session basis initially, just for that one album. But he was so good we soon offered him the gig full-time, and Pete stayed with us for the next three-and-a-half years. Apart from his playing, which was always spot on, his chief attributes were that he was all the things Spud wasn't any more: professional, easy to get on with – and sober.

It wasn't long, however, before another, more serious problem finally came to a head: the one between me and Alan. It began in 1983, when we were making the *Back to Back* album in Monserrat, and an argument erupted between us over which tracks should be released as singles. The track we both wanted to release as the first single from the album was a tune Alan had written called 'Ol' Rag Blues'. I really pushed for it with Brian Sheppard, saying I thought it would be a great single. Then, just as it looked like I'd persuaded the record company, Alan announced he wanted to sing it too.

I said, 'Well, you can if you want to but they'll never release it as a single if you do.' He was indignant, demanding to know why. 'You know why,' I shrugged. 'Because you're not seen as the singer. It's not my fault, you're just not.' But of course, being Alan, having opened his mouth he wasn't going to back down now and so it was agreed that we'd do two versions – Alan singing on one, me singing on the other – and let Brian Sheppard choose which one the record company released as a single. That's how ridiculous it got. We even did two different mixes; the first, what Alan called his Full Monty mix, at AIR Studios in London, which cost a fortune; the second, done by me, called the 'budget' mix, at a small, much cheaper studio outside London called the Factory. (I remember we had to be quick because Bonnie Tyler was booked in to record a new song called 'Total Eclipse of the Heart'.)

Then we played the tracks to Brian and guess what he said? The thing that really got me was how surprised Alan was. It really crushed him, because to Alan it was simple: Rossi sings the singles; Parfitt sings the singles; Lancaster should sing one of the singles, too. It's hard to argue with that kind of logic. Like Bill Wyman saying, 'Well, Jagger and Richards have done all the singing so far, it's time I sang one, too.' But why? You're the bassist; be a great bassist. Leave the singing to the singers.

It didn't necessarily mean that Brian or anybody else at the record company thought any better of my version, they just made the right commercial decision, as I had tried to tell Alan they would. As far as I was concerned, it didn't matter who came up with the songs as long as they were hits. Alan didn't see it like that. Even when the single went Top 10, it didn't appease him in the slightest. It even began to affect his relationship with Rick, as they jockeyed for position in the band. Silly arguments over who got the most close-ups on *Top of the Pops*. We were deep into Spinal Tap territory . . .

But the argument over 'Ol' Rag Blues' was as nothing compared to the firestorm of hell that rained down on me over a song from the album that I had written with Bernie called 'Marguerita Time'. Brian Sheppard was absolutely adamant we release it as a single in time for Christmas that year; predicting another big hit for us if we did. I was surprised. It hadn't occurred to me until then. But the more I thought about it, the more I could see Shep's point. Inspired by my own then unquenchable thirst for the stuff, 'Marguerita Time' was a wonderfully gleeful, country-flavoured tune full of singalong choruses, and I could see why it would fit right in on the radio over Christmas. Sure enough, it came out the first week of December and by the end of Christmas week it was Number 3. Alan, meanwhile, was aghast. He had always hated the song anyway. He wanted to keep the band as this macho, heavy rock outfit, and phrases like 'Christmas single' were enough to send him into a fit.

In truth, Alan wasn't alone among hardcore Quo fans in thinking 'Marguerita Time' lightweight compared to what we were usually known for. But it's now probably my all-time favourite Quo single. It also helped us reach a new audience, as we suddenly found ourselves being played on Radio 2 for the first time and appearing on more mainstream TV shows like *Little and Large* and *The Russell Harty Show.* (Rather bizarrely, the song also met with the approval of a certain mixed-up Brummy boy named Kevin Rowland, who felt moved enough to later cover it with his group Dexy's Midnight Runners.)

'We shouldn't be doing this,' Alan kept saying. 'How will I ever face my family again?' I was so angry, at first I didn't know what to say. Then I recovered my voice and we had a right old ding-dong. If Alan hated the song so much, then fine, I could accept that. If it had been a total flop, then double fine, he was right all along and we were fools not to listen to him. But it wasn't a flop, it was a big success, and while Alan continued to voice his distaste – refusing even to help promote the record with us (Jim Lea of Slade filled in for him when we did *Top of the Pops* that Christmas) – I noticed he had no problem taking his share of the royalties from its subsequent sales.

That was the last straw for me. For the first time since the days before 'Matchstick Men', when it looked like I was going to have to give it all up and become an ice-cream man, I began to think seriously about leaving the group. Rick and I had already talked about it once or twice. I remembered on the last tour how we had been at some airport in France, strolling round the departure lounge together waiting for our flight, talking about how fed up we both were and how it couldn't go on like this for much longer.

We talked about what we would do if we left and I said I'd probably go solo. As the front man, at least people knew my face and my voice, so that would give me a fighting chance of success, I reasoned.

Rick looked down. 'Yeah,' he mumbled, 'you always were number one with the fans. I'm fed up being number two.' I was taken aback. I hadn't meant it like that at all. I was merely thinking aloud, confiding in him. It was the first time I even realized he felt that way.

I had never seen Rick and me as competing; I still don't. To me, we complement each other. There are lots of things Rick did back then that I would never do – posing for books like Paula Yates's *Rock Stars in Their Underpants* or getting a custard pie in the face on kids' TV shows like *Tiswas*. He'd be a perfect candidate for *I'm a Celebrity – Get Me Out of Here!* I'm not saying stuff like that is beneath me, I just haven't got the showbiz nous to pull it off. Rick has, and that has made him much more famous than me on occasions. That's how the whole Rossi & Parfitt thing came about, as opposed to Rossi and those other guys, which it was for a while in the seventies.

I tried saying some of this to him that day at the airport but it simply didn't register. It seemed that, with the exception of Andy and Pete, none of us was happy with our lot any more. That, on top of all the hassle over 'Ol' Rag Blues' and 'Marguerita Time', was what finally pushed me over the edge and made me feel I had to get out. I wrestled with it in my mind all over the Christmas holidays and by New Year's Day I had come to my decision.

I didn't suddenly announce that I was leaving or anything dramatic like that, I began simply by saying I didn't want to tour any more. The others didn't like it, but they reluctantly agreed to go along with it on the basis that we did one last lucrative 'farewell' tour. Before I knew it, an announcement had been made in the press and tickets were on sale for what became dubbed the End of the Road tour. Officially, we were merely retiring from the road; there would continue to be Quo records released periodically. Unofficially, however, although I hadn't said anything yet, I had already crossed that off my list, too.

Maybe the others were secretly hoping I would change my mind later, I don't know. But there was no chance of that. I just didn't want to do it any longer. I had started to see continuing with Quo as a complete and utter waste of time. It wasn't just being in the band, it was everything else that was going on in my life too – the endless grams of coke and the empty tequila bottles piling up around me. But I wasn't ready to face that fact yet, I was still convinced that all my troubles began and ended with being in Status Quo. Now I wanted to put a full stop on it. To shut it all down. For it to finish and be gone. For good.

From the outside, the timing must have seemed very strange. Most bands wheel out the 'farewell' tour when sales are starting to dip. In our case, we were probably bigger, at that point, than at any time before. The record company certainly thought we were mad. I remember one guy there saying we would never sell any records if we didn't tour. That just spurred me on even more. He was wrong and I would prove it. I felt like that about a lot of people in those days. It's one of the hallmarks of long-standing coke addiction: victimhood and a messiah complex all rolled into one.

Symbolic of our contrasting fortunes, in April we had been presented with the Ivor Novello award for Outstanding Contribution to British Music. Four days later our farewell tour started, on 11 April, with two nights at Dublin's cavern-ous RDS Hall. The End of the Road tour comprised sixty-five dates across Britain, Ireland and Europe, including seven nights at the Hammersmith Odeon in London. The climax of the tour was to have been an open-air concert at Crystal Palace's Selhurst Park football ground on Saturday 14 July. But ticket demand was so great – all 27,000 tickets for the Odeon shows alone had sold out within four hours of going on sale – that we added one final show the following Saturday at Milton Keynes Bowl, where nearly 50,000 people turned up. Billed as Quo's Last Show, it was quite an occasion. Or so I'm told. I was so blotto for most of it, all I can remem-ber is falling over a few times. Bob Young came up and played harmonica on 'Roadhouse Blues', which was nice. Or would have been if I could remember it. I was into my full-blown coke-and-tequila phase, being carried to the stage half-conscious each night on the shoulders of a roadie.

It was the same after the Hammersmith Odeon shows in June, when we had a huge farewell party at Stamford Bridge, Chelsea's football ground. Hundreds of people came, includ-ing Roger Taylor and Brian May from Queen, John Entwistle from the Who, Lemmy from Motorhead, and Rick Wakeman from Yes, to name just a few. Again, I'm told a good time was had by all, though what I actually remember of it could be written down in two words: doing coke. Either it was a show day, in which case I obviously needed the toot to get me up for the performance; or it was a day off, in which case I was 'relaxing' and therefore deserved even more toot. I remember being in Switzerland, lying on the bed just as daylight was starting to peep through the curtains, waiting for it to stop; the fire singeing all the circuits in my brain. I lay there grinding my teeth, staring at the ceiling, muttering: 'I *must* get some sleep, I've got to get up again in a few hours. What can I do? I know, I'll have a little toot. That will sort me out . . .' That's the kind of bizarre, twisted logic you get into when you're a coke fiend.

Just to add texture to the backdrop, Elizabeth was now pregnant. Liz and I had developed a complicated relationship: part professional, part personal. She was dark and pretty and full of fiery Irish spirit, and though I was reluctant to commit to anything too serious in the wake of the collapse of my marriage, by the time she fell pregnant we had been together for almost five years and were very much a couple, whether I admitted it or not.

There was also no doubting she knew her gig, and the rest of the band were just as delighted as I was when she finally agreed to come and work for us in the early eighties. She had that kind of confidence and authority that ensured everything always went smoothly when she was around. By the End of the Road tour, however, her main job was looking after me, making sure I didn't walk under any buses.

Our daughter, Bernadette, was born exactly two weeks after the tour ended, on 3 August 1984. I was pleased as punch, especially so when I discovered I now had a daughter. At the same time, I took it in my stride. I already had three children; one more was good news but it didn't feel like such a big deal. Or maybe I just didn't want it to. In truth, I was still a mess, and those early days when Bernadette was a baby are mainly lost to me now. Sometimes Liz and Bernadette would be with me at the house in Purley; sometimes I would be in Ireland with them. Sometimes we weren't together at all. Being together and working together, I think we both secretly enjoyed the breaks from each other. Not that it can have been easy for Liz with a new baby to look after. I doubt

I gave that much thought, though, as I sat there chopping them out and pouring myself another drink.

Not long after Bernadette was born, I recorded one last single with Quo: a version of Dion's fifties hit, 'The Wanderer', which reached Number 7 in October. After all the promotional stuff for that was finished with, however, so were we. Alan went back to Australia, Pete Kircher and Andy Bown went back into session work, and Rick got into making a solo album. The label stuck a compilation album out – *Twelve Gold Bars Volume II* (following an earlier successful Quo compilation of the same name), which went Top 10, and I basically just stopped answering the phone for a while. Once it became clear that I wasn't interested in doing anything else, Alan and Rick even talked for a while about getting in a new guy and carrying on without me. I can't say that prospect thrilled me but I could see where they were coming from. My attitude was: fine, if that's what you want to do, go ahead and do it.

I was thirty-five and desperate to escape my past life in Status Quo. Nobody could have predicted then that we would still be going strong in the twenty-first century. Success back then was always something that was probably going to end tomorrow. I decided the time was right for me to break away; do a bit of writing; work on my own solo albums; maybe some other people's albums, too.

At least, those were the reasons I gave myself as I sat there alone in my darkened room, snorting coke and guzzling tequila. If I'd been less stoned and more honest I might have put it like this: I couldn't stand being in Quo any longer but without them I didn't really know what to do. A solo album seemed like the obvious place to start. Phonogram – who had now absorbed Vertigo – seemed agreeable, and a suitable advance was raised.

I called Bernie Frost. We didn't really know what we were aiming for, except that it was definitely going to be something different from Quo; more Everlys inspired, perhaps. But without the pressure of a band deadline hanging over me for the first time, instead of knuckling down in the studio we dawdled and spent far too long getting out of our heads.

I was the main culprit. I'd get in at about eleven in the morning and the first order of the day was to have a toot, make a few phone calls, have a cup of tea, another toot, then a few more phone calls ... Sometimes they were genuine business calls. Mostly, they would be drug calls. I was always on the phone trying to get more coke organized. By the time I'd done that it would be midday and now I'd have to leave the studio for a couple of hours while I went to get the gear.

Where most casual users might buy coke a gram at a time, by then I was buying it an ounce at a time – 28 grams – which would set you back about twelve or thirteen hundred quid. That would usually last me about a week. Working in the studio, however, chopping out lines left, right and centre to anybody who wanted some, it would all be gone in a couple of days and there I would be on the phone again, hustling around trying to get some more. In the end, the coke was costing me more than it did to make the album.

You couldn't get that amount of money out of a cash machine in those days, so you would have to go to the bank personally with your ID and get them to withdraw the money for you. No big deal, except that when you did that on practically a daily basis they would get very nervous and start checking and re-checking things, until the whole business became an ordeal. In order to avoid that hassle, I would drive around to two or three different branches, withdrawing four or five hundred pounds at a time. A substantial amount but not enough to draw attention, and never from the same branch more than twice in the same week. I would just keep driving until I found a new one, all of which ate into my time. Then, once I had the cash, I would have to go and score the coke. Another long, drawn-out procedure; the etiquette of such high-price coke deals being that you never just pick up and leave, you have to sit around shooting the shit for half an hour first before even broaching the subject of why you're really there. And then you have to sit there while they weigh it all out and listen to them prattle on about what a good deal they're giving you, etc.

By the time I'd get back to the studio with the coke it would be late afternoon. Meanwhile the clock's still running, the musicians and engineers are all waiting patiently because they're being paid whatever happens, and the whole thing just got ludicrous. I'd get back, split the coke up between whoever wanted any, which was most people back then, spend an hour at most, maybe, fiddling with some tune, then go home again, another good day's work done.

The next day the whole thing would start again. When you're doing that much coke, your whole life becomes devoted to it. We got as far as releasing a couple of singles I was quite proud of under the name Rossi / Frost – 'Modern Romance' and 'Jealousy', both of which crept into the Top 40 then crept out again – but as if to underline the futility of the whole project, when we did finally manage to put together enough material for an album, Phonogram declined to release it.

It was while I was working with Bernie, however, that one

day I got a call from Colin Johnson telling me he'd agreed for me and Rick to take part in some charity record that the singer of another Phonogram group called the Boomtown Rats was putting together. His name was Bob Geldof, and although he hadn't even written the song yet he'd told Colin there would be loads of other big name stars there – and that was good enough for Colin.

By the time Bob had put it all together and Colin phoned me back with a time and a place, I'd almost forgotten about it. But Bob and Midge Ure had now written the song. It was called 'Do They Know It's Christmas?' and all the artists appearing on it would do so under the umbrella heading of Band Aid. 'That way there's no fuckin' egos!' Bob had told Colin. I somehow doubted that, though, as he ticked off the names Bob had talked into getting involved.

I did wonder, in fact, what sort of reception Rick and I would get from some of the newer, younger artists that would be there. By then, Quo's proto-seventies rock had been superseded on the front pages of the music press, first by punk and now by what they called the New Romantics: new kids on the block like Spandau Ballet, Ultravox, Culture Club and Duran Duran – all of whom would be involved in the Band Aid record, too. I knew that as far as these kids were concerned, Quo were old farts. For my part, while I could see they looked great in their videos, I wasn't so sure any of these bands could actually play worth a damn. We were both coming at it from our own prejudiced positions.

But Bob had asked nicely and said that Phil Collins and Sting would also be there, so we wouldn't be the only thirty-somethings in the room, and Rick and I agreed to go along. That's where we discovered the great leveller, the common ground between old seventies farts like us and young eighties fops like them: drugs. Rick and I might have felt a little incongruous at first, milling about with all these eighties haircuts, but you know what they say: you're never alone with a bag of coke. Sure enough, our little corner of the room became the place to be and we ended up getting on well with everybody that day except for Boy George's friend Marilyn. He kept going in and out of the ladies' loo, making this big thing about being gay and not knowing if he was a boy or a girl and all this hoo-hah. It was so boring I got fed up and said, 'Look, why don't you just go into the men's loo and sit down? I'm sure you'll be more comfortable in there.' He looked at me as though I was taking the piss. I was.

Our only real problem that day was that by the time we came to do our vocals, Rick had already peaked and could barely manage a croak. I ended up having to do his part for him. I really did try to sound like him, too. Being Rick, though, he still managed to claim pole position when it came to the team photo at the end, elbowing himself in down the front next to Sting.

As we now know, 'Do They Know It's Christmas?' was a huge success, becoming the Christmas Number 1 in 1984 and inspiring a copycat Band Aid record in America, 'We Are the World'. By the start of 1985, plans were now afoot to stage a giant Band Aid concert at Wembley Stadium that summer. As we'd been on the original record, we were one of the first artists Bob spoke to about the show.

At first, I admit, I was sceptical; not about the concert, just our capacity to do it. Spending a day in the studio snorting coke with Rick and a bunch of other lunatics was one thing; resurrecting the band and actually doing a gig, even for such a good cause, that was another thing entirely.

I told him: 'We're not really together as a band any more.'

Bob said, 'It doesn't matter a fuck! Just get back together for the day. It doesn't matter what you sound like as long as you're there!' Which I thought was a bit too honest, but that's Bob for you. We somewhat reluctantly agreed to give it a go and at least contact Alan in Australia.

To my utter amazement, Alan agreed to fly to London at his own expense to be there. Now we didn't have any excuse not to do it. We called Bob and said: 'We're in.' Then the whole thing snowballed and all the big names came on board: Paul McCartney, David Bowie, Led Zeppelin, Bob Dylan, Madonna, Mick Jagger, Elton John, Queen ... So many, in fact, that it was decided there would be two Live Aid concerts, staged simultaneously in London and Philadelphia. Because of the time difference, the Wembley show would begin first.

It was one of those days that nobody who was there will ever forget, perhaps the greatest rock festival of all – that's what they always say about it, isn't it? Yet I'm amazed Rick and I have any shared memories of Live Aid at all, we were so out of it for the whole thing. I do remember the trumpeters and trombonists from the Guards regiment that played a few bars of 'God Save the Queen' just before we went on, then Radio One DJ Tommy Vance booming over the PA: 'It's twelve o'clock in London, it's seven o'clock in Philadelphia. This is Live Aid. Will you please welcome ... Status Quo!'

With Tommy's sonorous voice still ringing in our ears, we walked on stage at Wembley and opened with what became the event's unofficial anthem, 'Rockin' All Over the World'. Mike Appleton, then producer of the influential *Old Grey Whistle Test* TV show and the man in charge of organizing the BBC's live coverage that day, had canvassed hard for us to start the show with it, and he was spot on. 'Rockin' All Over the World' epitomized what Live Aid was all about. Within seconds the crowd was clapping and singing along. We finished that, then bashed through 'Caroline' and 'Don't Waste My Time' before saluting the crowd and walking off again. The whole performance lasted just twelve minutes.

But if our Live Aid set was the shortest we'd ever done, it was also, without question, the most significant. With over 70,000 fans in the actual stadium and over 2 billion, according to Bob, watching at home, I was told it was the largest event ever staged for a global TV audience. Suddenly we were famous in countries we'd never even heard of. And while Live Aid famously boosted the careers of several bands, most notably Queen and U2, it also rescued Status Quo, providing us with a publicity boost no manufactured PR campaign could possibly have achieved.

That said, in other respects Live Aid was no different to me from any other day back then. I had already done a gram of coke and half a bottle of tequila before we even went on stage. I think we did exactly one rehearsal beforehand. The feeling was, we're only doing ten minutes, we can knock that off. Quo didn't really exist any more, so who cared anyway?

We met up that Saturday morning at a pub in Battersea, near to the riverside apartment where Rick now lived. That would have been where I had my first quadruple tequila of the day. Then we were helicoptered off to Wembley Stadium. Looking out of the window as we came in to land you could see the place was already packed; everybody raring to go. What was different about this crowd, though, was that you knew they weren't there just to see you. They were part of the whole event, too. Stoned as I was, it gave an added aura to the event that was palpable.

Watching Quo from the Royal Box that day was the man at the centre of it all, Bob Geldof, in the company of

Prince Charles and Princess Diana. As Bob later recalled in his autobiography, *Is That It?*, Charles sat there tapping his brogues, then turned and shouted in Bob's ear: 'We're having a party at the palace next week. I don't think it will be like this, unfortunately.'

Before we knew it, we were being hustled off stage, to be replaced by the Style Council. There was the obligatory backstage photo and several interviews I garbled my way through, then it was off to the special Hard Rock Café enclosure backstage. It was nearly one o'clock and we had fed the world. Now it was time to start feeding ourselves. Rick went off in the helicopter back to the pub in Battersea, where they were having a special Live Aid party, while I stayed at the stadium.

Freddie from Queen came over and gave me a big hug, picking me up and swinging me round. He was so strong, the thought suddenly occurred: if he wanted to shag me right now, he could. There was no way I could have stopped him. Thankfully, I wasn't Freddie's type and he soon put me back where he'd found me – then went out there and led Queen through the best performance of the day. Like us, they had been through their ups and downs, but they had always been good guys and I felt proud as I watched them on one of the backstage monitors, because they really were the best thing all day.

With the exception of Elvis Costello, who it appears thought so highly of himself he refused even to speak to me when I tried to say hello, all the artists were friendly backstage. Nearly all of them were wasted, too. By the end of the day there were some real casualties walking around, not least yours truly. David Bowie astounded everybody by doing the opposite and looking better and better as the day wore on. By the end of the night, at which point I was a gurgling, bug-eyed mess, he was as fresh as a daisy. I said, 'How do you do that?' He leaned over and smiled. 'Ah, ha,' he winked conspiratorially, then walked off looking more immaculate than ever.

Finally, we were all gathered behind the stage, waiting to go on for the big finale. I had been sitting at a table with Bowie and Steve Van Zandt when suddenly the lights went out for some reason and the table collapsed, and we all had to scramble about in the darkness, trying to get to the stage. By now, Rick had returned from the pub on the helicopter and was even more shit-faced than me. The next day neither of us could remember being on stage for the end of the show. It wasn't until I saw the pictures in the papers and on TV that I was sure we'd actually done it.

It took a while for the magnitude of the occasion to sink in. Even longer for us to revive Quo again. But when we did finally resurface we found that Live Aid had transformed the band's reputation, and that we were now household names. Elder statesmen even; rock royalty that did a lot for charity. The irony was not lost on me as I sat there watching the telly and chopping out a few more lines.

It's strange how it worked for us, in that respect. Even before Live Aid – just at that moment, ironically, when our personal lives were starting to unravel – the band itself had begun to achieve a new-found respectability, through sheer dint of having been around for so long. It was over twelve years since 'Matchstick Men' had been a hit when, in June 1980, the Nordoff-Robbins Music Therapy Centre presented us with the Silver Clef Award for Outstanding Services to British Music at a special ceremony in London.

When we then became the first rock band to do a concert for the Prince's Trust Charity, in May 1982 – the first time we ever met Prince Charles: a decent bloke who stuck around longer than he had to just to have a drink and a chat with us – it threw a whole new light on the name Status Quo. We were spending less time in the music press and more time in the proper newspapers. Now, in the wake of Live Aid, that light had turned into a halo. Which is bizarre, given the shenanigans going on behind the scenes. Live Aid cemented our reputation as do-gooders just at that moment when we were at our most bad.

If there had ever been a perfect time to cash in, it was now. The only snag, of course, was that Quo no longer existed in any real sense. This minor detail did not deter our wily 'advisor' from making the moves that led to the band, albeit in altered form, getting back together in 1986. It always struck me as quite a coincidence, for example, that neither Rick nor I ever got to have our respective solo albums released. Instead, we were informed that contractually we still owed Phonogram one last album as Quo, and that in the wake of Live Aid the company was now pressing hard for it, even so far as threatening to sue if we didn't deliver.

I dug in and said I wouldn't do anything that involved Alan Lancaster. I was assured I wouldn't have to; that as long as the label had me and Rick, they felt they still had Status Quo. I believe Rick was told the same thing; that he could forget about the label cooperating with any solo projects until they had a Quo album first. It was a fait accompli. I wasn't happy, but when I spoke to Rick about it on the phone he sounded upbeat. He said he had been using an amazing new bass-and-drums partnership on his solo album and that we should try them out because I'd like them. I wasn't so sure, but reluctantly agreed to go along to a rehearsal.

To my relief, the two new guys were as good as Rick had

promised. Both were extremely experienced and competent, and because they were already a team, were immediately relaxed and easy to get on with, really doing their best to make *me* feel at home. It was strange but nice and I took to them straight away.

Even though he was three years younger than me, the bass player, John 'Rhino' Edwards, had done the lot, starting out in seventies bands like Rococo and the Spam Band before joining Euro-disco act Space (who had a hit in 1977 with the single 'Magic Fly'), then returning to the UK and working with everybody from Sandie Shaw to Judie Tzuke, the Climax Blues Band, and Dexy's Midnight Runners – in time for the latter's success with 'Come on Eileen'.

After that he had fronted his own group: a heavy rock power trio called Rhino – hence his nickname. But despite some good press they never got a deal, and by the time I met him he was working with the drummer, Jeff Rich, as a sort of gun-for-hire rhythm section. Jeff was another guy who had been around, starting in the sixties with Billy J. Kramer, followed in the seventies by stints in Jackie Lynton's band, then Stretch, who had a hit in 1975 with 'Why Did You Do It'. He first met Rhino when they played together in Judie Tzuke's band in the early eighties; now they were a session partnership. Andy Bown also joined us for rehearsals and the new line-up slotted together so well, so quickly, it wasn't long before we began to lay plans for our comeback.

Publicly, I was elated. We had even begun recording a new album – our first for three years. Compared to the last few albums the original band had made, it was an incredibly easy, almost effortless process. Everyone was so full of the joys of spring again, we couldn't wait to show people what the new band could do. Privately, however, I was still beset by doubts. Alan had predictably hit the roof when he'd heard of our plans to resurrect Quo without him. He tried to injunct us from using the name and the whole thing ended up in court. Even as we were making the album, none of us knew for sure whether we'd actually be able to release it as Status Quo.

We went to court and got a preliminary ruling in our favour that allowed us to continue until the whole thing could come before the high court. The case threatened to drag on all year. Meanwhile, we had finished the album but couldn't release it. Mercifully, Alan eventually saw sense and agreed to an out-of-court settlement. It was a desperate way to end what had been an amazingly successful partnership, but I didn't want to work with him any more and, true to form, instead of trying to settle our differences in an amicable way we ended up fighting. In the end, we paid him a six-figure sum for the right to continue as Status Quo without him; a vast sum of money for the time but worth every penny, from our perspective, just to get the chance to start again.

Ironically, right at the end, Alan came to me and said, 'I know you're the main bloke in this band.' I said, 'It's a bit fucking late to be telling me that now, isn't it?' But he was always that way, right from when I first knew him: stubborn to his own detriment. Alan officially resigned from Status Quo in January 1987.

In order to avoid a repeat scenario, some ground rules were established with the new band right from the off. The main one being that, while we wanted everyone to feel free to chip in ideas, Rick and I were now the ones calling the shots. It's all very well operating under the notion of a 'band democracy', but we needed leadership – and no more fights about which track would be the single. From now on it would be up to me and Rick, as the only surviving members of the original Quo, to provide that leadership.

The others were happy to go along with that and our first single with the new line-up – an upbeat rocker called 'Rollin' Home', produced for us by Dave Edmunds and written by his bassist John David – was released in May 1986. The first new Quo single for nearly three years, it jumped straight into the Top 10 the following week. It was the first time we did *Top of the Pops* with the new line-up and reaction was positive across the board. A few weeks later we set out on our first tour. We didn't want to play at home in Britain without making sure the new band was super tight, so we began with a trawl around Abu Dhabi, Bahrain, Yugoslavia (as it still was then) and Hungary.

Our UK début took place in July, when we appeared as special guests at four gigantic outdoor stadium shows with Queen: St James' Park, Newcastle, on the 9th; Wembley Stadium on the 11th and 12th, and Manchester City's Maine Road stadium on the 16th. All the shows sold out the same day the tickets went on sale and a fifth show was scheduled for Knebworth Park on 9 August. Again, I was so out of it I can't pretend I remember too much about it, but over 120,000 people came to the Knebworth show, and I'm glad at least to be able to say I was there. We didn't know it then, but Freddie was already ill and it would be Queen's last ever performance in Britain.

Meanwhile, we were back, I was sure. A second single, another Dave Edmunds-produced John David song called 'Red Sky', had also jumped straight into the charts. And a couple of weeks before the tour started, Rick and I took part in the Prince's Trust 10th Anniversary Party – joining an all-star line-up, fronted by Paul McCartney, for a short but sweet set comprised entirely of Beatles songs. The show was filmed and later broadcast by the BBC.

It wasn't until the release of our next single, though, that things really took off for us in a big way again. Until then we had merely been playing catch-up with the old band; now our career suddenly went into overdrive again as the new line-up contrived to produce the biggest hit Quo would ever have. It was called 'In the Army Now'. I first heard it on the radio in Ireland some time in 1982 and thought it was fantastic. I loved the whoa-oh-whoa vocal refrain, it really was like the wailing sound you'd make on your first night in the barracks. I thought it was going to be huge but I never heard it again. It stuck in my mind, though, and I tried for months to get hold of the track. I eventually discovered that it had been written by two Dutch brothers, Rob and Ferdi Bolland, who had released it under the name Bolland. I thought we could do a version for our next album, *Back to Back*. But when I played it to everybody they went, naw, not us, mate. Alan, in particular, was dead against it. He wasn't comfortable expressing doubts about the veracity of fighting wars. He thought it made us sound like wimps and conscientious objectors. It was only once the new band was together that we reconsidered it.

I knew it was going to be a monster. I had felt that way about other records in the past, only to see them die a death commercially. But this was something different, I knew it. What I liked best was that it had very little to do with the usual Quo 'formula'. If anything, 'In the Army Now' was a fairly morbid little pop ballad. But somehow we transformed it into one of the biggest-selling singles of the year, peaking at Number 2 in Britain but going to Number 1 in Germany and a dozen other countries around the world. As a result, our comeback album, released around the same time and also titled *In the Army Now*, was our biggest seller for years, spending over six consecutive months in the UK charts alone.

Now I knew we were back for sure. Behind the scenes, however, some of the problems we'd had in the old band still lingered like malignant tumours waiting to erupt. For a start, our manager Colin Johnson had gone, unhappy with the state we were in and the hangers on around us. And my personal life was about to be thrown into disarray again when a new woman entered my life. Her name was Paige Taylor and she was something else. Paige had been born in Delhi, but her family had emigrated to Manchester when she was a child. Now she was a young woman and from the moment I clapped eyes on her I knew I had to be with her. I've always had a thing for Asian women but Paige was simply the most beautiful woman I had ever seen, Asian or otherwise.

We had met on a speaking tour Rick and I did earlier that year. Although the new band was in place by then, everything had been put on hold until the legal wrangles with Alan could be resolved. So Rick and I agreed to do a short speaking tour: one of those 'Audience With . . .' type shows where we sat and told stories about our lives in Quo, then did a lengthy question-and-answer session. Some of these gigs could be quite bizarre. You'd get all sorts there, from obvious Quo anoraks asking obscure questions about the band's history, to hysterical middle-aged women throwing their bras and panties at the stage.

Rick and I were doing the show at the Portland Hotel in Manchester one night, and afterwards I went for a drink in the bar with Bernie Frost, who was also there. When we got there, Paige was there, too, sitting with a friend, this gorgeous blonde that Bernie immediately got the hots for. Which was just as well, as I couldn't take my eyes off Paige. I had spotted her as soon as we'd walked in. I was literally struggling for breath just looking at her.

Bernie and I wasted no time inveigling ourselves into their company, ordering champagne and inviting them out for dinner that night. And that was the start of my relationship with Paige Taylor – and the end of my affair with Elizabeth Gernon.

Despite having a baby, Liz and I had never really set up home together. I had certainly never encouraged any particular move in that direction, and of course I was at the height of my drug period and far too self-absorbed to check whether she felt the same way. I simply let the whole thing drift along. Thinking back now, it must have been hell for Liz, trying to do her job and bring up a baby, knowing I was always there and yet not always there. She was a wonderful, strong woman, and the truth is, if I hadn't met Paige, I would probably have stayed with Liz for ever. But I had met Paige. Wild, beautiful, wealthy, educated, do-anything-for-a-dare Paige, and for now I was absolutely smitten.

Liz understandably took the news badly. We had always agreed that if one of us should meet someone else we would always be honest about it, rather than go sneaking around behind each other's backs, causing even more pain when it eventually came out, as these things always do. So the first thing I did after meeting Paige was go and tell Liz about her. Big mistake. Always lie, that's my advice, unless you're sure you want to lose them. Up until that moment I hadn't really known what I wanted to do. Liz made my mind up for me by promptly quitting the band and cutting off all personal relations with me. She moved to Canada shortly after, taking Bernadette with her, and I didn't see or hear from either of them again for some years.

When they left I was upset but I can't say I was devastated. I probably just hacked out another couple of lines and got on the phone to Paige. The only thing that would have brought me to my knees at that point was if the coke had got on a plane and disappeared to Canada as well...

Paige now became my regular 'girlfriend', though I apply that term loosely. There were no ties; no vows. But we stayed together, on and off, for about two years. Paige was a very cosmopolitan girl and I always liked having her around. She was only in her early twenties and, quite rightly, all she wanted to do was have fun. Her father was a gold dealer who ran his own successful jewellery business, and she was always turning up decked out in forty-grand pearl necklaces and twenty-grand gold-and-diamond rings. She was a snappy dresser, too. When we started touring again, I quite often took her out on the road with me. She invariably brought more luggage than the rest of us put together; suitcase after suitcase stuffed with gold and diamonds and all the latest designer threads. They say opposites attract and that certainly seemed to be the case here. I was a grisly old rocker who did too many drugs, and she was young and fabulous and only drank champagne. For a while it was bliss...

The other thing that hadn't changed about the new band, of course, was the drugs. Rhino told me recently that when he first joined he couldn't believe how much booze and coke Rick and I were shovelling down our necks every day. Which is saying something coming from Rhino, a man who prides himself on his knowledge of the grape, as they say. Back then, though, we used to leave him standing. I was always passing out in strange places: under tables, in the gents', mid-sentence ... I remember waking up in a hotel in the Middle East once with the phone in my hand, having blacked out halfway through a conversation with someone back in England. When I checked out the phone bill was larger than the cost of the room!

Ironically, I always saw tequila as a very 'up' drink. Against the odds, the band was back and bigger than ever, and for a lot of the time I just put it all under the heading of Having a Good Time. In reality, however, I had got to the stage where if I wasn't sitting there with the curtains drawn doing coke, I was sitting there sweating on the phone trying to buy more coke. When I wasn't doing that I was running around like a headless chicken trying to earn the money to afford the coke. Those are the things I remember best about those days now. Not the so-called good times; but the very definite bad times.

Rick got much the same way during this period but he seemed able to leave it alone occasionally for a day or two. I wasn't capable of even that small restraint. I'd wake up in the morning and reach for the coke. I'd need a little toot just to get me from the bed to the shower. I could never remember what I had said or done the night before, either. Sometimes I couldn't even remember where I had been. I hated that. But I'd be sat there in bed chopping out a line as I thought about it, and it became like the movie *Groundhog Day*. I just went through the whole thing again and again, day after day, month after month, literally for years. I knew it was killing me. Yet I felt I couldn't possibly live without it. Even if there was a day when I didn't have so much to drink, I still had to have the coke – every day. It was an absolute must.

One thing I also couldn't do anything about, though, was

getting older. I was nearly forty now and my body was starting to rebel. My nose had been falling to bits for years; I had tried all sorts of nasal sprays to try to keep it going, even sticking a vitamin E capsule up there some nights. Now, though, the membrane separating my nostrils disintegrated completely. I was standing in the shower one day literally pulling bits of gunk from my nose, thinking I had the mother of all nosebleeds. I didn't realize I was actually holding bits of my nose in my hands until I looked in the mirror. To this day, I still have a large hole inside my nose where the coke rotted the flesh away. It's such a hollow shell I can't even pick my nose any more because there's nowhere for the bogies to congregate. It all has to come out of my throat now.

Even then, it didn't deter me. I was still maintaining my usual regime of two bottles of tequila a day and three grams of coke, plus I dread to think how many hundreds of cigarettes and joints. Was I unhappy in my personal life? Unquestionably. Was I running from reality? Absolutely. Was I deliberately trying to kill myself, though? Maybe. In retrospect, I certainly seemed to be going about it very methodically.

Ultimately, soft as it might sound, I think I missed being married. I like being among family. I don't like being on my own. Even when I was with Paige, I felt the emptiness sometimes. We were together for over two years in the end, but in all that time the only guy she knew was the coke-snortin' rock star, and I was slowly growing sick to death of that guy. That was when my relationship with Paige began to crumble. In fact, that's when everything began to crumble, including, to my surprise, my more deep-rooted relationships with both alcohol and cocaine.

The turning point came quite unexpectedly one night in September 1988, in the middle of a fourteen-night run at Moscow's Olimijski Zal stadium, of all places. For the first few nights I'd been drinking as usual right through the show. Then one night after we got back to the hotel, I found I had no desire to do anything other than go to bed. Usually I'd have gone to the bar with Rick and the others and stayed there until six in the morning. Not this time, for some reason. It wasn't like some big momentous decision – though I now realize my subconscious must have been working on it for some time – I just didn't fancy it. Then the following night I didn't fancy a drink until we got to the encores – very strange. The night after that I was barely drinking at all. Something inside had just snapped shut like a book and suddenly I wasn't into boozing any more. I didn't really question it – I was still doing plenty of coke so it wasn't like I was feeling saintly – I just went with it to the point where I found I had pretty much quit drinking completely by the time we got back to London.

Paige hadn't come with me on that trip. I had promised to call her when I got back, but I never quite got round to it. Which was strange. Our latest single, 'Burning Bridges', went Top 5 that Christmas and you might have thought I'd have been out on the razz with her to celebrate. In fact, I never heard from Paige again. I can only imagine she was as bored by the whole set-up as I was by then and simply let it slide.

The next thing to go, rather astonishingly, was the coke. Having broken the vicious circle by not drinking, the coke just wasn't working for me in the same way now. That didn't mean I could function properly without it yet. But that was partly because of the mindset I was still in. I had been unable to function without coke for so long that the minute I stopped taking it I fully expected to collapse. I knew my only chance was to try to taper off slowly.

Of course, it was never going to be that easy and I suffered from various strains of insomnia and depression for weeks afterwards. The trouble was I hadn't found anything yet to replace the coke; to fill the yawning gap it had left in my life. Away from the band, living on my own, I fell into a desperate sort of loneliness. I went to my chiropodist one day, a lovely Irish woman, and asked her to marry me. She thought I was joking and said, 'I'd love to, Francis, but I'm married already.' Then she looked me in the eye and realized with a start that I was serious. If she had said yes, I would have married her that day. I also asked a music teacher friend but she was already married too. Like I say, I was desperately lonely. I knew that was down to me; it had been my choice, ultimately, that things had turned out the way they had. But that didn't make me feel any less isolated and lost.

Some nights on my way back home in the car, I would think: shall I stop off in Balham and pick up a brass? Will that make me feel any better? No. All I really wanted was someone to talk to and no brass is interested in that. Either that or she's going to take me for a ride and sell the story to the newspapers: Rock Star Spills Heart to Tart from Balham! No, balls to that. Sex was no longer simple for me, anyway. I knew that just because you wanted to shag someone it didn't mean you wanted to be with them for the rest of your life, or even get to know them particularly well. What I didn't know yet was that the reverse was also true: that if you really love someone then sex doesn't really come into it at all. That there were more important things in life than instant gratification. Stuff like friendship, affection and support . . .

As I sat there on my own at night, flipping through the TV channels, trying not to think about coke, I realized belatedly that the only truly committed relationship I'd had for the last ten years had been my long-drawn-out affair with booze and drugs. I consoled myself with the thought that now, at least, that part of my life seemed to be coming to an end. It was time to move on. I just couldn't figure out how.

Then I thought of something. Someone . . .

Her name was Eileen.

FOUR

It sounds so stupid now, but I was overjoyed to find myself doing drugs with Francis and Alan again. Ever since I'd stopped smoking dope we'd been on different wavelengths. Now with cocaine we'd found a happy medium again. As a result, we were all pretty out of it, one way or another, for most of the eighties. Offstage was where most of the action took place of course, but even playing live, I would have done a gram of coke and knocked back half a bottle of Scotch before I even went on. I thought it was great; I thought I was great! But really we were living in a twilight world. Just getting off; that was enough back then. We didn't even know there might be more to it than that . . .

One of the side-effects of all the coke use was that me and Francis also became heavy drinkers. Francis would order a tray with something like thirty shots of tequila on it, then set it down on the table and work his way through all thirty shots just like that – bang, bang, bang! I wasn't into tequila but, unlike Francis, I had always been a boozer. It went back to those nights as a kid with my dad at the Working Men's Club in Woking. It was simple: if you were a man, you drank beer. In that respect, I had been a man since I was fifteen.

Now, though, with the coke to keep me going, I went completely over the top, going through a couple of bottles of Scotch a day, plus a couple of bottles of wine and two or three grams of coke. That would be a 'normal' day. On a 'special' day, like when one of our records went in the charts or we'd just sold out a gig, or any number of things – it's amazing how many 'special' days you find yourself having when you're on coke – I would get through even more.

I would try to have a couple of days off every week when I was at home, but on tour it was all day, every day. It made me a monster to live with. I would never go to sleep until daybreak, then I'd wake up all pissed off because the gardener had the audacity to be out there mowing the lawn at midday! Why he couldn't have done it at three in the morning, when I was up and about and wouldn't have cared about the noise, I didn't know. At that hour, I was usually so out of it I'd have probably gone out there and cut it with him! Sitting there bombing along in the old mower, completely zonked...

Once at Highland Court, drunk, I basically threw the entire dining-room suite into the swimming-pool. I thought it was rock'n'roll, but the next morning I had to sheepishly go and fish it all out again. I couldn't even remember doing it. I looked out of the window and went, 'What the fuck's all that in the pool?' Marietta said, 'You threw it in there last night.' I thought: how did I even lift it? Because it was everything – table, chairs, cabinets full of knives and forks and crockery and whatnot – all in the pool. The strength you have when you're drunk, it's frightening.

Inevitably, all this affected my family life terribly. But the band seemed to be getting bigger every year and the money kept rolling in, and by 1980 we had left Highland Court behind and moved into a huge new place called Hydon Ridge, near Hydon's Ball, one of the most remote and beautiful parts of Surrey. It was the sort of gaff that would cost several million now. I bought it for £192,000 at the end of the Rockin' All Over the World tour in 1978.

This was the place where we were all going to live happily ever after. The full-on rock star country mansion: eight acres of grounds with our own woodlands; six bedrooms and bathrooms; tennis courts; snooker room; swimming-pool; saunas ... I even had a twenty-four-track recording studio built where the band recorded backing tracks and demos for a couple of albums.

Again, as I had at Highland Court, I had all the garden areas lit up, front and back. Coming home in the car at night, down the A3 from London, you could see our place from about four miles away! It was situated on what turned out to be the highest point in Surrey. On a clear day you could stand on our back porch and look out over twenty-five miles of uninterrupted views all the way down to the coast. It was magnificent. Some nights, if the clouds were low, you would actually drive through them as you climbed the hill towards the house. We used to say it was like looking down on the world from heaven.

Roger Taylor from Queen lived in a similar-sized place literally across the next field and we used to hang out sometimes. We used to say we should get a couple of horses and ride them over to each other's gaff, because they can't nick you for riding a horse drunk.

It should have been an idyllic life, and it was, before I started fucking things up, first with my boozing and then with the coke. That was when the dark clouds started to appear, including one gaseous monstrosity that would submerge my family into the deepest possible gloom when my two-and-a-half-year-old daughter, Heidi, died in a tragic accident at home in August 1980.

First of all, I want to make clear that what happened to Heidi had nothing whatsoever to do with drink or drugs or unruly behaviour on my part. The band was off the road, putting the finishing touches to our next album, *Just Supposin'*. It was the weekend and I was at home enjoying a nice, chilled-out Sunday afternoon with the family. Heidi had been with Marietta, who was in the kitchen cooking lunch. I was in the lounge watching TV with Richard. Then Marietta came in and asked where Heidi was. I said I didn't know, that I'd thought she was with her.

There was no panic yet. I just got up and went to help find her. I remember us walking round the house calling out, 'Heidi! Heidi! Where are you, darling?' No response. Now a bit of panic started to creep in. If she wasn't in the house, she must be outside. There were eight acres of grounds out there and she could be anywhere. We ran outside and started calling her again. Still no response.

Now the real panic began. Then it went through me like a thunderbolt – the swimming pool! As soon as I thought of it, I already knew. I dashed round the side of the house to the pool and there she was, floating face down in the water. I didn't have time to think – that would come later, when it seemed like I had an eternity to do nothing else – I just dived in and got her out of there, then laid her down and tried to resuscitate her. I didn't have any training, I just knew from watching TV that you had to pump the chest first to get the water out of the lungs, then try with the mouth-to-mouth.

It didn't work. I tried and tried until I was gasping for breath and nearly sick, but still her inert little body refused to respond. Marietta was screaming hysterically. We called for an ambulance but I already knew she was gone. I walked around with her in my arms while we waited for the ambulance to arrive, still just kind of hoping that somehow this was all a big mistake and someone would be along in a moment to rectify it. Only no one was.

Our son, Richard, was speechless. He was only five and couldn't really comprehend what was going on – just that something terrible had happened that was making Mummy and Daddy scream and shout. The ambulance arrived and we followed it in the car to the hospital, which was about five miles away. The whole journey we were just praying they had been able to do something for her in the ambulance, but when we got to the hospital she was still unconscious. They took her inside and tried everything they could to bring her back but it was just too late.

I will never forget that terrible moment when the doctor came in and asked if we would like to see a priest. It was simply the most crushing moment of my life. Then, as if to rub salt into the wound, they said that one of us would have to come and identify 'the body'. Marietta was in no fit state so I did it. It was mind-blowing. You go in and they pull the sheet back and you take a look at your little girl who an hour ago was at home playing and ... I went completely numb. I didn't know *how* to react, what to say, anything. I was just frozen with horror-stricken grief.

Going back to the house afterwards was another nightmare. Unless you have lost a child yourself, I don't think it's possible to understand what that feels like. To see her bed still unmade and all her toys and dollies spread about the room where she'd been playing with them ... the dinner Marietta had been cooking still in the oven, waiting to be eaten ... the swimming pool rippling peacefully outside in the sunshine ... It was soul-destroying; the pain was unbearable. Our daughter was dead. What in God's name were we supposed to do now?

Well, first of all you have to make some phone calls, letting the rest of the family know what has happened. Can you even begin to imagine what that's like? Seeing your wife having to ring her parents to tell them their youngest grandchild is dead? Then having to take the phone from her, still sobbing, and ring your own parents to tell them the same? Unless it's happened to you, the answer is: no, you can't.

Marietta's parents were fantastic. They just jumped in the car and drove all the way to England. Twelve hours later, they were with us. Other friends and family rallied round too. Kevin Godley from 10cc, who was a close friend, came over with his wife, Sue, and stayed with us for a few days. Dave Watson, the England footballer and another close friend, also came down with his missus, Penny. People were there for us, but it was impossible for any of them to really pierce the deep sense of despondency that now descended on us. Although life obviously did go on, I have to say that some of that deep sense of despair has never really left me. Life has simply never been the same again. How could it? I lost my baby girl, and nothing can ever make that right in my mind.

It sobered me up overnight. I had the pool emptied and we never went near it again. Then I began asking questions, confronting God. 'Why have you taken my little girl away from me? You bastard! Why have you done this to me?' It just didn't make sense. Why did this have to happen? What had I done wrong? I might have been a bit of a rocker, a bit of a raver, but I hadn't killed anybody; I didn't deserve this, surely?

Being religious, Marietta had her beliefs and her Bible

classes to fall back on. It didn't mean she felt any less pain – she probably felt it even more than I did – but she did have a network of support behind her which I completely lacked. At one point she actually brought a priest up to the house to talk to me. He tried to give me some words of comfort but I wasn't really listening. Unless he could bring back my little girl I couldn't see the point in anything he was saying.

When that didn't work, Marietta even got Cliff Richard to come and visit me. I remember asking him if I would ever see Heidi again and he said something like, 'If she looks like a milk bottle in heaven, you'll look like a milk bottle in heaven, too. You'll see her for exactly what she is and be closer to her than ever.' That was his line to me, more or less. I tried to take it on board but it didn't really help.

Finally one night I'd had enough. I was in a terrible state: my head felt like it was in bits. I ran out into the garden and ripped my shirt open. I don't know why I did that, maybe to let God see my broken heart. I stood there with my chest exposed, glaring up at the night sky, and begged him: 'Just give me a sign – anything – that my little girl is all right.' God had taken my little girl away from me and I wanted desperately to believe there was some hidden purpose behind it. 'Just to let me know she's all right!' I screamed. 'Just one small sign, anything, please, anything at all . . .'

I stood there waiting for hours, the tears running down my face, but of course no signs came. Not one. I went out there again the next night and made the same speech, then again the night after that and the night after that. I waited and waited for a sign, some small crumb of comfort I could cling to in my hour of need.

Nothing.

I have been a staunch atheist ever since. I had never really believed in God anyway; now I definitely knew he didn't exist. That's when I slammed the door on organized religion for ever. To this day I still think the whole thing is a complete fucking farce. I can't believe that people even pray. And what's the end result? You don't have to be a historian to know about the wars and the bloody tyrannies that have occurred throughout the ages in the name of religion. It's still going on today.

I often think now that if I ever had to go to court again and they asked me to hold the Bible and solemnly swear, I'd say, 'What do I want to do that for? That's just a fairy story, swearing on it would mean absolutely nothing to me.' The only time I use a Bible now is when I'm on tour and I'm smoking in my hotel room. I use it to put on top of the ashtray, to kill the smell.

Having given up on God, I began to blame myself for Heidi's death. I should have known better, I told myself. We should never have had an open pool with the kids around. The same thing had nearly happened to Richard at Highland Court a couple of years before. He had been going round the pool on his bike and had caught an uneven paving stone and toppled into the pool.

We were lucky with Richard, though, and I had been able to fish him out in time. Now, in my grief, I looked at the two accidents and convinced myself that malign forces were afoot. I seriously wondered if it was the Devil trying to get one of my kids. I got past that eventually with the realization that if I didn't believe in God then I couldn't believe in the Devil, either. So many strange things go through your head, though, when you lose a child. I had lived a charmed life for so long,

I wondered if it was just time something really bad happened to me. But that didn't seem right, either. It wasn't fair on the memory of Heidi. For once, this wasn't about me.

We had a service for her in the church in the village of Hambledon, where we lived, though Marietta and I had said our own private goodbyes to her the day before at the undertakers. We went to see her in her tiny white coffin before it was closed. She looked so beautiful we both broke down. Walking away, I literally felt myself go weak at the knees. I forced myself to keep going though, guided by Marietta, knowing that if I stumbled and fell I might not be able to get back up again.

The next day at the service I was only a bit steadier. That is, until it came to the moment when the coffin had to be carried to the grave. That was my job, my privilege, and as I carried the small white coffin to its last resting place, I did so with as much dignity as I could muster, holding my daughter as gently and carefully as if she were merely sleeping ...

Mourning Heidi was one thing, carrying on with my life again was something else. I thought getting back together with the band would be the hardest part, but in fact it turned out to be the thing that finally saved me. At first I couldn't handle it at all. The new Quo album, *Just Supposin'*, was just about to come out and there had been the usual lengthy world tour planned to promote it, but I just wasn't up to it. The guys understood and cancelled everything until I felt ready to come back again. Meanwhile, the first single from the album, 'What You're Proposing', came out and immediately shot to Number 2, making it our biggest hit since 'Rockin' All Over the World' three years before. With the band suddenly inundated with requests for TV and radio appearances, I agreed to come along and help promote the record for a couple of weeks. I shouldn't have gone back so soon, but there was simply no way to promote a single in those pre-MTV days without making personal appearances on various shows. I remember prancing around on *Top of the Pops* and several other copycat shows around Europe, to this very upbeat, jolly-sounding tune, and the whole time I was doing it all I could think about was Heidi. I don't think I smiled once throughout the whole campaign.

Somehow Marietta and I managed to get through that first Christmas and New Year without Heidi. Finally I told the band that I wanted to get back to work, and Quo returned to the road again in March 1981, in time for the release of our next album, *Never Too Late*. At first everybody treated me with kid gloves. But I had talked to Marietta and she felt that the best thing for me was to get back to work. She was right because that tour saved me, it really did. The album was another big hit and I suddenly had other things to deal with. Until then, I had actually been thinking of suicide. The only reason I hadn't gone through with it was because of what it would do to Marietta and Richard. Then I went away with Quo and it stopped me thinking like that. I didn't have time for introspection, I was too busy trying to adjust to being back in the band.

It took more than just one tour to do it, of course, but working hard with Quo over the next few years really did help me through my grieving period, until I was finally able to accept that Heidi had gone and that I was never going to see her again. Once I was able to do that, my grieving ended. She would always be in my heart, but I had finally accepted that what happened had been an accident. Ask any parent, children are always getting into trouble. You're forever taking things out of their mouths, pulling their hands away from electrical sockets, making sure they don't run into doors. But you can never stop them having accidents. They say it's how they learn, and ninety-nine times out of a hundred it's true. So neither Marietta nor myself could accuse ourselves of being to blame for Heidi's death. It was an accident and, tragically, it was that one time out of a hundred where it resulted in a death. The children were forbidden to go near the pool. But I think one of the dogs we had, a little terrier, may have led her there because he was very fond of the water. She knew she wasn't supposed to go there, but she was only two and a half years old. You don't think like that at that age, you just follow the little dog . . .

Rather poignantly, I've actually got some beautiful video footage of Heidi in the pool; on one of those happy days when the whole family was with her, splashing around having fun together. I can now watch it and use it to go back in my mind and remember her, but for many years I couldn't even think about watching it. At one point I even thought about destroying those tapes. I'm so relieved I didn't, though, because it does bring her back for me now – at least, in my mind.

It took a while for me to get to that stage, though. Meanwhile, it didn't stop me acting quite differently once I got off the road. Suddenly that whole countryside scene was way too quiet for me, and what had once been a warm, friendly retreat began to feel increasingly claustrophobic. Heidi had gone, and whatever delight I had once taken in the house had gone with her. My marriage was hanging by a thread and I really didn't know what to do with myself. Inevitably, it wasn't long before I was back on two bottles of Scotch a day and endless grams of coke. We carried on living together like that, trying to be a family, for another year or so, but by then things had completely fallen apart.

I would disappear for two or three days at a time, boozing it up and bingeing on coke and anything else I could get my hands on. Then I would come home, still driving the Porsche even though I was barely able to walk. It's a terrible thing to admit, because I wasn't just putting myself in danger but seriously imperilling the lives of other road users, too. But try telling me that back then . . .

I started having flings with other women. Mainly stoned drunken grapplings out on the road that I refused to even think about the next day. It was gross and unfair to everyone involved and I make no excuses. I had turned into a really horrible bastard. I just didn't care any more. I should have done, because I still had Richard and Marietta to look after, but that was the state I was in. I no longer took any responsibility whatsoever for my actions. To me, it was like I had died, too.

I could probably a write a book just on all the stupid, crazy things I got up to during this period. One particular evening springs to mind, though. A supposedly quiet night at home in which I managed first to nearly electrocute myself, then to completely destroy my beloved Porsche!

We'd just finished some shows in Europe and were taking a short break before starting work on the next album, which was going to be recorded out in Montreux. Nearly a year had passed since Heidi's death, and though we were still totally screwed up about it, life went on and we were starting to socialize a bit again in a vain attempt to get back to some sort of normality. One Saturday night we had Kevin and Sue Godley over for dinner. Although I was sneaking off to the toilet every now and then for a crafty toot, as far as everybody else was concerned it was a nice, normal dinner party and we shared a few bottles of wine.

The drunker and more coked-out I got, though, the less normal the evening became. I had recently got into photography and suddenly decided to take a picture of us all. Next thing I'm grappling with all this elaborate equipment I've bought: lights, tripods, coloured gels, different lenses ... It was exactly the sort of great idea you have when you're high – and a complete pain in the arse for everyone else. I had a perfectly good flash I could have just attached to the camera but, no, not me! I'm out of my skull and I want to get the arc-lights out ...

There must have been a loose connection somewhere, though, because as I was plugging these big arc-lights in I suddenly got the most terrific electric shock! They were 240 volts apiece and I was holding one in each hand, standing there shaking like a leaf while they all sat there laughing because they thought I was putting it on. If it hadn't been for the fact that one of the bulbs burst, breaking the current and freeing me, I would have sizzled to a crisp!

I slumped to the floor with my veins popping out of my neck and my hair standing on end. That's when the others realized what had happened and came running to help me. Needless to say, I never did get that picture ...

But that was only the start of the night. Having recovered from nearly killing myself, I came back from the toilet with an even better idea. I wanted to go for a drive. As Marietta and the others were quick to point out, there were two main obstacles to this plan. The first: I was completely drunk. The second: I was actually banned from driving at the time. I had a ready answer to both of those questions though.

'Bollocks,' I said, and got in the car.

Before Heidi died, I had been in my full-tilt rock-star car-buying phase. I had dozens of them: a couple of Mercedes, a couple of Porsches, a Studebaker Hawk, a Corvette Stingray ... you name it, if it was flash and expensive I probably owned one at some point, right down to a miniature Range Rover for Richard! I was even going to have traffic lights put in my drive because it was about 400 yards long and on a curved, high-banked slope literally carved out of the hill. At one point there was a dog-leg and you couldn't see what was coming in the opposite direction, so I thought the traffic lights would be a good idea. Plus, I thought it would be very rock'n'roll. But to the relief of everybody I mentioned it to, I never quite got round to it.

Of all the cars I owned at the time, my favourite was my Porsche Turbo 3.8. I had two Porsches: one for Marietta, to go with her Merc, and the Turbo for me. It was such a fantastic-looking car. Just to sit in it was exciting. It became like my pal. I'd talk to it and I swear it would talk back! I used to call it Percy – as in Percy the Porsche. The name didn't really suit a sleek-looking mean-machine like that, but that's what it was. I used to get to the bottom of the hill where we lived, take him gently out towards the motorway, then fasten my seatbelt, put my leather driving gloves on, and say, 'Right, Percy, it's you and me, baby, here we go!' Then I'd grip the wheel, put my foot down and start shooting up the A3 towards London at 100 miles an hour. Nothing could touch us; we were a team, me and that car, and I loved him dearly.

Recently, however, I had been banned for twelve months after being convicted for drink-driving. (Something for which I would become a serial offender over the next few years.) Now Percy was just sitting in the garage waiting until I could legally drive him again. I had a chauffeur but, being a car nut, I really missed being able to drive myself, particularly in my beautiful Porsche.

Now I decided I could wait no longer. It may have been the early hours of the morning but that would only work in my favour, I decided with the impeccable logic of the very drunk. We lived at the top of a steep private road, at the bottom of which lay the village, through which came one policeman on a bicycle maybe once a week. All I wanted to do was drive my Porsche to the bottom of the hill and back – who would know? What harm could it do? The fact that I was drunk as a skunk and pumped up to my eyeballs on coke was a mere detail . . .

So off I went in my beloved Percy. It was a long, winding road with only a few other big houses besides ours on it, and I absolutely steamed it down to the bottom of the hill, no trouble at all. Then I steamed it even harder back up again. There was a sharp left-hand corner at one point but I remember thinking, 'It's a Porsche, it was built for fast turns,' so I put my foot down and went for it. I must have been doing about seventy. In the split-second I had to think as the car swung round the corner, I saw there was a Mini parked outside one of the houses which I hadn't noticed on the way down. Now suddenly it loomed all too clearly before me. I didn't even have time to hit the brakes, I just ploughed straight into it . . .

I clambered free of the wreckage and dusted myself down. I was fine because I was in the Porsche and those things are built to withstand impact. But the car itself was badly smashed, and the Mini was a complete write-off. If anybody had been sitting in it they would have been killed, no question. When I surveyed the scene I saw that I had also taken out a red post-box, which I must have hit before I even got to the Mini. Oh, dear . . .

Then the guy who owned the house – and the Mini – came outside, all pissed off in his pyjamas and dressing-gown. That was all I needed. I'd probably be banned for life this time. They might even throw me in the nick. I had to think fast.

I knew the guy slightly as a neighbour, so I said, 'Look, let's settle this without any formalities. I'll buy you a new car, to replace this one. Any model you like, just name it.' He thought about it for a moment then slowly nodded his head. 'All right,' he said. Phew! All I had to worry about now was what car he wanted. I was praying he wouldn't ask for a Rolls Royce. Luckily, he didn't. Instead, he asked for a Singer Vogue, which happened to be his favourite car. I'd never fancied them myself, but I said I'd have one delivered to him that same week.

Because I had mates in the motor trade, I had his Mini towed away to a breakdown yard at the crack of dawn, where it was mashed into a cube and the logbook burnt. They literally made it vanish. Then I had my lawyer, my manager and my accountant all come down that Sunday morning to draw up the relevant documents, along with a confidentiality clause, for my neighbour to sign. In return for which, I got to cover the whole thing up and he got a new car. The only thing that had to be explained to the village was the destroyed pillar-box, which we put down to a rogue hit-and-run accident by some 'loony' driver. Sadly, poor old Percy was never the same again, though, and I had to sell him. It broke my heart, but there you go. Another rock'n'roll casualty. There are millions of 'em . . .

The really stupid thing is that the next day it would all

kick off again. I'd even be quite chirpy about it. 'Well, I nearly killed myself, smashed up my Porsche, then had to buy the bloke next door a new car, but what the hell – who fancies a toot?'

Another annoying habit I had back then – although this time the only person who really suffered because of it was me – was giving away my gold records. By the start of the eighties Quo had been presented with over 100 gold records from around the world just for our albums alone. I was very proud of them all, but for some reason I got into this thing of giving them away to so-called close friends. Anyone I would meet on my travels, if we hung out together long enough and I got stoned enough, they would get a gold record. How I regret that now, especially when I go over to Francis's house and see all his gold records on the walls. I look at how many he's got and realize I must have given away more than half my collection over the years.

For instance, I was hanging out quite a lot back then with the snooker player Alex 'Hurricane' Higgins. Though obviously not in Alex's league, I was a pretty good snooker player myself. As a teenager I had been captain of the Working Men's Club B team, while my dad had captained the A team. So I used to go to tournaments occasionally, which is how I met Alex. This was in 1982, when he was world champion and at the height of his hell-raising stardom. A legendary boozer, it's no secret that Alex was also a bit of a trumpet merchant and, needless to say, we made a good team. We also hung around with other snooker-playing mates of his like Kirk Stevens and Jimmy 'Whirlwind' White. We were all big party animals but Alex was by far the biggest, and I ended up giving him at least two of my Quo gold albums. I would literally get up in the middle of some marathon drinking session, jump in my car and drive sixty miles home to pick up the record, then drive back again, completely shit-faced, in the Porsche at three in the morning. Well, he was my best mate in the world, wasn't he?

Once, I remember, it was the night before he took part in the World Doubles championship. It must have been about five in the morning by the time I came back with this gold record for him. I can't even remember which one it was now but it seemed very important he have it at the time. Alex accepted it gleefully and called for another round of drinks. He was a dreadful mess by the time we sent him off for his doubles match. Needless to say, Alex was not at his best and his side lost heavily that day.

I just couldn't get enough of it: the drugs, the carousing. I was always bringing people I barely knew back to the house in the middle of the night. Or my pet hate: waking up to the sound of the doorbell ringing, only to look out of the window and see half-a-dozen people I'd barely recognize standing there; people I'd met the night before and invited over for lunch the next day. It was unnerving how often that used to happen.

Meanwhile, Marietta was going through her own kind of hell. I'd be off out again and she would be left at home minding Richard, alone with her thoughts. It must have been dreadful for her to begin with, but she started finding her own way through it. She was a ballet and opera lover and had started hanging out in this very theatrical circle that I had no part of. Used to me bringing home all sorts of weirdos, she took to having her ballet and opera friends over, too. I would get home at three o'clock in the morning and be surprised to see all the lights on in the house. I'd go inside and she would be there with her new chums: all these dancers and artists and theatrical types swanning around calling each other darling and drinking pink champagne. Marietta had become this kind of tragic diva figure to them, particularly the gay ones, who loved her because they saw her as this Marlene Dietrich type, with her voluptuous figure, her German accent and her long cigarette holder.

I will never be a ballet or opera lover, but these days I can at least appreciate the artistry involved and how much joy they bring some people. Back then, though, it was all too much for me. I came in once and there was a bloke doing a pirouette across the kitchen floor. I was like, 'What the fuck's going on here?' He looked me up and down and went, 'Oh, you must be *the husband*.' The uncouth yob Marietta was married to. I took the bait of course and immediately reverted to type. 'Fucking right it's me, mate!' I snarled. 'Now fuck off the lot of you!' And much to Marietta's embarrassment they all left.

Poor Marietta. How she was expected to cope with all this, I don't know. She put up with it for a while but in the end she was only human. Finally, I came home one day from another three-day bender and she announced that she was divorcing me.

I was stunned. 'All right,' I said, 'I'll stop all this. I'll stop right now.' But she just looked at me witheringly. 'You've said that before,' she said. 'I know, but this time I mean it, I'll stop!' She shook her head. 'No, you won't.' She was right: I wouldn't have done. I wouldn't have known how. I moved out the very next day. She helped me pack.

I was devastated. I was so used to being away – either because of the band or, more recently, because it seemed like I would rather be anywhere but home – that you might think perhaps that leaving Marietta and Richard behind would not have hurt me as much as it would a father who was used to coming home from work each day and being with his family. But to me it felt like it hurt even more. It made the sense of blowing it all the more palpable. I was never at home much anyway, and when I was there I was so despicable to live with that my wife and son now wanted me to leave. Stoned or not, that's some hard information to try and absorb.

I have wondered since whether the marriage might have survived if Heidi had not died. But something like that should have brought us even closer together; the fact that it didn't tells you where the marriage was at. Not because of Marietta; she was prepared to try to heal the wounds as best she could. It was me. I had already been into my full-blown wild man of rock phase before Heidi died. Now I had gone from bad to worse.

I gave Marietta the house as part of the divorce settlement. I didn't contest it at all, I just gave her everything she wanted – that she deserved, as I saw it. While it was all being sorted out, I rented a small cottage a couple of miles down the road in Chiddingfold. It's a lovely part of the world, but it was the middle of winter and the cottage was like something out of *Wuthering Heights*: a cold, dark, creepy little place with no gas. It had electric lights but no central heating, and the cooker was powered by Calor gas cylinders that you had to keep replacing. The only heat came from a big open fire which you had to build yourself. It was nice to sit in front of once you got it going, but it never quite got the whole place warm and the bedrooms would be damp and freezing. It was a terrible place to be on your own, but I wanted to be somewhere close to the family, even though I was banished from the household, and this was the best I had been able to come up with at short notice.

It was the winter of 1983 and the band was off the road at the time, taking a break before beginning work on the *Back to Back* album. I had absolutely nothing to do and the loneliness was terrible. I would spend whole days and nights sitting on my own in the Crown. A picturesque pub restaurant where Marietta and I had gone sometimes in the old days, its chief attribute now was that it was less than 100 yards from the cottage, so I didn't have to drive to and from it. I could just stagger . . .

What saved me from sinking into total depression was the arrival of someone new in my life. Her name was Deborah Ash – sister to the actress Leslie Ash, who later became famous in the TV comedy show *Men Behaving Badly*. Debbie was a dancer in Hot Gossip, the 'saucy' dance troupe that appeared on the *Kenny Everett Video Show*, then the hottest new thing on TV. We had met when Quo appeared on it once.

I took an instant shine to Debbie because she was more like me back then: wild. Marietta was straight and didn't do drugs, didn't really drink except for a glass of wine occasionally. She was friends with Cliff, for crying out loud, how straight can you be? Debs was the opposite. She just didn't care.

She was also just getting divorced from her husband, Eddie Kidd, the stunt bike rider, and she had a flat in Clapham, in South London, which she invited me to move into with her. I jumped at the chance. Marietta was refusing to see me at all by then, and I had become so cocooned inside the cottage that I couldn't tell if it was day or night without getting up to look out the window. Mostly, it seemed to be night. Where I was, you never saw anyone new. Some days you never saw anyone at all. That just wasn't me. I've always been an outgoing person. Even now that I'm older I don't think I could endure that kind of isolation. Back then it nearly drove me up the wall.

Then Debbie came along and all that changed. She was right on my wavelength: out at the clubs every night, stacks of make-up, always tarted up. She looked like a pretty China doll and loved to get loaded – my kind of gal. So I left the gloomy little cottage behind and went to live with her in Clapham. She and Eddie had a young daughter named Candy who lived with us too. She was a beautiful little girl, and of course it doesn't take a rocket scientist to see why I would enjoy being around someone like that again. There was a housekeeper, too, so Candy was well looked after whenever Debs and I went out on the razz. It was nice to be in that sort of family environment again. At the same time, it was weird because Eddie was the one out of the picture – just as I was with my own family – and I understood what he was going through, though I tried to keep out of their business as much as possible. The agreement was that I could live there rent-free as long as I looked after Debbie and Candy in every other way financially, which I did.

Meanwhile, life just carried on getting crazier. It just went fucking mad and stayed that way for the next two and a half years. It eventually went pear-shaped between me and Debbie, but by then everything had gone pear-shaped. All my good luck appeared to just run out at once.

It was strange. Before I got involved with drugs, people used to say that if I fell into a pot of shit I'd come up smelling of roses. It's kind of a nice thing to have said about you but it's also kind of dangerous too, because you start to believe it. Up until Heidi died, I had felt that things would basically always turn out for the best. So I would go out on a limb: buy that car on an impulse; chase after that girl I'd only just met; join that strange rock'n'roll band from Butlin's ... I think I thought I was pretty indestructible.

My mum always used to say to me: don't tempt fate. But I *was* tempting fate, and sure enough, it got me back. For a long time – years – it was like everything the band touched just turned to gold. Now all of a sudden it was like we were being presented with the bill. One thing after another started to go wrong, like cracks in the ice suddenly appearing. Then suddenly there was an avalanche and the whole edifice came crashing down around us ...

The signs were there for all to see when John Coghlan left during the making of the *1+9+8+2* album in Montreux in 1981. The pressure was starting to tell on us all by then. There were lots of arguments between Alan and Francis, as there always had been, only now they assumed a new edge. Like me, they were both doing a lot of coke and it just made their fall-outs even more manic. To his credit, John wouldn't allow himself to get drawn into all that. For a start, he didn't do coke or any other drugs. He was strictly a boozer, so that meant he was always on a different wavelength to the rest of us anyway. I felt I knew where he was coming from better than the others, because I had also felt somewhat ostracized when I'd stopped smoking dope. Now that we were all doing coke, though, I was back in the inner circle with Francis and Alan, and I suppose John began to feel more and more outside of things again.

You might have thought success would provide him with its own compensations, but the bigger the band got the worse things seemed to get for John. He had reached the stage where he was walking through hotel foyers slashing furniture with a knife. He had also started to put on a lot of weight and really let himself go. I think he saw himself as this tragic Keith Moon-type figure, but to us he was just a pain. It was such a shame, because he was basically a really good guy who just wanted to do his own thing. But success did something to him – to all of us – and in the end he couldn't handle it at all. He would lock himself in his hotel room and sit there sobbing his heart out. We would stand at the door listening. We had no idea what to do. We were always in the middle of a tour so we just carried on as best we could.

It finally came to a head in Montreux. John came in the first day, did one roll round the kit, then went into a tantrum and kicked the whole thing apart, sending bits of it flying all over the studio. Francis and I stood there fuming. Then we turned as one and said: 'Right, that's it, Spud. You can fuck off. We've had enough of you.' He must have had enough of us, too, because he didn't protest, he just got up and walked out.

John went home and in his place we got this mild-mannered guy called Pete Kircher: an ace drummer and all-round good guy. After all the traumas with John, it was a real pleasure to have someone like that in the band again. It was only a temporary peace, however, and by the time I'd met Debbie and we were ready to release the *Back to Back* album in 1983, tensions between Francis and Alan had reached such a tumultuous stage that they now threatened to bring down the band itself.

In retrospect, there were probably several turning points in their relationship. The straw that broke the camel's back, though, involved a song Francis had written with Bernie Frost called 'Marguerita Time'. It was a cheerful, old-fashioned-sounding tune, almost folksy, that the record company decided would make a perfect Christmas single that year.

Being the out-and-out rocker that he was, Alan hated the idea. He thought it was far too namby-pamby and not right for Quo at all. Francis naturally took this badly. As usual, I was stuck in the middle. Like Alan, I saw myself as a rocker, and Quo as primarily a hardcore rock band. But because of my cabaret upbringing, I was also able to see it from the other side, and there was no question that 'Marguerita Time' had 'hit' written all over it.

Like Francis, I was also keen to spread the band's musical wings a bit. We'd had an unbroken record of chart success for over ten years, and if we now wanted to do something a bit different, why not? Like ballads. We'd never had a ballad as a single before we came up with 'Living on an Island' in 1979, but that didn't prevent it being a hit. I liked that because it meant it wasn't just diehard Quo fans buying our records; they were now appealing to people across the board. It was the same thing for me with 'Marguerita Time'.

Alan wasn't happy with that direction at all, though, to the point of saying, 'How am I going to play this to my friends? They're gonna laugh at me!' As soon as he said that, I looked at Francis's face and thought, oh no, here we go . . .

It caused such a huge row between them that Alan refused to even help promote the single, which was a pity because 'Marguerita Time' turned out to be another big hit for us. But by then I don't think either of them cared any more. Francis knew it could be Number 1 for a year and Alan would still hate the song. I think that's when Francis made up his mind he'd had enough.

He didn't come right out and say he wanted to fold the band, at first he just said he didn't want to tour any more. But I think I knew even then. It was the way he said it. I'd never seen him so serious and determined before.

I was shocked, but I knew what it was all about. I was finding Alan hard work, too. He would get uptight because people always recognized me and Francis but didn't always recognize him, unless he was standing next to us. He especially didn't like it that I had co-written and sung a few of the hits, like 'Whatever You Want', 'Rain' and 'Living on an Island' – something Alan would love to have done. He took all these things so personally, but it wasn't about personal choices. It just came down to good commercial sense and we'd have been fools not to capitalize on it. But Alan just saw it all as terribly unfair on him.

That said, I never saw splitting up as the answer and I was gutted by Francis's decision. We had moaned and groaned to each other in the past, but I never thought he would ever seriously want the band to end. Next thing I know, we're doing this huge 'farewell' tour – the End of the Road tour we called it. I was so dismayed I didn't know what to say. It seemed like the time for saying things had passed.

Although we played to some of the biggest audiences we had ever known, I hated that tour. The whole thing was awful from start to finish. I especially disliked the final show at Milton Keynes Bowl, in July 1984. There may have been 50,000 people there that day, but to me it felt like the loneliest place in the world. I remember standing there thinking as we got to the end of each song, 'Well, that's the last time I'm ever gonna play that then.' As each number ended for the last time – 'Caroline', 'Down Down', 'Rockin' All Over the World', 'Whatever You Want', on and on like a recurring nightmare – it all started sinking in, layer by layer. We were pelting through all these great songs that we were apparently never going to play again and I just thought: but why? How had it come to this?

When we finished the set it was so strange. I still couldn't quite believe it was happening, that this really was the end of everything. It didn't really hit me until we were sitting in the helicopter flying us back to London, looking down on all the thousands of sad Quo fans below. I said to myself: 'I'm just like them. I don't want this to end, either. Yet it has and there's absolutely nothing I can do about it.' It all felt very low. I don't even remember talking to the others much as we sat there. A kind of blankness descended on us ...

Straight after the tour was over, we recorded one more single together – a version of 'The Wanderer', which went Top 10 in October – but after that I didn't see or hear from Francis again for months, and the idea that we might carry on recording together as Quo was quietly shelved. I can't say that really surprised me, but Alan was distraught. Whatever his problems with Francis, Alan hadn't wanted the band to end any more than I had. But we'd given up phoning Francis. He just wasn't returning our calls.

It was disheartening. I felt I deserved more than that. But all contact between us just ceased overnight. Francis wanted to get completely away from Quo, I realize now. As far as he was concerned, the band was definitely over. Whereas, for me, the band had never truly ended. I just saw it as a temporary blip. I don't know why, all the evidence certainly pointed to the contrary, but I just didn't feel like the band *should* end, I suppose.

I confess, I also missed the spotlight. Being in Quo, you knew you could never be number one with the fans because that would always be the singer, as it is with most bands. Ironically, however, Francis was always the one who appeared to seek the limelight the least, maybe because it just came naturally to him. Meanwhile, Alan and I would fight over who would get the most attention after Francis. I knew I was flattering myself by wanting to be number two – Alan had started the band with Francis and by rights he should have been number two in the minds of the public. But I was also aware that people tended to recognize me as much as they did Francis. And I liked that and cultivated that. For me, fame was the name of the game. I felt if I could get on kids' TV shows like *Tiswas* and have baked beans poured over my head, it would make up for the fact that I never got the main spotlight in Quo. Francis would rather cut his arm off than do stuff like that, but I love it! I used to do *Tiswas* most weeks, at one point. I was mates with the presenters, Chris Tarrant and Sally James, and just used to turn up and let them put me in the cage. I have fond memories of standing in there with people like Michael Palin while they pelted us with eggs, flour and all sorts of gunk.

Now all that was gone. Without the band I'd lost my calling card. Worse still, I'd also now lost my only available source of income. Within months, I was broke. The divorce had cost me roughly a million pounds, including the house and court costs – virtually all that I had. Now, with the band no longer working, I had nothing coming in bar the twice-yearly royalty cheques, which were enough to live on but not much more than that. Whatever money did come in was never like the amount you expected anyway. (Something we'll get to later.)

I didn't know what to do. In the past, if I was skint, I knew that as soon as we went back on the road I'd be making money again, so I never worried about how much or how little I might have in my bank account. If I wanted something, I just went out and got it. Now I didn't have that option. My relationship with Debbie was also on the rocks. She had got fed up with me because I was doing so much coke that I could hardly get a hard-on any more. She told me to leave and suddenly not only was I broke, divorced and unemployed, I now had nowhere to live.

As usual, when faced with an insurmountable problem, I did what I always do and threw money at it. I hailed a taxi and told it to take me to the Holiday Inn in Chelsea, where I promptly checked myself into a penthouse suite. Not that I had the money to actually pay for it, I just blagged it on the back of being a famous face. I really didn't know what else to do and eventually stayed there for about three months, racking up a huge bill that I had absolutely no way of paying. I kept putting the hotel management off by giving them the big rock star act and for a while they bought it. After three months, however, they were starting to seriously hassle me for at least some of the bill to be paid and I found myself literally creeping in the back way. I was living in a luxury five-star hotel, virtually penniless, and I felt at that moment as though I didn't have a friend left in the world. Everybody had gone and there I was, truly on my own for the first time in my life.

Thankfully the cavalry was on the horizon in the shape of Colin Johnson, who saved the day when he negotiated a solo deal for me with Phonogram. I got £100,000 in advance and went, 'Whoopee!' That wasn't the word I actually used but you get the picture. I was absolutely flat-arsed broke at that point. Now I was able to pay my hotel bill and find myself my own place to live in. Suddenly I could breathe again.

After spending days walking around looking at cold, dank flats in Victoria, thinking, 'No way can I possibly live in a place like that,' I finally found what I was looking for when I went to see an apartment in a building called Valiant House in Battersea, on the south bank of the Thames. As soon as I walked in I knew it was the pad for me: panoramic views overlooking the river; huge lounge; two good-sized bed-rooms; nice kitchen and bathroom; dining table in an alcove ... I couldn't believe my luck. Best of all, it was situated between a wine bar and a pub! As I didn't own a car now – I was banned again, and had ended up selling them all anyway for the cash – it couldn't have been more perfect.

I rented it for £400 a month. It didn't have much furni-ture, just the basics, but despite my taste in flash cars and expensive drugs, I discovered that when it comes right down to it I don't actually need a lot more to survive on than a TV and a sofa. I still had my guitar and a portable cassette player, too, so really I had everything I needed. Everything, that is, except someone to share it with.

I wasn't rich again by any means, but after laying down a deposit on the flat and paying off the hotel, I still had most of that hundred grand advance burning a hole in my pocket. If I'd been sensible I would have tried to eke it out by booking a small, cheap studio to make my solo album in. But of course that wasn't my way, and I ended up booking a top-notch studio in London and hiring Quo's producer Pip Williams to work with me. By the time we'd finished, we'd racked up a bill for £110,000.

But if the short-term financial cost was high, the long-term benefits proved to be incalculable. For it was while making my solo album that I first met bassist John 'Rhino' Edwards and his drumming sidekick, Jeff Rich. Pip was the one who recommended them to me. He'd first met them when they were in Judie Tzuke's band, and had used them since on other sessions he'd done. The idea was that with me on vocals, rhythm guitar and a bit of keyboards, Pip on lead guitar, and Rhino and Jeff on bass and drums, we would be able to make the album reasonably quickly, which is exactly what happened.

John and Jeff were such a good team they made the whole thing very easy and enjoyable. They were that rare thing: really top session players who don't take themselves too seriously. Jeff, by his own cheerful admission, was a real wanker. I mean that in the literal sense of the word. The fact was, Jeff had to have a wank at least four or five times a day – absolutely *had* to. His sexual libido was just such that he couldn't stop himself. Rhino had forewarned me, but I thought he was winding me up until we got to the studio and I saw the makeshift screen Jeff had erected next to his drum kit, so that whenever he felt the need he could go behind it and wank himself off. Inevitably, it became known as Jeff's Wanking Booth. He'd have his magazines in there and some cushions and tissues and whatnot. He was a fairly irrepressible character anyway, shall we say, and I dread to think what he would have been like if he hadn't been allowed to have his daily wanks. He'd probably have exploded . . .

Slowly things were starting to look up again in my personal life, too, with the unexpected news that an old girlfriend of mine was coming back on the scene: Patty Beeden, my old flame from the days of Mary.

She had been in Australia for over ten years by then. Now I'd heard from one of her friends that she was coming back, and my mind began working overtime. By now I was living in Battersea, shagging a couple of birds on the side but nothing serious, and for the first time in ages I was starting to feel positive about things again. I was off the drugs for the simple reason that I couldn't afford them any more, and a few home truths had sunk in. I was starting to think more seriously about my situation. Being in Quo, there had never been time to sit and think before, you were too busy just going out there doing it. Now I had all the time in the world.

I arranged to meet Patty at the airport. I'd only seen her once during those ten years, on the Australian leg of the Rockin' All Over the World tour, and she was so nervous about seeing me she had drunk the plane dry by the time it landed! She still looked good, though. Very good. She was in her early thirties now but she still looked like a twenty-one-year-old.

She had opened a clothes shop in Sydney that had done well for her, so when she sold up and came back to England she had money – just nowhere to live. She was going to stay at her parents' house. I suggested she stay at my place, until she found somewhere of her own. She laughingly accepted and that was the start of what would become the last great love affair of my life. As I write this – twenty years, one child, one divorce and one reconciliation later – I'm still waiting for her to find a place of her own. I hope she never does, though, because she has become the most important woman in my life.

But I'm getting ahead of myself. All that deep stuff would come later. At first it was just fun and exciting to be with her again after so long. It was like coming full circle. She wasn't working, so we spent all our days and nights together. It was like making up for lost time. I even wrote a song for my solo album specifically with Patty in mind, called 'Show Me the Way'. When I played it to her she cried . . .

It was while all this was going on that I got the call one day from Colin Johnson asking if I wanted to take part in a one-off charity record that Bob Geldof of the Boomtown Rats was organizing under the heading of Band Aid. I was told Francis had already agreed to be there and so I said yes. Alan was in Australia, so it would be just the two of us.

It was strange seeing Francis again after so long. It was the first time we'd even spoken since the band had stopped working. Any tensions there might have been between us, though, dissolved the minute we arrived at the studio. Suddenly we were in the midst of all these eighties bands that we appeared to have absolutely nothing in common with. It was all a bit peculiar. No one even really spoke to us at first, so we just sloped off together down the corridor and got the coke out. Suddenly we were the most popular guys in the room! It was outrageous. I hadn't been to bed the night before and was actually feeling pretty shit until then. Now suddenly I was at the centre of Party HQ!

The trouble was there were so many people in the studio you had to wait around all day to do your bit. There was a pub across the road and that was fatal, too. Poor Trevor Horn, the producer, was desperately trying to organize everybody but it was like a mad, debauched circus. By the time Francis and I got to do our part, I'm ashamed to say that I was so out of my tree I couldn't sing in tune. Actually, it was worse than that – I was so gagged on coke I could hardly speak, let alone sing! It was embarrassing. I had waited all day for this, only to suffer the ignominy of having Trevor say, 'Don't worry, love, we'll get someone else for this part . . .'

Talk about blowing it! Francis had to come to my rescue and do the part for me. I've still got my triple-platinum disc for it up on the wall at home, though, just to prove I was there in spirit, if nothing else. I'm very proud of it, too, even if I'm not sure I quite deserve it. The important thing was that the record, 'Do They Know It's Christmas?', was a huge success and raised nearly a million pounds for the starving people of Africa.

As we now know, the next thing was Geldof had arranged a big concert at Wembley Stadium to raise even more money – Live Aid. Bob asked us if we would open the show for him and we said, 'No, of course not. We're not even together any more.' He said: 'It doesn't matter a fuck, just be there!' He was most insistent, as they say, so we said we'd make some phone calls. I knew Pete Kircher and Andy Bown would be up for it, but I had no idea how Alan would react. To my surprise, however, he agreed at once.

Not that the wounds between him and Francis had healed. They would do the gig, they said, but that didn't mean anything had changed between them. As a result, I don't think we even did one rehearsal, just a quick ten-minute soundcheck the day before the show. But it was like Geldof said, it really didn't matter. It was just being there that counted.

The fact that he also asked us to go on first and start the show off was a bonus to me. Some of the others didn't see it like that at first – they thought it meant being bottom of the bill. But I saw it as one of the best spots we could possibly have. I sensed it would be special. Plus, I didn't want to be stuck in the middle with the likes of Paul McCartney and Elton John because we would have been swallowed up.

We met on the morning of the show at Battersea heliport, which was just a few hundred yards from where I was living with Patty. We came towards the stadium on the helicopter at a few hundred feet, then circled round, just to get a better look. It was an unbelievable sight! It wasn't even midday, yet the place was already packed. That was when I felt the first tingle go up my spine. Until then I had been too preoccupied with the stresses of dealing with Francis and Alan again. Now, as I looked out of the window of the chopper, the full enormity of the occasion started to dawn on me. I began to feel very nervous.

Backstage we hung out at a specially erected Hard Rock Café enclosure, for all the artists and their entourages. What was amazing was that everyone went along with it. There were a lot of big egos there that day, but everyone knuckled down and got into the spirit of things. There was no complaining about the flowers in the dressing-room, it was just go on, do your gig, then get off again.

As we made our way to the side of the stage ready to start the show, the atmosphere was quite different from anything I'd ever experienced at a gig before. It was midday and the sun was shining high in the sky and you could not have wished for a more vibrant setting. As we walked out on to the stage, an enormous roar went up from the massive crowd and the hairs literally stood up on the back of my neck. We went straight into 'Rockin' All Over the World' and the place just erupted! After that, everything went so fast we seemed to be on and off again in seconds . . .

As we came back towards the dressing-room, Bob Geldof was there waiting for us. He thanked us, then said, 'OK, now go off and have a good time – just make sure you're back here for the finale!' Francis stayed at Wembley with the rest of the guys. I was with Patty and we decided to jump in the helicopter and fly back to Battersea, to the local pub, where it was all, ''Allo, mate. Just been watching you on the telly. What are you having?' We stayed there for the rest of the day, with the show on the telly in the background, getting completely drunk and coked-out until it was time to go back again.

By the time we fell out of the helicopter back at Wembley that night, I was completely gone. In fact, I didn't need the helicopter to fly back to the gig! When we got there, I said to Patty, 'You've got to come on stage with me!' She was going, 'No, no, I can't do that!' I said, 'Yes, you can! Come on,' and just dragged her up there with me. If you watch the video you can see us standing over by Elton as he's tinkling the ivories, these huge stupid grins on our faces. I remember looking out at the stadium, over this sea of people, and the feeling was extraordinary. It was dark by then, and everybody was holding lighters aloft like stars in the sky. To stand there and see that, while sharing the stage with McCartney, Bowie, Elton and all the rest, was something I will never forget. Which is just as well, as I certainly can't remember much about the rest of that night . . .

If Live Aid is now regarded as the defining moment of eighties rock, it was also a major turning point in the fortunes of Status Quo. Ironically, just as the band was at its most fractured, we were suddenly more famous than ever before. A fact not lost on Phonogram, who now began making noises about wanting another Quo album.

At first, I was indignant. 'How the fuck are we going to make a Quo album?' I cried. 'There isn't a Quo any more!'

I had also just finished recording my solo album and wanted that to come out. I had called it *Recorded Delivery*, and when it was finished I was convinced I'd done my best work since Quo was at its height. Now, suddenly, I couldn't get anybody to talk to me about it. I couldn't understand it at the time: why would the record company want to sit on something that had cost them so much money? It was weird: Francis couldn't get his solo album released, either. Or at least, I thought it was weird at the time. I can't help wondering now whether the label simply decided to hold both albums back until they could squeeze at least one more Quo album out of us. They hadn't wanted to know before Live Aid. Now we were front-page news and they started to apply real pressure.

According to our managers, they had us by the balls. Even though the band didn't exist any more, technically we still owed them one more Quo album under the terms of our old contract. There was even talk of them suing us if we didn't comply. Being skint at the time, that was all the persuading I needed to give it a shot. Francis was in a stronger position than me financially because he still had his house, but he didn't fancy having Phonogram trying to take him to the cleaners either, so he very reluctantly agreed to at least sit down and discuss the possibility.

His only stipulation was that he would not work with Alan again. This made things especially difficult for me, as Alan was over from Australia and staying with me at the time. But the powers that be at Phonogram had made it clear that while they were happy to continue with the band as Status Quo even if it meant just having me and Francis from the original line-up, they were not interested in the band if it was just me and Alan, or any other permutation that did not include Francis.

The way I saw it, I was left with a straight choice between staying with Alan and starting all over again with a new band but no record deal. Or going with Francis and having my bread well and truly buttered with Quo. I didn't have to sit around thinking about it for very long. Needless to say, Alan went ballistic when he found out and that's when things ended up in court. Which was a great pity for everybody, because there was only one side that was ever going to win that battle, and Alan should have recognized that and saved himself a lot of grief. But of course that wasn't his way. Alan was a born fighter and so he chose to fight us to the bitter end.

The whole thing was extremely unpleasant. He got on the phone to me at one point and threatened to wring my neck the next time he saw me. Indeed, he still disputes everything he can with us to this day. It's a great shame, because Alan was once an important member of this band, as was John Coghlan, and in an ideal world they would both still be with us. But human nature is far from ideal, and Francis and Alan had known each other since they were schoolboys. They were men now, husbands and fathers, and their personal relationship had simply not survived the changes they had both been through. Put it down to irreconcilable differences, either way, Status Quo was no longer a town big enough for both of them. In the end, we reached an out-of-court settlement with Alan.

With Pete Kircher having now settled into semi-retirement, we would need a new drummer as well as a new bass player if we were to make a new Quo album. I suggested using Jeff and Rhino. 'You'll like 'em,' I told Francis. He was sceptical. 'Oh, all right, if we have to,' he mumbled.

We arranged for a getting-to-know-you rehearsal down at this little studio in South London called Candlelight. There was me, Francis, Andy, Jeff and Rhino, with Pip Williams overseeing the sessions. At first Francis feigned indifference, leaning with his back against the wall, playing along desultorily. But we sped through a few numbers and suddenly his whole attitude changed. Within a few days he was up and running again. He said to me, 'You were right, these two guys are great!' We found we had a real vibe going again. It was established now that Francis and I were in ultimate control, eliminating all the niggly arguments we used to get in the old line-up, which left us free to get down to the business of making music with real pleasure and enthusiasm again.

Once it looked like Francis and I were going to get Quo back together, Phonogram issued us with a nice hefty advance and suddenly I had a few bob to play with again. I still wasn't what you could remotely call rich but the first thing I did was buy Patty a fur coat, which she looked absolutely stunning in. Then the next morning I went out and bought myself a Rolls Royce Silver Shadow! Oh, yes! Rockin' Rick was back! It was a two-tone champagne-and-walnut-coloured Roller and I fell in love with it the moment I set eyes on it. It was second-hand but in mint condition, and I paid about fifteen grand for it. I couldn't afford to buy it outright the way I had in the old days, I got it on the drip, as they say. But I did get it. I may not have been a millionaire rock star any more, but that didn't mean I had to stop looking like one.

I was serving my latest ban at the time – four years for drink-driving – so Patty acted as my chauffeur. A mate of mine in the motor trade had a great numberplate – Tax 1 – which he lent me, and suddenly I found myself sitting in a Rolls Royce with this gorgeous blonde in a fur coat at the wheel, driving around with what looked like 'Taxi' on my number plate. All the cabbies in London were sounding their horns and giving me the finger. 'You flash bastard!' I was delighted. I thought: I'm back! I wasn't home free yet, but at least it now *looked* like I was, and I knew how important that was in this business, where appearances mean everything.

After the business with Alan was finally cleared up, we were ready to go. We started off in 1986 with a couple of typical Quo-sounding type singles that came out that summer – 'Rollin' Home' and 'Red Sky' – both of which became our first chart hits for three years, much to our relief. But the one track the new line-up recorded that really brought us back into the spotlight was a song called 'In the Army Now'. It was also the title of our big comeback album, released in August that year, and when both single and album were huge hits it was like getting the ultimate seal of approval for the new line-up. The new Quo era had finally begun in earnest, and suddenly there was that feeling again of, uh-oh, look out, here we go again . . .

That said, I have to hold my hands up here and admit that at first I wasn't totally convinced by the song 'In the Army Now'. Originally by an obscure Dutch group called Bolland, Francis had wanted to do it before the original band split up. But it was another one of those songs that Alan had decided he just couldn't live with. It was about the horror of being conscripted into the army and being sent off to fight, and Alan didn't fancy that at all.

Now things were different Francis felt free to suggest it again. I had no problem with it, in principle. To me it was just a song, not a personal philosophy. I just wasn't sure at first whether it was a hit single. It was catchy but it also had a dark, plaintive quality that I thought might put some people off. It was pretty dire subject-matter, after all. But I knew how strongly Francis felt about the song, so I kept my mouth shut and let him get on with it.

Then John Deacon from Queen came over to the flat one day and helped me see things differently. I had always been a bit in awe of Queen, musically, because they were such a fabulously gifted group of individuals. (The funny thing was that they loved us as well, particularly Brian May.

Unbeknownst to the fans, he's been sat at the side of the stage, banging his head, at countless Quo gigs.) Anyway, when John came to visit me one day in Battersea, I played him the demo of 'In the Army Now' and he flipped out! He said it was a sure-fire hit and that we would be mad not to do it. That persuaded me to think again and, sure enough, John and Francis were right. 'In the Army Now' was not only a hit, it was the biggest-selling single Quo would ever have.

We had also done our first tour together that summer, starting with some shows in the Middle East, playing to a couple of thousand ex-pats every night. It was a useful way to ease the new band in without being in the spotlight the way we would once we played in Britain for the first time. The plan worked a treat, and by the time we were ready to come home again the band was really rocking. It was such a relief. Apart from the money, I desperately wanted to be a success again. Now at long last it looked like I was going to get my chance.

We toured Britain that summer with Queen, culminating with a huge outdoor show to over 120,000 people at Kneb-worth Park. It was a hell of a platform on which to make a comeback. And the more shows we did together, the better it got. By the time 'In the Army Now' was sitting pretty at Number 2 that autumn, the fire in our bellies was well and truly lit and we were off again, ready to conquer the world. Everything in the garden, it seemed, was rosy again.

We didn't know our troubles had only just begun . . .

FIVE

I first met Eileen Quinn, as she was then, back in 1973. I was still married to Jean but the band was on tour in America and were taking a short break after a show in New York. Bob Young and I took off on our own for a couple of days to visit my cousin Patrick Arnone, who lives in Elmsford, in what they call Upstate New York – not the city itself but the beautiful countryside that lies hundreds of miles to the north of it. Patrick is gay and has never had a girlfriend, but Eileen was a close friend of his and so she happened to be there too. I remember thinking how easy she was to get on with; always with something nice to say for everybody. When we left a couple of days later she came to wave us off and I remember feeling sorry that we would probably never see each other again.

Our paths did cross again, however, when, some years later, Eileen accompanied Patrick on a holiday to London. I invited them both to stay with me at the house for a few weeks and that's when I really got to know Eileen well. It was now the mid-eighties, Jean and I had long since split up, and I had just started seeing Paige. I would loll away an afternoon sitting in the garden talking to Eileen about anything and everything, then run off at night to see Paige. The two relationships were quite different in my mind: I was still at that stage where I was confusing sex with love.

Eileen had never really left my thoughts, though. Three years on, alone at home and confused in the wake of the Moscow shows, starting to worry less about where my next gram of coke was coming from and more about where my life was actually going, I suddenly found myself thinking about Eileen all the time. The stick-on good looks of celebrity meant that I had never had a problem attracting sexual partners. True love, however, and all the things that go with it like mutual understanding, emotional support and, above all, simple companionship – that was something I now doubted I had ever known seriously.

That's when my thoughts about Eileen suddenly transformed themselves into action. Something just clicked into place in my mind as I realized, belatedly, that she was exactly the sort of person I wanted to be with. Someone whose beauty ran more than skin-deep; someone straight up and sincere – and not messed up on booze or drugs or any of the other trappings of the so-called rock'n'roll lifestyle. All at once, I knew I had to try to do something about it.

I was due to start another British tour with Quo at the end of October 1988, so I had to move fast. A few days before the first show, I flew over to America to see Patrick. I didn't bullshit him, I told him exactly why I had come. He had bad news for me, though. Eileen had married someone else just a few months before! Moreover, she was pregnant!

I sat down and put my head in my hands. Too late! I couldn't believe it. All my hopes and dreams gone, just like that...

Then I thought: no, wait, this isn't over yet. Not until

Eileen says so, anyway. I knew I couldn't just fly all the way home again without at least seeing her. And if I saw her, I knew I wouldn't be able to stop myself from telling her how I felt.

With Patrick's encouragement, I arranged a little get-together for us at this old-fashioned American diner in town. Just the three of us. As soon as Eileen arrived, Patrick made some excuse and left us alone together. It must have been so obvious something was going on that I dropped the whole pretence and came straight out with it: I was in love with her and wanted her to come back to England with me.

It sounds a bit much, said all in one go like that, and I suppose it was. Considering Eileen was a recently married, not to mention pregnant woman, I wouldn't have blamed her if she had thrown her cup of coffee in my face and stormed off. But she didn't. Instead, she stayed and we talked, as we always had done, freely and easily to each other for hours.

It turned out she had always had feelings for me, too, but I had apparently ignored all the 'signals'. To my astonishment – I don't think I really believed she would say yes until she didn't say no – by the end of our conversation Eileen had agreed to come back to London with me. She would have to go home and talk to her husband first, of course, but she insisted she would be ready to leave with me later that same day. She told me to go back to Patrick's place and wait for her.

I went back and told Patrick what had happened and we both sat there in shocked silence. I still half expected her not to come: for there to be some inevitable complications her end that prevented us from simply running off together. Only a couple of hours had passed, however, before suddenly there she was: packed and ready to go. I nearly dropped down with relief. I still couldn't quite believe it was happening; that things might turn out all right after all. Before I knew it we were sitting next to each other on the plane on our way back to London – and the start of a whole new life together.

Inevitably there was a bit of commotion among her family and friends when she first took off with me. Eileen comes from a large Irish-American family with lots of brothers, all of them giants, and at first they must have thought she'd lost her mind – leaving a stable, ostensibly happy marriage to run off with a drug-crazed, long-haired rock star from England! But as time went by and they began to see how seriously we both took the relationship, they were able to put all that behind them. As long as Eileen was happy, that's all they cared about, and you could hardly blame them for that. I realize now that I had some front even asking her to come with me. But then she could have said no and that would have been that. Except she didn't; she said yes. We both sensed a connection there, so we decided to trust our instincts and go for it. We didn't want to hurt anybody, we just wanted to have our little shot at happiness.

I didn't have a problem with the fact that Eileen was pregnant with another man's child. She had the baby – a beautiful dark-haired boy she named Patrick – in February 1989. It was decided he would live with us and although we brought him up to know his real father, too, I have always felt Patrick was as much my son as any of my other children. Eileen feels the same about the kids from my previous relationships.

Nevertheless, it can't have been easy for her. No sooner had we arrived back in London than I was off on tour. Although I returned in time for our first Christmas together, come the new year I was off with the band again. This time to Compass Point studios in Nassau for two months to make our next album, the prophetically titled *Perfect Remedy*. I would have understood if Eileen had started to have second thoughts at that point, but she just took it all in her stride, the way I've since learned she does everything. Nothing is ever a problem for Eileen, and that gives me strength too. Which was doubly good, as right then I needed all the strength I could muster. For Nassau was also where I finally managed to get to grips with my cocaine addiction.

I had been slowly tapering off since Moscow. Having Eileen there meant I didn't have much chance to think about coke when I was at home now anyway. Being away from her, though, gave me all the opportunity I needed to get right back into it. Especially in a place like Nassau: a tropical Bahamian paradise where the coke is as plentiful as the coconuts. Nevertheless, it was against this backdrop that I finally began laying my coke demons to rest. Even though she made no demands in that direction, I wanted to be true to Eileen by getting off the stuff completely; not just when I was with her. There was a new baby to consider too; a new life for us all to share together. I didn't want to start out on the wrong foot.

I forced myself into a routine of only having coke on the night before a day off. That way I was only doing it once or twice a week, and when I did, the coke hangover would be gone by the time we went back to the work in the studio. Then one night before another day off, I suddenly thought: I don't actually want a toot tonight. I just want to go back to my room, have a bowl of cornflakes and watch the news on TV.

That's when I really started to let go. It wasn't like telling myself I couldn't ever have it again; that would have been too hard. It was real one-day-at-a-time stuff. Strangely, I actually found having it so readily available made it easier to say no to. By the time I got home to London I had got into the habit of saying no. It was the first time for years that I realized I actually had a choice. Not long after that, I stopped completely. Occasionally I would succumb again, on a night off on tour maybe. Nothing like what it had been, though. I'd simply lost the taste for it.

One of the last times I ever did coke, I was with Eileen in Amsterdam and somebody – a well-wisher, let's say – passed me a little gram packet as we shook hands on the street. I didn't want it, but there was somebody with us who I thought would and I decided to give it to them. I was trying to buy ice-cream for the kids at the time but I said, 'Won't be long!' and left them with Eileen while I dashed back to the hotel. Of course, the temptation was too much and I had a quick toot myself before handing it over. First time for ages, fantastic!

Then as I got halfway back down the stairs it hit me. 'Shit! I shouldn't have done that . . .' My body had gone so numb I had to stop off in the hotel bar and have two or three shots of tequila just to try to calm down again. Then I went back to Eileen and the kids. I felt so terrible, like I'd let myself and everybody else down. I thought, fuck this, I hate it. That's the last time, I swear! And it was.

Once my head was clear, I started to look around at the rest of my life, and not a moment too soon, as it turned out. For it was then that I first discovered how much trouble the band was in financially. We shouldn't have been: despite a two-year gap in the middle, the eighties had been even more successful for us sales-wise than the seventies. But somehow we seemed to be broke.

Again, for legal reasons I cannot spell out exactly what had happened to us. All I will say is that I was one of the few people who didn't laugh when it came out a couple of years later that Sting had been ripped-off for millions he never knew he had. It's more easily done than people think. You're a musician; money is not what you're good at. So you hire managers and accountants and all sorts of consultants and financial advisors. If one of them then decides to rip you off there are a million clever ways they can do it that would never occur to you as you sit there trying to work out the chorus to your latest song. So when people take the piss out of Sting for not noticing he was down a few million quid, they don't know what they're talking about. Look at it this way, if it can happen to a clever bloke like that, it can happen to anybody. It certainly happened to us.

In retrospect, the signs had been there for all to see for some time. Alan Lancaster, in fact, was the first one to start asking awkward questions. But Alan was always moaning about something, and we were so out of our heads all the time, neither Rick nor I took it seriously. One of the reasons we still didn't twig quite how much shit we were in financially was the PR debacle of our ill-starred trip to South Africa.

On bad advice, the band had performed ten shows at Sun City in October 1987. We had all heard of apartheid, of course, but none of us knew the up-to-date situation and simply took people's word for it when they said it was now cool to play there again. We were told of all sorts of other groups that had done it and that we could even hire black stage hands and have a strict non-segregation policy for all the shows. Foolishly, we took it all at face value, not understanding that ticket prices would be so high most black South Africans wouldn't be able to afford them. We remained blissfully unaware of all that as we played to sell-out shows each night. It was a beautiful country to visit as well and we thought it was a fantastic trip.

But when we returned to London it was to a sea of condemnation in the media. Overnight we found ourselves publicly chastized by the United Nations and blacklisted in parts of Europe and Scandinavia. In the end we had to issue a written apology to everybody concerned. Probably we deserved it – on the basis that ignorance is no excuse for doing something wrong. But while there had been outcries before about various musicians and sportsmen playing in South Africa, I couldn't recall any other group receiving the level of negative publicity Quo got for it. These days I wonder if the press had even been tipped off as a smoke-screen.

It took me a long time to figure all that out though, and for the next year or so we just sort of carried on regardless. By then our tour manager, Iain Jones, was running things for us. Iain didn't have an established organization behind him, though. He didn't even have an office; he was just a good guy doing his best to help out. By the time we were recording *Perfect Remedy* in Nassau, however, it was apparent to all of us that we would need heavyweight help to help get us out of the mess we were in.

Enter, in a very loud voice, David Walker. Whatever Rick and I might say about David now, he was definitely the right man at the right time. He owned a group of entertainment-related companies called the Handle Group of Companies. On the management side he was mainly looking after producers like Pip Williams – which is how we first met David, briefly, when we were working on the *Ain't Complaining* album with

Pip in 1987. Before that, David had managed bands like the Sweet and the Bay City Rollers, and, more recently, Barclay James Harvest. Coming from a marketing background, he was much more business-minded than any other manager we had known. Exactly the sort of person, we decided, to sort out the mess we were in.

We hired him after a typically boisterous meeting in Nassau, at which he not only promised to sort out all our problems in one fell swoop but to charge us a fortune to do so. He actually came out with the immortal phrase: 'Remember, I don't come cheap.' True to his word, he didn't. But then he did keep his promise about sorting out the mess, too. And what a mess it was – beyond our worst nightmares. Once David had been through the books, even without being able to trace every penny, he reckoned we had lost something like £6 million!

We could have gone to the police, I suppose. But they weren't going to get our money back and we would have been tied up in legal wrangles that held us up for years and cost us another million for our trouble. Better to deal with it privately, we decided. Draw a line under it and get on with our lives. Which is what we did. You have to move on or you would literally end up stuck in one place for ever. Plus, we were broke and needed to make some money – fast.

Fortunately, from that perspective, we had David. One thing he definitely knew how to do was make money. As a result, the next ten years were some of the most successful Quo would ever have. On the other hand, they were also some of the least satisfying, from an artistic perspective. It was the beginning of the era when Quo would become more a commodity than a musical happening; no longer merely a band but a 'brand'. David taught us that word. He was one of the people who helped invent that whole language.

While I was pleased to see the money going into our bank accounts again, I wasn't always sure how much I liked what we now had to do to get it. But then we didn't have much choice. The nineties was sink-or-swim time for Quo. David knew that, and was determined to keep us afloat no matter what, and at first Rick and I saw him as something of a saviour. Not only did he sort out our dire financial situation, he was very protective. Yet another in a long line of father figures, he would blow up at anybody he thought was fucking with the band. He was a serious coke fiend as well, which was the worst thing he could be as he was so hyper already. The combination could be frightening, and even though he wasn't a tall guy, he could be an extremely intimidating figure to have to deal with.

What really put the ball in David's court in the nineties, however, in terms of guiding the band's career, was the relative failure of *Perfect Remedy* when it was released in November 1989. None of the singles from it were hits and the album barely scraped into the Top 50. I don't know why it did so poorly. You could argue that the scene had moved on, but it had only been twelve months since 'Burning Bridges' went to Number Three as a single. Was it simply down to the quality of the material then? As the guy who wrote most of it, that's a hard question to answer. Put it this way: I wouldn't put any songs forward for a Quo album that I didn't think were good enough. The album did well in Europe and Australia, but we were back to square one in Britain. Ticket-wise we were still strong; still doing multiple nights at places like the NEC and Wembley Arena. In the end,

I was content to write it off as a 'blip' and carry on with the next album.

David saw things differently, though, and decided we would need, in his words, 'more than just another bunch of Quo songs' if the next album was to escape a similar fate. He felt our 'old formula' had 'dried up' and that we needed to 'try a new tack'. It came as a bit of a shock to be spoken to like that. I didn't necessarily agree. On the other hand, considering the relative failure of *Perfect Remedy*, it was hard to argue with him, so we agreed to try it his way for the next album. First though we took a long break during the first half of 1990, during which Eileen fell pregnant with our first child together, born in September that year: another beautiful dark-haired boy, who we named Fynn. By then, however, David's plans for the next album were well under way and it wasn't long before I was off with the band again.

We had regrouped in June for some outdoor shows in Germany. We also took part that month in the Silver Clef Award Winners charity concert at Knebworth Park, in front of over 120,000 people. The show featured us, Paul McCartney, Elton John, Eric Clapton, Robert Plant, Pink Floyd and Genesis, and the whole thing was filmed and later broadcast by the BBC. The following month, it was announced we would be embarking on our twenty-fifth anniversary tour – using as its starting point the season at Butlin's in 1965 when Rick and I first met. Billed as the Rockin' All Over the Years tour, to accompany it, instead of a new Quo album, there would be a greatest hits collection – also titled *Rockin' All Over the Years* – along with David's big idea for 'the longest single ever'. He thought he was being brilliant; I couldn't believe he was serious. But he was.

The track itself – an extended medley of us doing a long list of old rock'n'roll classics like 'Let's Dance', 'The Wanderer', 'I Hear You Knocking', 'Lucille' and several more – would be so long, in fact, we would have to stretch it over *two* singles. Despite my misgivings, the first, titled 'The Anniversary Waltz Part One', was released the same month Fynn was born, and became our biggest hit for years, reaching Number 2. The *Rockin' All Over the Years'* album came out a few weeks later and also went flying to the top of the charts. Apart from our live album in 1976 and the brace of 'Gold Bars' compilations in the early eighties, there had been a host of dodgy compilations released over the years by Pye to cash in on our success. So we really wanted this to be special. A double album containing all our biggest hits, I was amazed at how many there were – well over forty by that point!

To kick the whole thing off, David arranged for us to perform a special one-off show at Butlin's in Minehead, on 10 October. A special Quo Express was laid on to take a party of over a 100 press, TV and radio people down there from Paddington – along with some mates of ours like the DJ Chris Tarrant and Alan 'Fluff' Freeman, and actress Vicky Michelle from the TV comedy show *'Allo, 'Allo*. The train left at 9 a.m. and everyone was served scrambled eggs, smoked salmon and champagne for breakfast. I was already down at the site rehearsing with the band and by the time the train arrived that afternoon everyone was steaming!

That night we played in what was once the Rock'n'Roll Ballroom, since renamed the Grand Ballroom. Afterwards there was a big party, and all the media were booked to stay the night at the camp, while the band and I stayed at a local hotel (we'd had our fill of holiday camp chalets, thank you!). That said, I don't think anyone actually went to bed. I remember a very 'happy' Chris Tarrant being put into a car at two o'clock in the morning, in order to be driven back to London in time to do the Capital Radio breakfast show that morning.

The next day, everybody, including the band this time, clambered back on board the Quo Express for the trip home. Even though I wasn't drinking at all at the time, the champagne flowed once again. When everybody was suitably refreshed, Rick and I did back-to-back interviews in a special carriage together. I say 'interviews'; the more the booze kicked in the quicker the hangovers evaporated and soon the whole 'interview' idea had deteriorated into a simple booze-up.

As a result, not only did we get the biggest blitzkrieg of media coverage we'd had since Live Aid, but the album went to Number 2 and sold over a million copies in the UK alone, giving us a triple-platinum album in the process! Part Two, as it was officially billed, of 'The Anniversary Waltz...' single came out in time for the British tour in December and also went Top 20. Compared to the total lack of interest that had greeted *Perfect Remedy* just a year before, you'd have to say David had been proved right. He wasn't the sort of person who refrained from saying 'I told you so,' either, and from here on in, he was unstoppable.

In February 1991, Quo appeared at the Brits, where we were presented with a special inaugural award recognizing our twenty-five years in the business. It was a great night. We knew what we were getting – they told you in advance – so we arranged something special as a party-piece. When we went up to receive our award we were all dressed in smart-looking dinner suits. But they were special 'theatrical' suits we'd had made, and as soon as we finished thanking everybody, we ripped them off to reveal our usual jeans and T-shirts underneath! It was something I'd thought of years ago that I thought maybe we could do at the start of a gig, but somehow we'd never quite got round to it. Then came the Brits and the perfect opportunity for a one-off gag like that. The next day the *Sun* ran a picture of us tearing off the suits on its front page and called it 'the highlight of the show'.

A week later Rick and I were invited on to the *Michael Aspel Show*, along with the actor John Hurt and the comedienne Dawn French. Rick and John hit it off immediately, rambling on about cars, while Dawn teased me about how thrilled she was, as a teenager learning the guitar, to discover that 'Caroline' really was just three chords! We spent the whole time doing these things now. On 3 April, Rick and I visited a prison workshop at Pentonville Prison – pictures of which were all over the papers the next day. Then on 1 May, we attended the official unveiling ceremony of our two waxwork dummies at Madame Tussaud's. We were placed in the Rock Circus section. Why that should make me feel in any way proud, I don't know, but for some reason it did. (I just wish I still had as much hair as the dummy me!)

That June we did an outdoor festival tour co-headlining with Rod Stewart – big football stadiums like Parkhead in Glasgow, Old Trafford in Manchester and, biggest of all, Wembley Stadium in London. Just before the tour started, the band flew to Monaco to attend the World Music Awards, where we were presented with the award for Outstanding Contribution to the Rock Industry by Prince Albert of Monaco. Then we flew back to London, ready to start the Rod Stewart tour. We did a couple of weeks of shows together in all and by the end of it we had played to over a quarter of a million people.

Somehow, in the middle of all this, Eileen and I found time to get married. It was 19 June 1991 – bizarrely, almost

Above. Rick's parents, showing off their new son.

Right. Rick aged about four with his first boat!

Above. Rick's grandmother Maude, outside her cafe in Woking.

Right. Rick at the Sunshine Holiday Camp, aged fifteen.

Above. Rick winning the Butlin's Junior Talent Competition in 1960.

Below. In 1962, Rick also won a week's holiday.

Above. The 'Canaries' at Sunshine Holiday Camp, Hayling Island, in their yellow and white uniforms. Rick is standing on the far left. Gloria and Jean Harrison are in the front row with their beehives.

Above. Rick, at the back dressed as the infamous Captain Thunder, had to help out with children's activities.

Above. A different look for the evening, singing a number for the *Variety Show*. Rick is second from the right.

Right. Ricky Harrison with Gloria and Jean in The Highlights, playing at Butlin's in Minehead, 1965.

Left and below. Rick at his German wedding to Marietta, in 1971.

Rick at Silverdale Avenue, Walton-on-Thames.

Cars have always been a passion. Rick with his Messerschmitt and, *below*, his Porsche 3-litre turbo convertible.

**Richard and Heidi
in 1980.**

Heidi Marie Elizabeth
PARFITT

10th August 1980

'Whoever is a child of God, does not continue to sin,
for God's very nature is in her, because God is her father.'

1 John Ch. III, v. 9

Hambledon Church, 17th August 1980

Rick and Patty on their wedding day, 1989.

Left. Rick and Patty at the Formula 1 show, 2003.

Below. Rick with Richard and Harry 2002 on the Heavy Traffic tour.

the same date I had married Jean nearly twenty-five years before. Unlike that occasion, however, I didn't see marrying Eileen as anything more meaningful than tying up the formalities. I wanted her to have all the legal privileges of being my wife, but that was all. We didn't need to go to some strange room and repeat a lot of strange words to prove our love to each other.

We did the deed at Croydon Register Office. We left home that morning at 11.30 and were home again by 12.30, in time for Eileen to cook lunch. I had hired a driver for the day, and he and our regular house-cleaning lady acted as our witnesses. I didn't have a best man. Don't be daft. I'm just not into that any more. In fact, I can't deal with weddings at all, not mine or anybody else's. I went to so many as a kid and they were always the same – they always started with everybody smiling and ended with everybody fighting.

We didn't have a honeymoon, either. Not because we didn't want to spend time together, but because we have never felt the need to be anywhere other than at home. We went to Portugal for a holiday once but after a few days we got sick of it. We were paying a fortune to stay at a place not half as nice as the one we'd got at home, so we packed our bags and left the next day. Of course, we're lucky having a house that allows you to feel that way. We know that, which is why it's so hard to prise us out of there sometimes.

When Quo finished with Rod, we took off on our own festival tour of Europe. Then David had another brainwave and came up with the idea of us doing four shows in one day. He even had a title for it: Rock 'Til You Drop. Organized, ostensibly, as a charity event in support of both the Nordoff-Robbins Music Therapy Trust and the Brits Performing Arts, each of which would receive twenty-five per cent of the box-office receipts from the four shows, David also arranged for the Britannia Music Club to sponsor the event.

All four shows took place on Saturday 21 September 1991. The event officially began the day before, however, when we attended Newbury racecourse, where the Nordoff-Robbins people had arranged a special Music Therapy charity race day. Quo were official sponsors of the two o'clock race, the Rock 'Til You Drop Stakes. The BBC broadcast the race live and Rick and I were shown handing over the Rock 'Til You Drop trophy to the owner of the winning horse.

The real race – or should I say, marathon – kicked off at noon the following day, when we appeared on the BBC 1 Saturday-morning kids' show *Going Live*, where we explained all about the events we were staging that day and performed a special medley of hits. From there we sped down the motorway to RAF Northolt, where we were helicoptered up to Sheffield, in time to go on stage at the International Centre at 2 p.m. sharp. We played for an hour then got straight back on the helicopter and flew up to Leeds airport, where we transferred to a plane which took us to Glasgow, where we were due on stage at the SE&CC Arena at 4.30 p.m. We got there with just fifteen minutes to spare, played for an hour, then helicoptered back to Glasgow where we got another plane, this time bound for Birmingham, where we were due to appear at the NEC at 7.00 p.m. Same drill as before: we did an hour then jumped on a plane – bound for the last show in London, due to start at Wembley Arena at 9.30 p.m. Again, we made it with mere moments to spare, played for one final hour – and that was it. We were done. In every sense. I don't think I have ever felt so tired in my entire life. At the end of the Wembley show we were joined on stage by Norris McWhirter, who presented us with certificates proclaiming our entry into the *Guinness Book of Records* for performing the largest number of British arena shows in under twelve hours. Best of all though, we had raised over £250,000 for both charities.

The real 'unexpected' climax to the four shows was to have been Michael Aspel strolling on stage at Wembley to surprise Rick and me with a joint *This Is Your Life*. But we got wind of it at the last minute and cancelled it. It was complicated. We would have been happy to do it if it had been focused on our careers with Quo, but the producers wanted it to be solely on Rick and me and our personal lives. Fine, in principle, only we weren't ready for the microscope to be turned on us quite so closely yet. Rick, in particular, was left in a quandary. I can't remember if he was seeing Patty or not at the time, or possibly someone else – I've never been able to keep up with Rick's love life – but let's just say the thought of having surprise guests from his past suddenly thrust upon him was not one Rick welcomed gladly at that point. Me neither, frankly. I still had too many skeletons rattling around my closet that I hadn't dealt with in my own mind yet. Anyway, by the time we'd actually finished that fourth set, I could barely stand up straight, let alone pretend to be delighted when Michael Aspel came wandering on with his big red book under his arm. Maybe another time, Mike . . .

The *Rock 'Til You Drop* album was released a few days later and was an immediate hit. A compromise between what David felt we should be doing and where Rick and I felt we should be going, *Rock 'Til You Drop* was a collection of half new Quo songs, half cover versions – 'Let's Work Together' by Canned Heat and 'Bring It on Home to Me', the soulful Sam Cooke ballad, plus a couple of re-recordings of earlier Quo tunes such as '4500 Times', which originally appeared on *Hello* in 1973 (and is probably our most popular song among Quo diehards). As a result, *Rock 'Til You Drop* managed to keep both sides happy by giving us another hit, reaching Number 10 – our highest position for a 'new' Quo album for five years.

The next few years would follow a similar pattern. Heavy touring, regularly interspersed with high-profile promotional activities engineered by David and our PR man, Simon Porter, to ensure plenty of TV and newspaper coverage. In June 1992, we headlined the End of Race show at the TT races on the Isle of Man. A month later we performed 'Roll Over Beethoven' with Hale and Pace on an ITV Saturday-night special called *Comedy Night Out*. Then in August, we played at the twenty-fifth anniversary party for Radio One, before over 125,000 people at the Party in the Park concert in Sutton Park, Birmingham. It was also around this time that Bobby Davro started doing his impersonations of us on TV. We could hardly object. It was all done in fun and, if anything, it just made us even more of a household name. When Rick and I turned on the Blackpool Illuminations, in September 1993, more than 25,000 people turned up to see us do it – their biggest crowd for over thirty years! We also did a Radio One roadshow that morning and a *Daily Star* roadshow later the same day. We were no longer just rock stars. We were part of the furniture.

As if to prove the point, there were even Royal Doulton mugs produced that year with Rick's and my faces on them. That's when you know you're famous – when they immortalize you in a high-quality Toby jug! Usually the company concentrated on famous politicians or members of the royal family. I was amazed to discover that the only other rock group they had ever done, in fact, was the Beatles! Designed by Royal Doulton's main sculptor, Martyn Allcock, they were launched in October in limited editions of 2,500 each at the Royal Doulton Fair, held that year at London's Park Lane Hotel. Both Rick and I went, of course, and signed hundreds of mugs for all the Quo fans that had suddenly descended on the place. The regular Royal Doulton patrons had never seen anything like it before, though I noticed there were more than a few of them in the queue for signed mugs, too.

A few months later the band travelled up to Manchester to make a record with the Manchester United football squad, who were then on the verge of their first Premiership and FA Cup double. The idea was to re-record 'Burning Bridges', retitled 'Come On You Reds'. The team's then striker, Brian McClair, had seen us at Old Trafford on the tour with Rod and it was he who actually came up with the idea of adapting 'Burning Bridges'. Not knowing anything about football, I turned the task of writing suitable new lyrics over to Rhino and Andy, who are the big footie fans in the band. They were the ones who came up with the new title. Not being a sports fan myself, I couldn't tell you if it was a good record or a bad one, but when it came out in April 1994, it went straight to Number 1 and stayed there for three weeks – our first Number 1 single in Britain since 'Down Down' almost twenty years before.

That same month we did another Prince's Trust gig, at the Albert Hall, with Prince Charles in attendance. Billed as the Appointment, the event raised over £70,000 for the charity. While meeting Charles afterwards we presented him with two miniature Rossi and Parfitt look-alike Fender Telecaster guitars, for his then still quite small sons, William and Harry, as well as a Tele signed by the whole band for auction in aid of Capital Radio's Help a London Child appeal.

David's thing was being able to transform each new Quo record into 'a media event', and you have to say he was pretty damn good at it. When the next Quo single, 'I Didn't Mean It', came out in July that year, however, we didn't need any help turning it into an event. Our performance of it on *Top of the Pops* on 4 August was an historic occasion – our hundredth appearance on the shows. I didn't know it until then but we had now been on the show more times than any other act in the programme's history; a record we still hold to this day. 'I Didn't Mean It' went into the charts two days later – at which point we were informed that that was our forty-sixth Top 30 hit single! I was truly amazed. I still felt like we were trying to make it, to keep going. And in many ways we were. Our new album, *Thirsty Work*, released in August, was our first proper Quo album since *Perfect Remedy* had bombed five years before. We desperately wanted it to do well; to prove we still had something more to offer than just cover versions and novelty records. But although it went Top 20, it only got as high as Number 13. Good but hardly great. Certainly not by David's standards.

Fortunately, from David's point of view, 1995 was the thirtieth anniversary of the band. All the ammunition he needed to cook up his next scam: an album of cover versions from the last thirty years. We had recorded a version of 'Don't Stop' by Fleetwood Mac for the *Rock 'Til You Drop* album, but had abandoned it at the last moment when we ran out of space. Now we resurrected it. We even called the album *Don't Stop*.

Released as our official thirtieth-anniversary album in February 1996, *Don't Stop* was our first release under a lucrative new deal David had done for us with Polygram TV. Backed by a costly promotional splurge including a TV ad campaign, it was another huge success, reaching Number 2 and selling over 300,000 copies (making it 'platinum') in the UK in the first month alone. Featuring an array of guest turns – including our old mate Brian May of Queen (on Buddy Holly's 'Raining in My Heart'), Maddy Prior of Steeleye Span (on 'All Around My Hat') and, not least, the Beach Boys (on 'Fun, Fun, Fun') – whatever misgivings we had behind the scenes about doing a bunch of cover versions, once again David had been proved resoundingly right.

When we then released our version of 'Fun Fun Fun' as a single we suddenly found ourselves doing masses of promotion with the Beach Boys! They flew to London and we embarked on a high-profile promotional tour, appearing together on everything from *Top of the Pops*, to *GMTV*, *The Shane Richie Experience*, *The Des O'Connor Show*, *Cilla Black's Surprise Surprise* ... you name it, we did it. They were a great bunch of guys too, and the whole experience was an extraordinary one, to say the least.

We first met them in 1994, when we both appeared at the Last Tattoo concert in Berlin; a huge event to celebrate the withdrawal of the last British and American troops from the city, in the wake of the collapse of the Berlin Wall five years before. We'd all gone out together afterwards and at the end of the night done that typical muso thing of saying how we should work together one day. When, a year later, David suggested inviting them to join us on a track on the covers album, we thought there would be no chance. But then he contacted them and they said they would love to do it! I was so knocked out he had to tell me three times before I would believe him.

I wouldn't describe the Beach Boys as heroes, but I did like a lot of their songs. I used to sing 'Wouldn't It Be Nice' to

Jean when we were first going out together. Finding one of their songs that Quo would sound right doing, though, was not exactly easy. We tried all sorts before deciding on 'Fun, Fun, Fun'. We did the backing track then sent the tapes to America where they recorded their vocal parts, then sent them back to us. For something done so piecemeal, the finished version sounded incredible. The first time we played it and heard their voices come soaring in on the backing track, it sounded so lush it gave me goosebumps. When they actually agreed to come and help us promote the single, it was unbelievable: who in their right mind would ever dream of having the Beach Boys as their backing vocal group? They really got into the spirit of things, though, and we had a great time together.

The only one who was a little bit strange was Brian Wilson. Famously reclusive since the late sixties, I've since heard he's fine now, quite lucid. But at the time he was still pretty foggy. Those were his first public appearances with the Beach Boys, in any guise, for something like twenty-five years, and the whole situation was clearly hard for him to take in some days. You'd be chatting to him normally one moment, then the next he would just switch off and start staring into space, and his wife would have to come and take him off for a lie down. When we were introduced, I said: 'Hello, mate. How are you?' He just looked at me and went, 'Who are you?' It was class. 'Who are you?' That put me in my place . . .

In between times, we still tried making some original music. I also released a solo album later that year called *King of the Doghouse*. It was a good album – or would have been if it hadn't been scuppered by the production. One day I would come in and everything would be fine, the next day the producer would be tearing the track apart and starting again! It was a pity, but at least I managed to get some new songs out there; something that was occurring with much less frequency now in Quo.

Then something happened that put the whole thing into perspective. The year 1997 had started well for us. In February we did our first tours of Japan and Australia since the Rockin' All Over the World tour in 1978. Then in March, we flew from Sydney to Los Angeles, where we also did our first US shows since the seventies. Even though we'd never been big there, the people at the shows seemed to know all the songs and we went down a storm each night. It was strangely gratifying. We knew we'd never be big there now, but at least we seemed to have left some sort of mark.

We were back in London, in April, taking a break before setting out on another summer tour of Europe, when I got the phone call that nearly upset the whole applecart. Rick had been admitted to hospital for major heart surgery. I'll leave him to fill you in on the grisly details, but for a while, I confess, I thought he might be a goner. Not Rick, though. Where something like that would have totally changed the lives of most men his age, Rick just treated the whole thing as though he'd put his engine into the garage for a service: as soon as the job was done, he was off roaring down the road in a cloud of dust again.

He was back on stage with us, in fact, just three months after his operation. He made his comeback in suitably grand style when we did an open-air show on 2 August at Norwich City's Carrow Road football ground. There were over 25,000 noisy Quo fans there that day but by far the biggest rounds of applause were reserved for Rick. There were 'Welcome

Back!' banners and flags everywhere. I remember one in particular which made me laugh. It read: 'Rick Parfitt's got more by-passes than Norwich!'

Two months later came the release of *Whatever You Want – The Very Best of Status Quo*; the latest of David's great ideas for quickfire success. Though it didn't do as monstrously well as the *Rockin' All Over the Years* compilation seven years before, it was still another sizeable hit for us, and the band was back touring harder than ever. If Rick had been given any doctor's orders about slowing down or changing his lifestyle, I can't say I noticed it. We had a short break at the start of 1998, then in March we went back to Australia, where the band was now bigger than ever, for more shows. We spent the rest of the year doing our usual lengthy round of European and UK tours. John Coghlan turned up backstage when we played at the Oxford Apollo in December and Bob Young came to the show at the Brighton Centre. It was the first time I'd seen either of them properly since they left the band and, to my surprise, it felt good to speak to them both again. Particularly Bob.

From the outside then, things were looking good again. But while the success we enjoyed with David was undeniable, somewhere along the way the music had stopped coming first. Instead of being a means to an end, the endless promotion and high-profile media stuff now seemed to have become an end in itself. I was happy enough to go along with the success his ideas brought us, but I hated to see our new music so neglected. As time went by, David and I started to clash about it more and more.

Like the argument I had with him over the *Under the Influence* album. Released in March 1999, it was the first authentically new Quo album (eleven originals; only one cover) since *Thirsty Work* five years before and I desperately wanted it to be taken seriously. The plan began to unravel, however, before we'd even released the record. It started with the sleeve. They had all these different ideas for the cover mocked up for us to look at and the one we all liked was of a bent fork on a white background. There was just something very enigmatic and intriguing about it. But David said, 'We'll never be able to work up a marketing campaign around that.'

I said, 'That's not my problem. Tell them to use their imagination.'

He said: 'What about a pub sign with a picture of you and him [me and Rick] on it?'

I nearly got up and walked out. As usual, David was going for the lowest common denominator, but the phrase 'Under the Influence' had nothing to do with boozing. The song itself was actually about an erotic dream I kept having about this girl I once knew – and two of her friends! I used to wake up in the night sweating; they really affected me for a while. Hence, 'Under the Influence'. The melody was one I actually wrote on the piano when I was thirteen. For David to then suggest bringing all that down to the level of a pub song was disheartening, to say the least.

We gave in, though, in the end. We always did. And even though I still hate that album cover, the promotion David organized off the back of it was very successful. Sponsored by the *Sun*, who ran a competition under the heading 'Get Quo to Play in Your Boozer', we actually did a ten-date tour of various pubs around the country (plus a similar series of high-profile pub shows in Germany and Holland). The publicity we got for it was amazing, but in truth the whole thing was a nightmare. Even though there were only 250 tickets available for each gig, it didn't stop Quo fans in their thousands descending on the pubs. Inevitably, there were scuffles – some of which ended up being shown on the TV news. Nevertheless, people still talk about it today; so again it was hard to argue that David was wrong. He said it would work and it did – if you like that sort of thing.

By complete contrast, that autumn the band made its first appearance on the Night of the Proms tour. Starring a number of different artists from across all fields of the music spectrum, backed by a full classical orchestra and choir, the Night of the Proms was an idea originally staged in Belgium in the early nineties, and is now one of the most popular annual touring shows in Europe. Both classical and jazz artists are featured, as well as rock artists like us, Simple Minds, Meat Loaf, Bonnie Tyler, UB40 and several others that have taken part over the years.

Personally, I found it to be the most fun I'd had on tour for ages. We did something like thirty shows in all; beginning with a dozen shows back-to-back in Antwerp, before moving on for similar runs in Germany and Scandinavia. We did four songs each night: 'Rockin' All Over the World', 'Whatever You Want', 'In the Army Now' and 'Twenty Wild Horses', one of the new tracks from *Under the Influence*. Even though we had a fully booted-and-suited orchestra thundering away behind us each night, we all went on dressed as usual. It really was tremendous fun, having this huge orchestra thumping out the riff to 'Rockin' All Over the World' Because there was so little travelling involved, it meant I could also establish a nice routine wherever we were. Rather than a hotel, I'd rent a small apartment and find out where the nearest gym was. I'd take a bicycle and a couple of guitars with me and I'd be sorted.

By the start of 2000, however, I was back home fretting

over our future again. Although our ticket sales and publicity value remained unaffected, the impact of the David Walker years on our longstanding hardcore audience was undeniable. We may have been all over the telly and the papers but our albums of original material just weren't selling like they used to. Our new records weren't even played on the radio that often any more. In fact, the only place you heard Quo songs regularly in the late nineties was on the telly. I expect most people in Britain will recall how 'Whatever You Want' was used for years in the Argos TV ads. But that was only the tip of the iceberg. 'Down Down' became the music to a Kwik-Fit ad, while 'Whatever You Want' also provided the musical backdrop to the 1999 Hoseason's summer catalogue campaign. Before that, it was the theme tune for a big new Saturday-night TV show the BBC launched in 1997 called – you guessed it – *Whatever You Want*. Did we mind? Not when we first saw the royalty cheques. But later ... maybe. It was all right being a household name, but that didn't mean I wanted the band to turn into a box of soap powder.

In fairness, it wasn't all down to David. Rick and I were to blame, too, for allowing him to push us so far in that direction. But David could be a very intimidating figure to have to deal with; he was always so convinced he was right. Rick used to have this expression which we all used: 'He's been Walkerized!' He'd give you a right fucking talking to and that's when you knew you'd been Walkerized.

The last straw, for me, was the *Famous in the Last Century* album which we released in March 2000. It had David's fingerprints all over it. To 'celebrate' the millennium, he decided we should release an album containing twenty of our favourite hits from the twentieth century. Or, put another way, another bloody covers album! We went along with it, as usual, but inside I felt like a fraud. *Famous in the Last Century* may have gone Top 10 and given us another gold album in Britain, but for me it was the worst Quo album there had ever been – or ever will be!

For a while it left me feeling terribly depressed. I remember sitting at home one winter morning just before it came out, staring out of the window. Here we were, at the start of a new century, and instead of feeling fresh and renewed and ready to go forward, I felt more lost – artistically – than I ever had before. I felt like there was no point writing new songs any more; nobody was interested, not even my own manager and record company.

In the end I forced myself to snap out of it. From the outside, maybe it did look like we were selling out – *selling* being the operative word. Perhaps some of them weren't the right moves, but at least we were still in business. One thing's for sure, I doubt I would be sitting here now, recounting the story of my life in this book, if we hadn't made those moves. Because Status Quo would have been finished a long time ago.

And so things might have stayed, had fate not taken a hand in things. David died suddenly of a heart attack in August 2001. He was fifty-seven. It was a great shock and terribly sad. He had just come back from a spell in rehab and was looking good again. He had been in before but this time he was determined to stay clean and sober. In fact, he had become very anti-drink and drugs. But life at the sharp edge of the business had obviously taken its toll. It wasn't just the drugs, it was his whole lifestyle. He didn't exercise and he would lie in his bunk on the tour bus at night eating sweets and chocolates. He was a smoker, too, coughing his lungs up every morning.

That said, if David hadn't died, I think we would have

parted company with him sooner or later anyway. A couple of days before he died, he actually said to Rick: 'You realize that you two have probably only got a couple of years left and then it's all over.' Rick was very put out when he told me about it but I believe now that David was probably thinking more of himself. He was the one who only wanted to give it a couple more years before jacking it in. He just didn't see us continuing without him.

I didn't feel that way, though, and neither did Rick or the rest of the guys. In fact, if anything, David's death freed us to explore new possibilities again. If David had still been around I'm sure the next album we made, *Heavy Traffic*, would have been very different. He would have hated the cover for a start – a picture of us being chased up the street by a herd of elephants – and he'd almost certainly have pushed us into throwing in a few more cover versions.

Instead, after David died, our longstanding PR, Simon Porter, took over. Simon is a great guy who has been with us now for almost twenty years. During the last few years of David's life, Simon had started to take over more of his duties anyway. David had become phobic about flying and was always asking Simon to deputize for him on trips abroad. When he died, Simon seemed the logical successor. And so it has proved. The first thing he did as our manager was engineer a new deal for the band with Universal Records. Brian Berg, their MD, really liked the new demos we had made, it was as simple as that – we had a deal.

It wasn't until we'd actually begun recording *Heavy Traffic* that someone at Universal above even Brian decided they would also like an album of cover versions. They had obviously checked the sales of our two previous covers albums. Another one now would at least guarantee them a hit, they reasoned, while the album of original material was more of a gamble. I went ballistic. I really thought we'd finally left all that behind us. But no. As soon as Simon walked in I knew something was wrong just from the look on his face. Then when he told us what it was I walked out. I couldn't deal with it at all . . .

But I got over it. I went home and sat in the garden with Eileen and talked about it and decided, well, fine, if that's what we've got to do then that's what we've got to do. We recorded the covers album – titled *Riffs* – as soon as we finished *Heavy Traffic*, then forgot about it while we got on with the business of promoting the latter, which we launched in August 2002 with a big promotional party on the decks of the navy aircraft carrier HMS *Ark Royal*. The first single, 'Jam Side Down', went to Number 15 and *Heavy Traffic*, released a few weeks later, also jumped straight into the Top 20, going on to become our biggest-selling album of original material since the eighties! For once, the critics were largely kind and the general opinion seemed to be the one we were seeking, which was that Quo was back to its rocking roots again. We had clawed back some of our lost credibility and our by now annual winter tour of Britain was one of our longest and most successful for years, culminating with two sold-out nights at Wembley Arena a week before Christmas.

Apart from occasional breaks, we carried on touring throughout almost all of 2003. When the *Riffs* album was finally released in November that year, backed by a TV ad campaign, I confess I had mixed feelings. The first time I actually sat down with the CD and played it at home, I was surprised by how likeable it was. Unlike our previous covers albums, the material on *Riffs* was more eclectic, ranging from vintage old classics like 'Tobacco Road' (by the Nashville

Teens), 'On the Road Again' (Canned Heat) and 'All Day and All of the Night' (The Kinks) to more modern, left-field fare like 'Pump It Up' (Elvis Costello) and 'Real Wild One' (Jerry Lee Lewis via Iggy Pop), plus re-recordings of some of our own best-known tunes like 'Caroline', 'Whatever You Want' and 'Rockin' All Over the World'.

It was all very listenable, but when the CD finished I put it back in its sleeve – and that's where it's stayed ever since. At the end of the day, it's just us doing those tunes. It doesn't mean anything. As a result, where *Heavy Traffic* did unexpectedly good business – right album, right time – *Riffs*, despite all the costly promotion, didn't do half as well as the record company expected it to. Wrong album, wrong time. It's obvious. Well, it is to me and Rick, anyway.

The other big difference about *Heavy Traffic* was that it saw me back writing with Bob Young again. Being Bob, he'd never held a grudge. As mentioned earlier, he had even come along to a Quo show recently. Now I decided to try and bury the hatchet. So I called him on the phone one day and, gentleman that he is, he immediately agreed to a get-together.

He came round and we sat in the garden chatting, and that's when it all came out, all the lies we had been told. The worst part was that we had fallen for it so easily. All those years spent apart ... for nothing. It's probably the one thing I regret most about my time in Quo. At least Bob and I are back together now. He comes round the house and within twenty minutes he's left me to go and talk to Eileen, or he's in the kitchen getting something to eat. Sometimes we go to my music room to write and the pair of us end up snoring on the couch together. It's marvellous, really: the kind of intimacy not even a twenty-year separation can dent.

Best of all, since Bob and I have started working together

again I feel like I've been given a new lease of life as a songwriter. Of course, the music scene has changed a great deal since we were starting out in the sixties. A lot of the music, particularly in the nineties, felt alien and machine-like to me; the charts swamped by acts that made great videos but whose records sounded cold and contrived. The great thing about the pop business, though, is that it's constantly going in cycles. Which is why a band like the Darkness can come along now and be flavour of the month. You can see why that might please me – they look like they should have been on *Top of the Pops* with us in 1973 – but it's not just for that reason. The Darkness have not only brought long-haired rock'n'roll back into fashion, they have brought fun and personality back too. And they can play! Call me an old fart – you would hardly be the first – but how many new pop sensations can you say that about?

The most important ingredient for success, though, is luck, and I've had more than my fair share. Every time I look at the gold and platinum records on my wall I realize that. Undoubtedly my greatest stroke of fortune, however, was meeting Eileen. I couldn't have got through the David Walker years if it hadn't been for her. She doesn't have to say or do anything, just knowing she's there is enough. She's just incredibly bright, and musical – she plays more instruments than I do! And so easy-going we have never even had an argument. Some people say it's not a real marriage if you don't have arguments but that's rubbish. I might get a bit heated-up occasionally – what middle-aged father doesn't find things to rant and rave about sometimes? Eileen just shrugs and leaves me to it. She knows that whatever's bugging me it's never her. She's the one who smoothes all the bugs out.

Since Pat, we have had three more children of our own:

Fynn, born in September 1990; our daughter Kiera, in December 1993; and another boy, Fursey, in September 1996. Fynn is an incredibly bright young man (he's currently learning Japanese) and a good musician, too. Not that that makes him better than anybody's else children. It's what's inside that counts and Fynn, like all my kids, knows that. Kiera was conceived on the roof of a flat Eileen and I were living in, in Amsterdam, one wonderful spring night in 1993, during another tax year out. Even though Kiera and my son Simon have different mothers, they look exactly alike. While Fursey is still just young enough for me to call him my baby.

Kiera and Fursey were each originally one half of sets of twins, but in both cases the other twin died during the pregnancy. People expected us to be devastated but Eileen and I were actually quite fine about it. Eileen comes from a long line of twins; she herself is a twin. So there was no mystique about having twins for her. The way we saw it, we still had the two beautiful children we were left with, and that's what you have to think about. Not what might have been but what is, here and now.

Of my three sons with Jean, the eldest, Simon, is in his mid-thirties now. He's gay and works in the theatre. He's a singer, too – a hell of a lot better one than his dad, I might add. He trained as an opera singer; his tutor was keen for him to pursue a professional career. But he was always more in love with the idea of the theatre. He did a Youth Opportunities course when he was sixteen and they sent him to work backstage at the Dominion in London, when the Dave Clarke musical *Time* was on there. Simon said the minute he walked in and found himself surrounded by all these poofs in make-up running around screaming at the tops of their voices, he had 'never felt so at home before'.

These days, Simon is an actor / singer in his own right. He had a part in the hit film *Scandal*, starring John Hurt, and several other small parts in films and West End stage productions. Right now he's 'resting', as they say in his trade. The important thing is that he appears to be happy. He has a regular partner he's lived with for a few years now who I always refer to as his husband; he's a business journalist on the *Financial Times* and they make a wonderful couple.

My other two boys with Jean – Nicholas and Kieran – have followed in their old man's footsteps even more closely, forming their own band, Little Egypt. Nicholas sings and plays guitar and Kieran plays bass and does backing vocals. They have been together for a few years now and they're a good little outfit – that's why I've had them support Quo on a couple of tours. I wouldn't have done so if I didn't genuinely think they had something. It looks like I might be right, too, as there are a number of record labels sniffing around them now, including one of the majors. I don't want to say any more than that in case it jinxes them, but let's just say I'm keeping my fingers crossed for the boys.

The nice thing is that we are all still close. Even Jean still comes over at Christmas. We have a big family party every Christmas Eve which everyone is invited to. There's lots of food and lots to drink. It's a very Italian sort of Christmas – except we don't go to Mass at midnight.

The only one of my children I have hardly any contact with, sadly, is Bernadette, my daughter by Elizabeth. She's still in Canada with her mother, where she is currently studying at university. I know she loves music, and animals; she rides horses and has won a couple of equestrian events, I believe. Unfortunately, that's all I know. Now in her early twenties, Bernadette has decided she doesn't want anything to do with me. I don't think she believes I actually love her. But I do. Whatever the circumstances, she is still my daughter and I can't love her any more or less than I do my other children. After Liz moved to Canada though, there was no contact between us for years – mostly my fault, I admit. It wasn't until I got together with Eileen and started putting my life back together that I started thinking seriously about Liz and Bernadette again. We went to court in the end and had it all sorted out legally. I made a lump sum payment and arranged to pay child support, etc. I didn't mind at all. I only regret we didn't sort something out sooner.

She and Liz came to stay with us once, when Bernadette was twelve. An amazingly generous gesture by Eileen, I thought, but to her they were family, and she wanted to welcome them as she would any other family members. They stayed for a couple of weeks and it was a little strange at first, I suppose, but nice. We all got on fine. That was the only time they have been here, though. After that, they more or less disappeared from our lives.

I realize I might be partly to blame for that, too, as I don't send birthday or Christmas cards. But then I don't send birthday or Christmas cards to my other kids either. I don't even send them to Eileen. In fact, I don't even know what date Eileen's birthday is exactly. And I don't do presents. I just don't see it as part of my duty the way most people do. It's got nothing to do with being miserly. I'm quite happy to splash out on things for my friends and family. But only when I want to, or they need things, regardless of what time of year it is.

I'm not a great keeper of photographs, either. There are thousands of the band in storage somewhere, and I have hundreds of the family locked away in a cupboard at home.

But I don't have a lot of framed photos around the house. It just doesn't interest me. Like videoing the kids. It's not something I ever wanted to do. Maybe I'll regret that as they get older and I want to relive the memories of them as children, but I doubt it. I just don't think like that. I'm happy with what's going on now.

Ultimately, whatever mishaps have befallen me, I'm glad, because if those things hadn't happened I wouldn't be where I am now. These days I get told I'm boring because I don't go to parties. But I know who the really boring ones are. I'd rather sit in my garden, having a cup of tea with our housekeeper, Bernadette Bachelor, or nattering to our gardener, Stan Cannon, than go to yet another boring music biz party.

The last time I looked, the official Quo website listed my hobbies as 'collecting koi carp, eating pasta and clay pigeon shooting'. But the pasta-eating's been reduced considerably over the past couple of years and I sold the carp to a friend of Rick's because the kids got too upset every time one died. But when I have the time I do still like to go clay pigeon shooting. There's just something about being outdoors with the dogs and trying to hit moving targets. It requires skill but also relaxation and good mental and physical reflexes.

Each shoot is different, they set the traps in various ways to imitate certain birds. As the clay fires out, you have to pick it up and follow it with your eyes. If it's falling away you come underneath it and if it's still rising you go above it. You have to work all that out in a split second. But if you succeed and actually hit it, it's such a fantastic feeling! There are other musicians I know who are into it, too, like Mark Knopfler. Suzi Quatro has asked me to go shooting with her a couple of times, too, but she's shit hot, championship material.

Apart from keeping fit by going to the gym every day and

eating the right foods (I don't eat bread at all any more and I only recently started eating meat again, for the protein, after abstaining for eleven years), the other change I've made in my life recently has been my attitude to dope smoking. Having smoked marijuana and cannabis in various forms for most of my adult life, I never felt 'addicted' in the way I did with coke, which had a total stranglehold on me. But it's like the old joke goes: 'I've been doing drugs for thirty years and I'm still not addicted!' How can you tell?

As an experiment, I stopped completely for about six months recently. Even though I still wouldn't describe it as physically addictive, nevertheless, the first two nights without dope I soaked the bed sheets through as the toxins gushed out of me. By the third night I was having the most outrageously vivid dreams. After a few days, however, it all settled down and I began to sleep really well again. That's the downside of dope. Do it all day and your mind is still running like a rat on a wheel even as you try and sleep.

I have since started having the occasional joint in the evening after dinner. Purely for relaxation, though. It's not something I do all day any more, or even every day. I certainly don't do it when the band are working. Once upon a time skinning up a fat one was my first priority as soon as we came off stage. These days my only thought is to get showered and changed, then sit down to a good meal on the tour bus. After that I might watch a movie, or get my little palmtop computer out and play a bit of Patience, or maybe just do the crossword. Then go to sleep. I'm much more alert that way and I need to be. I can't just sleepwalk my way through the band like I used to.

As for Quo, that too has never been in such robust health. 2005 is our fortieth anniversary year, and from what I'm told we will be on tour for most of it. After that, Rick and I both feel it might be nice to stop for a while – or at least slow down a little. I definitely want to take a break, just so I can write some songs. There's the stuff you come up with when you know you've got a new Quo album to do, and there's the stuff that just comes naturally when you're not thinking of anything else, and those are often the best songs. In order to get there though, you really do have to get off that treadmill for a while.

Right now, apart from finishing off the last pages of this book, I'm also busy recording a new solo album. Mainly songs written with Bob, both old and new, the plan right now is for it to come out after the fortieth anniversary tour, some time in 2006. I've been thinking about putting it out via the Internet, like Chris De Burgh did recently. I heard that because there are no huge costs, he only had to sell 6,000 copies of the album to make as much money as he would have done if he'd sold 60,000 with a major record company. That kind of arithmetic is hard to resist. It means I'd be more than content if I sold 10,000 copies, which is the minimum I would expect to do if I released it on a major label.

In terms of where Quo go next, that's easy. We have already done demos of four new tunes that Bob and I have written; one or two of which may even have seen the light of day by the time this book appears. Or we might decide to keep them until 2005 and the anniversary tour. We'll see. One thing's for sure, the story of Status Quo is far from over yet.

As for me, I'm too content with what I have now in my personal life to want to look too far ahead there. Of course, nobody's life is ever perfect, and while these past fifteen years with Eileen have undoubtedly been my happiest, things on the domestic front have still had their ups and downs. My mother, for example, who spent her last years living at the house with us, was quite a burden to bear. Madly religious right to the end, for the last ten years of her life she wouldn't even let me call her 'mum' any more. I was to call her Annie, she said, because she felt more like a friend to me now than a relative. It was the same with her grandchildren; they all had to call her Annie.

She was always coming out with stuff like that. One day she told me she'd been cleaning the bathroom and discovered that – shock, horror! – I hadn't been using my flannel. I said, 'Well, I don't always.' She scolded me: 'Well, you should because you're giving them a free feel!' I said, 'Who's "them"?' She said: '"Them", "those", the evil ones!' I said, 'But I might want them to have a free feel.' She would look at me as though there was no hope for me. Or like the whole business about me being born by immaculate conception. I would point out that my father might have a different opinion and she would fly into a rage. 'He never came near me! Never!' I'm just glad she never came out with this stuff when I was a kid. It was bad enough having to listen to it as an adult – like being disowned, in some way. Mind you, it could have been worse. My brother Dominic was an ordinary conception, apparently. Poor sod. She never forgave him for that . . .

Don't get me wrong, I never stopped loving my mother but when she died in November 1997, mainly the feeling was one of relief. She was ill with osteoporosis and various cancers; she needed to die. She even asked me once to help put her out of her misery. 'You know about drugs, give me something.' I said I would but there was no way I was going to prison and getting shagged up the arse by large hairy men just for her. That brought a smile to her face.

It was about seven-thirty one morning when she finally went. I was asleep in bed, but Eileen was with her and she was the one who woke me with the news. I said, 'Oh, good,' because I knew she was better off, then turned over and went back to sleep. When I woke up properly a couple of hours later I went and saw her. I stood there for a while then reached out and touched her face. As soon as I felt her skin, I thought: no, that's not who I knew. That wasn't my mother lying there. That was her body but she – the person I knew – had moved on. Once that became apparent to me I was fine about it.

I was going to bury her in the garden. I really was. I even told her so before she died. She laughed and pointed out that it would devalue the house, and of course she was right. So instead we had a 'proper' Catholic funeral for her. People kept coming up saying how sorry they were that I had lost my mother and I would make a joke. 'I ain't lost her. She's in that box.' Not because I was feeling chirpy, but because I just can't deal with all that emotional wallowing. As a result, I have often been accused over the years of being cold. Maybe I am, but these events that people find so crushing, I'm just not sure they should be always. It's just the way we've been brought up to respond to them. Is death necessarily such a terrible thing, in the bigger picture? According to the Catholics, you've gone to a better place anyway, so what are we getting so upset about? It's how it's meant to be, isn't it?

I didn't cry at her funeral. I used to cry easily as a youngster, and some things can still set me off now: watching *ET*, perhaps, or listening to certain pieces of music – anything from Shania Twain to Pavarotti. Real-life situations don't have the same effect on me, though. I didn't cry when we lost the twins, either. I got a bit worried when Eileen was in hospital once, but I don't know if I cried even then. It's not a macho thing. If I want to bawl my eyes out, I will. I just don't find myself doing it when it comes to the real thing.

Is it a defence mechanism? Probably. There has to be some of that in there, I suppose. But that doesn't mean I suddenly break down when someone presses the right buttons. I can't afford to sit around crying. I sound like my father when I say that but it's true. I want to be a responsible husband and father. That means I've *got* to keep it together. Very occasionally I do have a weak moment when I know that if I'm not careful I could quite easily crack. But I get hold of them and contain them and they soon pass.

It was the same when my dad died just after Easter, 2001. We were on tour and I got a phone call in my hotel room. 'Oh, shit,' I said. 'Poor old dad.' Then I put the phone down and got ready for the gig. I was sad but at the same time not sad. His time had come, that's all. Just like mine and yours will, too, one day. I did the show that night then a few days later I went to his funeral. It was quite a hilarious occasion, actually. The priest had just arrived from Africa and could barely speak English. He kept mispronouncing my father's name and someone started giggling. Next thing, the whole church was in fits of laughter. Much more preferable to all that crying. Dad would have preferred it that way too, I'm sure.

Oddly, however, my mother's extreme take on religion did have one positive effect on me in that it helped propel me towards my own current understanding of the whole 'God' question. She was so over the top I began to realize how ridiculous so many teachings of the Catholic Church – and all other religions – really are when you look at them cold on the page. For a long time, the old guy with the long white beard had haunted me. Now, in my mind, the whole shaky edifice began to crumble.

I had started going back to church on a semi-regular basis in the eighties. Paige was a Catholic, too, and we would go to Mass together sometimes. Then later, after I married Eileen, who also comes from a Catholic background, we started going to church regularly every Sunday morning, as much for the kids as anything. Which was ironic as the kids used to be bored stupid. But you have children and suddenly the whole thing is back on the menu again. They were all enrolled into Catholic schools, too, so the whole thing just fell into place.

By then I had begun questioning things, though: something the Catholic Church does not welcome. I still received Holy Communion, for instance, but I couldn't put myself through the farce of Confession again. I'd had enough of that as a kid – sitting in the little black box trying to think of something sinful I had done to please the priest. ('Lying' was always a good standby.) It was ridiculous, I knew it even then. Now, however, even things like the Lord's Prayer began to seem hollow to me. Not the words but the fact that everyone says them in church then goes out and does the complete opposite. And I remember getting very pissed off one day when one of the kids came to tell me that I wasn't his father because God was his father. I said, 'Oh really? Then maybe God could find somewhere for you to sleep tonight, too.' I discussed it with Eileen and our attitude was: how dare they teach our children this rubbish? Or I'd be standing there in church taking Holy Communion, thinking, 'So we're teaching our kids that they're eating the body of Christ and drinking his blood? This is class . . .'

It was around then that I read the first of a wonderful

trilogy of books called *Conversations with God*. It was the homeopath who helped look after my mother when she was ill – a wonderful Malaysian woman named Tina Wong who has since become a close family friend – who first told me about it. At first I was like, 'No way! I've had enough of God!' But she slammed the first book on my chest one day and said: 'Read that! Trust me, you'll enjoy it.'

So I gave it a go and I'm so glad I did. I've now read all three and they're all fantastic. I recently started reading the first one again – it's my fourth time and it never lets me down. I keep trying to get others to read them, too. Eileen and I used to buy dozens of copies and hand them out to people. They usually turned very polite and started nodding their heads like it was the most interesting thing in the world – then ran a mile as soon as we weren't looking.

What's it all about? You'd have to read the books themselves for the proper answer to that one. In my case, the main appeal is that they cut through all the crap most religions feed you. It doesn't deny the presence of God – quite the opposite – it just takes the story out of the hands of the religious fanatics and gives it back to you straight, in a way that makes perfect sense. And I needed that in my life right then. Even though I used to come out of church seething sometimes, I still had a certain faith in God. I still do have faith in God, but not the one that is going to frown and punish you if you do something wrong. The way I look at is, we are all *part* of God: humans, animals, even tables and chairs. When you break us all down to our molecular structure, we're all made of the same thing – energy. Particles. Life-force. Or God, if you like.

I suppose I've always felt that way, basically, but reading *Conversations with God* was what really crystallized those ideas for me: that life is purely an experience; there is no judgement; there is no learning; we are all born perfect beings. It really is up to us what we want to do with all these treasures, for good or ill. Religion teaches you the opposite: not that we are equal but that some (the ones who follow that religion) are better than others (the ones who don't follow that religion). What kind of God goes along with that?

It was shortly after reading the first book that we stopped going to church completely. Since then, interestingly, nobody from there talks to us any more, that's what good Christians they are. And of course we took a bit of flak from the heads of the various schools the kids were at. But we had made our decision and we stuck to it. Ultimately, once our children are old enough, they can decide whether they want to be Catholics or not. But for now we do things the way Eileen and I think best.

I know what you're thinking: I'm going on a bit. You're right, so I'll stop here with one final thought. I love blue skies as much as anybody, but I also love the rain – and the wind and the cold. I even love being on the tour bus sometimes, or at the very least moaning about being on the tour bus. I love making music, I love eating, I love shagging, I love swimming, I love working out . . . In short, I love being alive. That, to me, is what God stands for now. Getting the most out of your day, come rain or shine. As it says in the first book: 'Love is the ultimate reality, it is the only, the all. Your feeling of love is your experience of God. And the highest truth is that love is all there is, all there was and all there ever will be.'

It seems to me that most religions contain a thread of that simple truth, but it's been fucked with, to keep people grovelling in fear of God. To keep them in line. In other words, the opposite of love. I also like the bit about fate being an acronym for From All Thoughts Everywhere; the idea of a collective consciousness and how it can work both for and against you – hence the idea behind meditation, prayer, and just wishing. I read that and went, yes!

All right, I promise, that's it. Just do yourself a favour and check out *Conversations with God* one day. As the old cliché goes, it will make you think . . .

Getting back to more earthly matters, in terms of where Rick and I go now, with or without Status Quo, the fact is, we're at that stage now where it doesn't pay to look too far ahead. We're both going to be sixty soon! Retirement age for most people. Fortunately, Rick and I have never been most people.

Why keep going at all, you might wonder? Surely we've made enough money by now to never have to work again? But while it's true that if the band ended tomorrow I would still be financially secure for the rest of my life, that doesn't mean I'm going to turn down the chance to earn some more if I can, the same as anybody. Then there's the fame. While I could definitely live without it some days, it is, after all, what we have worked so hard to achieve all these years. As Rick says, it's when they *don't* stare at you when you walk in the room that you're in trouble in this game.

Neither of those things are the real reasons we keep going, though. We keep going because we wouldn't know what else to do. I love being at home, and there are times when I feel I could happily hide away here for ever. But I know that sooner or later I would miss the buzz of going on stage with the band; the thrill of coming up with a new tune. The whole excitement that goes with being in one of the biggest, best-known rock bands in the world. It's the one drug I don't think I'll ever be able to kick.

I'm proud of what we've done and who we are, too. We could so easily have ended up as just another faceless rock band from the seventies. Instead, Rick and I became the cheeky chappy and the blond one. For some reason people just took to us. It's got to the stage now where we've become like a double-act. Nobody wants to book one without the other. We're like the mad uncles of Ant and Dec. That can get on people's tits, and I admit, it gets on my tits, too, sometimes. But it's too late to turn back now even if we wanted to.

It's funny, Rick and I still talk about what we're going to do when we get old – forgetting that we *are* now old. All that stuff we used to talk about, taking it easy, getting a few rounds of golf in, they never seem to happen. But then we've always been different as people – opposites almost – and the older we get the more different we become. I like to plan and think ahead; Rick lives totally in the moment. It's one of the things that makes him so endearing, his impetuousness. It's also what drives you crazy sometimes, because it means he only ever sees things his way. Like his love of expensive cars. Because it's one of his big passions, he immediately assumes everybody else feels the same way too. Now, while I like cars, and appreciate the comforts of my BMW, other than how to drive one, I've got no deep interest in them. You'd think Rick might have twigged that after forty years, but no. Knowing I like BMWs, he said to me the other day, 'Why don't you get that new BMW that's coming out this year?' I said, 'I don't need to. I've only done twenty thousand miles in the one I've got.' He just grinned: 'Go on, you know you want to . . .' 'No,' I said, 'really, I don't . . .' I ended up having an argument with him about whether I wanted to buy a new car or not!

But that's Rick. As he says himself, 'I never know what I want, do I?' Rick will say, 'Look, it's great over there!' and he'll go and stand over there. Then within minutes he'll go, 'Shit! It's terrible here! I should have stayed where I was!' and he'll come back again. Then he'll go, 'No, it *is* better over that side,' and go all the way back again. And so it goes . . .

You've got to love him, that's all. He's the Peter Pan of rock. Even though he's six months older than me, I have always been the older brother of the relationship. He still comes to me for reassurance sometimes.

'We're gonna be all right, aren't we?' he'll say out of the blue.

'Yeah,' I say, 'We're gonna be all right . . .'

And we are.

FIVE

On the surface, the late eighties was a great time for me, both personally and professionally. After the huge success of 'In the Army Now', Quo was more popular than ever. Our next album, *Ain't Complaining*, in 1988, had been another sizeable hit for us. I co-wrote and sang the title track, which became a Top 20 single, while Francis and Andy Bown came up with an even bigger hit in 'Burning Bridges', which went to Number 3 that Christmas.

Even my personal life was back on track. I married Patty at the start of July 1988. We had secretly planned the wedding while the band was recording at Chipping Norton Studios a few weeks before, but had decided to keep it quiet. We didn't want a big do, we just wanted it to be one of those almost spur-of-the-moment things. We set off from the flat one morning and took the Rolls-Royce down to Richmond registry office. Both sets of parents were there but that was all. We didn't have time to tell anyone else, we just went and did it.

Within three months Patty had become pregnant with Harry. We were in the Roller one day when she told me. It was the first time I'd actually driven it since getting my licence back, so I was already flying. Then when Patty suddenly said, 'I'm pregnant,' I nearly skidded to a halt. 'Fantastic!' I cried. What with becoming a father again *and* being able to drive, I was happier than a dog with two dicks!

By the time Harry – Harrison John, to give him his full name – was born in June 1989, life had become almost idyllic again. We had moved out of Battersea and into a fabulous new place I'd bought for £160,000 at Key West, in Teddington. Key West was another riverside apartment but it was much more luxurious than the one in Battersea. Spread over two floors, it had two big double bedrooms, two bathrooms, plus a huge lounge and kitchen. It also came with its own mooring on the river – your own private parking space for a boat. Being me, of course, I thought, right, well, I better get aboat then! It was the start of what has now become another of my great passions, alongside cars and guitars.

As luck would have it, there was a chandlery – the place where they sell all the gear you need for boating, from ropes and buoys to the boats themselves – next door to the new flat and I got to know the bloke who owned it, Malcolm, now a good mate. It was he who loaned me the first boat I ever took out on the river, which I nicknamed the Bathtub. It was actually called a Doory, but it was made of fibreglass moulded into what resembled a bathtub, with a small outboard motor down one end where the taps would be. We used to go out for hours on it: me and Patty, putt-putting down the river. I loved how you could totally change your day just by jumping on the boat and taking off somewhere. You don't even have to know where you're going, just for a ride . . .

Of course, it wasn't long before I started noticing other, much bigger boats on the river. Luxurious-looking motorized yachts with people sunbathing on the decks, sipping their gin and tonics. I'd be thinking, 'Wow, look at that! I want one of those!' Then we were out on the river one day when we happened to pass a boat sale. We decided to go and have a gander, not with the idea of buying anything yet, just to have a look at what was on offer and how much it all cost. We walked around gawping at all these beautiful vessels. Then we found one that really caught the eye – a twenty-one-footer that really looked the part. It had a cabin, a half-deck, bunks to sleep in, a galley to cook in and a fridge to put all the beer and vodka in. I realized that going from the Bathtub to something like that would be like going from an Austin Metro to a Porsche! That's when I knew I had to have it. It was priced at just under fifteen grand, as I recall, and I bought it on the spot. I named it *Shy Fly*, after one of the early Quo tracks.

We took it out for a ride the moment it arrived. Patty was five months pregnant at the time and I knew nothing about proper boating yet. All I knew was I'd got a throttle in my hand and I was gonna use it! It had an inboard V8 engine and for a boat it really rocked. That first trip we found ourselves going all the way past the Houses of Parliament, up to Tower Bridge. speeding along like the novice I was, getting knocked from side to side by the wake of passing ferries. To me it was like a ride at the fairground but Patty begged me to slow down. You could hear all the crockery and glasses smashing in the galley . . .

We ended up travelling for miles that day. We passed HMS *Belfast* and got nearly all the way to Greenwich before deciding to turn back. Of course, not really knowing what I was doing, I hadn't given any thought to stuff like high- and low-water times, I just blithely sailed on; though I did notice how few other boats there were out there with us on the journey back. It was now early evening, coming into what I was about to discover was low-water time. Suddenly it was getting dark and we were literally running out of water to float in! The propeller started churning up mud from the riverbank and I had to lift the leg of the prop so that it was almost facing out of the water just to prevent it from getting stuck. By the time we got home it was gone midnight and we were crawling down the centre of the river in about three feet of water. You could have paddled faster. Patty was cursing me.

I learned my lesson, though, and after that I took the whole idea of boating much more seriously. I started reading books and talking to Malcolm about it, and that's how I learned. It's like owning a car; it's all right to have fun and enjoy yourself in them, but you need to know how to drive first and what the rules of the road are.

I only had *Shy Fly* for a few months, however, before exchanging it for something even better. I had been to the Southampton Boat Show and seen this monstrous machine with a thirty-six-foot bow; a fly-bridge; lower and upper decks; two bedrooms; big galley; a bathroom and a shower. It was painted silver-grey on the outside and decorated in blue suede throughout the inside, and it had all the onboard luxuries you could think of. It was powered by two 350 Volvo turbocharged engines and, needless to say, I was smitten immediately. I simply *had* to have it! The thought of being on the water with twin turbo engines under me was just too much to resist. It meant it could do about thirty-two knots, which is approaching forty miles an hour – fast out on the river.

It was called *Silver Sun* and was going for £80,000. I did a deal and part-exchanged *Shy Fly* for it. A couple of weeks later it was driven up to London on the back of a huge transporter.

Me and Patty went to meet it in the car out on the M4. To see this thing on the motorway was staggering. It was so massive it looked like the *QE2*! I was almost creaming myself following it back in, the orange lights of the transporter flashing. I thought, that's mine! Mine! Amazing! We drove down to Kingston, where it was gently hoisted by a crane back on to the water. It was an awesome sight. Ten tons of boat swaying in the air. Then one of the previous owner's captains accompanied me on the trip up the river back to Key West, during which he showed me how everything worked.

We had the most amazing times on *Silver Sun*. We were always going up and down the river on her. I even took her out to the Channel Islands once, me and a mate who acted as map-reader while I steered. Sailed her down to Dover, refuelled, and set off for Guernsey. Flat out across open sea, four hours. It was so wonderful; up on the fly-bridge, riding out through the open sea, just kicking arse! Rather poignantly, however, it was on that trip I received the news that my dad had died. He had been ill for some time with emphysema and was in a nursing home. If I had known he was on the point of dying I would never have left him. But he had seemed quite stable and when Patty phone me with the news it was hard at first to take in, stuck out there on the boat in the middle of the ocean. Ironically, my dad always fancied himself as a bit of a sailor, too. So we stopped the boat, turned the engines off – I remember it was very calm and sunny – and I took a large tot of scotch over to the side of the boat and tossed it in. Like a final salute from his son. I think he would have liked that . . .

Mainly, though, I just puttered around the river on it with the family. I remember how we were able to open a hatch on deck and look down to where Harry used to sleep, so we were able to keep an eye on him. The whole lifestyle at Key West was just lovely like that, and that really should have been the happy ending to my story.

Except, of course, it was all about to go wrong again. The root of it was that I went back to my bad old ways: the drinking; the drugs; the womanizing. As soon as Quo got back together and started having success again, I started going off the rails once more. It was the same for Francis. In fact, we were both going for it so much in the late eighties we couldn't see what else was going on under our noses, so to speak. Namely, the fact that we were being taken to the cleaners.

When it all came out, I felt utterly betrayed. As long as the band was doing all right and I had enough dough to maintain my cars, my boats and my coke, I didn't really give too much thought to anything else. Especially not anything complicated...

The scales started to fall from my eyes, however, after a visit to my accountant's office one day. I'd just bought myself the new Porsche turbo convertible and he wasn't pleased. He said: 'But you have a bill from the tax man for forty grand.' I said, 'So what? Pay it!' He shook his head. 'You don't understand. I can't pay it. You haven't got enough money in your account.' I was gobsmacked. I was certainly spending money, I knew that, but not so much it would actually leave me broke, I felt sure. I went home that day and phoned Francis and that was the start of us gradually putting two and two together.

Then came South Africa. Unfortunately, me and Francis were totally green on the ethics of playing in South Africa at that time, and we were told everybody did it now – Queen, Black Sabbath, even Cliff Richard. We thought if they'd all done it, it must be all right. Famous last words . . .

When we got home we were greeted by some of the worst press we had ever had: 'Quo Defy Apartheid Ban!' was probably the kindest headline. We apologized to everybody we could but the damage had been done. Then when we brought in our new manager, David Walker, some months later, we became aware of the sheer size of the hole we had been left in, financially. We were appalled to discover that somewhere in the region of six million quid had been siphoned off from us over the years! At which point, life became a nightmare. There I was living this palatial lifestyle, thinking my troubles were over, and suddenly I was broke again. For a while I thought I was going to have to sell everything again.

Fortunately, however, we had David there to help guide us out of the financial maze. He was an astute businessman who specialized in squeezing every last drop of promotional juice out of any given situation, and though we may not have released some of the best Quo records in the nineties, we certainly released some of the most successful. Nearly all of them were down to David's ideas and drive, so he must have been doing something right.

Behind the scenes, however, things between me and Francis were not going so well. We seemed to be travelling down two different roads for much of the early nineties. He had met his soon-to-be second wife, Eileen; a lovely woman who helped him get his life back together. While I, by contrast, appeared to be going in the other direction, my personal life starting to spiral out of control again. In any event, Francis now started to exert much more control over the band. He was already doing the majority of the songwriting. I was still coming up with the odd little gem but, in truth, my lifestyle had started to impact badly on me and my writing suffered accordingly. Prolific, I was not. Meanwhile, Francis was coming out with reams of new stuff and the contrast between us, both onstage and off, could not have been starker.

We both became quite annoyed about it, at one point. I didn't see that what I was doing was so bad. Francis had been even worse than me at one point, surely he of all people could understand what I was going through now? Looking back, of course, I realize now that he saw only too well. My life had become a mess again but, as usual, I was the last one to get to grips with that uncomfortable fact. It wasn't just the drugs. By then my whole world had been turned upside down again when Marietta had suddenly walked back into my life.

It had begun with a chance meeting back in the summer of 1990. By then Patty and I had moved out of Key West and into a beautiful country mansion. We had always intended moving back to the countryside; Key West was originally supposed to be no more than a stopping-off point for us. We had also bought a dog by then, a King Charles Spaniel we named Henry, and with Harry now running round the place too, we decided we needed somewhere bigger with a proper garden. It meant moving away from the river and I thought, well, if we're going to do that, then it better be to somewhere really cool. So we rented a big place in Walton-on-Thames, one of the most affluent suburbs of London.

The house was one of the finest in a beautiful street called Silverdale Avenue. It had once belonged to Mike Yarwood, the comedian whose impersonations of Harold Wilson and Ted Heath made him a TV superstar in the seventies. It had its own tennis courts, swimming-pool, sculpted gardens, the works. The rent was four grand a month. Crazy, really. The house was on sale for £750,000 and, bloody hell, how I regret not putting that rent money into a mortgage for it instead. It's probably worth five times that now.

Not that I could really complain. After David had cleared up the financial mess the band was in, we were living in fine style again. We stayed at the house in Silverdale Avenue for about eighteen months, during which time *Silver Sun* was moored at Walton Marina. I kept Key West on, too. I used to let friends stay there sometimes, or I might stay over myself if I'd been working late in town or whatever. Mostly though, I forgot I even had the place and got into enjoying life at Silverdale. Without a boat to mess around in outside my door any more, I began a new car collection. I'd sold the Roller by then and got the Porsche. I'd also bought a Range Rover, which we used as the family car, as well as a bright red Jag that we called the Fire Engine. My passions were all coming alive again and life was good. Then I saw Marietta and everything changed just like that...

Me and Patty were having dinner one night at Langan's, a place we often used to go in those days. I'd been on stage earlier that afternoon with Quo, performing at the Silver Clef Award Winners charity concert at Knebworth Park, in June 1990. We hung around for a couple of hours afterwards soaking up the atmosphere backstage, then Patty and I grabbed a bottle of chilled champagne from the dressing-room, jumped into a chauffeur-driven limo and headed back to London. By now it was early evening, so we drove straight to the restaurant, told the driver to wait for us and went inside. We were sitting there still having fun when Patty suddenly said, 'Look who's over there.' I looked and it was Marietta. It was the first time I'd seen her for years and my eyes nearly popped out of my head! She looked ravishingly beautiful. I couldn't stop looking at her. I thought, oh dear, I'm in trouble here . . .

I went over and said hello and she looked pleased to see me, too. We sat and had a drink and at the end of the conversation we swapped phone numbers – and that was the start of us getting to know each other again. Patty had no objections, in principle, because she knew that I saw getting to know Marietta again as a way of getting back in touch with my son Richard again, too. After the divorce, Richard hadn't wanted anything to do with me and it had been almost ten years since we'd last even seen each other. At one point, as a child, he'd contracted Crohn's disease and been very ill, but even then he'd refused to see me. I suppose his mum hadn't painted a very pretty picture of me when he was growing up. To be fair, there wasn't any pretty picture to paint. Richard had seen quite a lot of the madness, too, as a child, from me wrecking furniture to bringing strange people back to the house.

So when, not long after bumping into each other at Langan's, Marietta phoned to tell me she thought it was time I got to know my son again, I couldn't have been more thrilled – or surprised! She was thinking of moving back to Germany, she said. She had sold the house not long after the divorce and started her own interior design business. But then that faded and now her father had offered her a top job working for him at his company, back home in Germany. She had more or less made up her mind to go, I think, but she wanted to make sure Richard still had a home to go to in England. He was fifteen now, away most of the time at boarding-school. While he could obviously go to his mother's new home in Germany during school breaks and holidays, she knew he would prefer to live somewhere closer to all his friends in England.

She asked me what I thought and I said I was all for it – it just depended on how Richard felt. We decided the best way to find out would be to arrange a little visit. I agreed to put on my Sunday best and go up to where they were living in Guildford. Driving over with Patty, I was a bag of nerves. I missed my son so much, yet now I was going to see him again, I didn't know what to think. I was so nervous I was worried I was gonna blow it.

Thankfully, though, everything was fine once we arrived. He'd obviously grown up a lot and was already halfway to becoming his own man. But he also had a wonderful sense of humour, very prankish and full of fun, and we got on almost immediately. At first I couldn't take my eyes off him, watching every move out of the corner of my eye. He was a good-looking boy, clearly intelligent. And so tall now and handsome! It really brought it home to me how much I had missed of him growing up. I had never stopped loving my son, though, and I suppose, somewhere in his heart, he had never stopped loving his bad dad. Whatever the reason, it felt great to be in touch with each other again.

Yet again, Patty, bless her, was very supportive, even though it was clear that Richard would take time to get used to her. She readily agreed to more visits, with a view to him becoming a full-time family member at some stage, because she knew how much it meant to me. What I didn't tell Patty, I'm ashamed to say, was that my relationship with Marietta now went beyond the 'friends reunited' stage. As chance would have it, Marietta had moved to a house in Addleston, the next town along from Walton, so seeing each other was easy. Too easy. Once it had begun, it didn't stop. Suddenly we couldn't get enough of each other. It was terribly unfair on Patty, but I was lost in a drug-induced haze again and, apart from the sexual allure, there was still a lot of unfinished business between me and Marietta. To have her and Richard back in my life again after so long apart ... well, it just felt right somehow.

That doesn't mean I was oblivious to the wrong I was doing. I realized that, in a strange way, I was back where I'd been in the seventies – doing drugs and cheating on my wife. The only difference was, Marietta was now the other woman. When Patty found out – as she'd been bound to do sooner or later, discretion never having been one of my stronger suits – she was understandably furious. She said she felt betrayed in every sense and I couldn't deny it. Then she packed her things and walked out, taking Harry with her.

I didn't take it well. In fact, I must have gone straight to the rock'n'roll medicine chest, because the next thing I knew I was waking up with a sore head and a very distressed-looking Marietta standing over me. She said I had rung her, boozed and coked out of my mind, to tell her what had happened. Then when she'd tried to call me back later and I didn't answer, she'd become worried and had decided to drive over and check on me. She told me that when she arrived she found me unconscious on the floor of the lounge, the front door of the house wide open.

Marietta got me on my feet and drove me back to her place, where she looked after me for the next couple of days. The minute I left her, though, I went straight out and got blotto again. I was in self-destruct mode. This was true rock'n'roll; not the glamorous kind you see in videos, but the real nitty-gritty. When I finally went home to Silverdale, the only reason I didn't smash the place up was because it was rented. Instead, I concentrated on trashing myself. A pretty good job of it I did, too. For a while I didn't even know where Patty and Harry were. I still don't. It was like when I left Marietta and Richard all over again. I don't even recall how long they were gone for. By then I had abandoned the house completely and had fled back to Key West. I was in such a state that days and nights flashed by like the lights of a passing train. All I knew was that I was in trouble. I thought the courtroom was looming again ...

Fortunately Patty eventually calmed down enough to forgive me, if not entirely forget. She came home one day and said she was giving me a second chance. I didn't deserve it but that's the kind of generous-hearted woman Patty is. Not long after that, Marietta finally left for Germany and Patty and I got back to a semi-normal life again. For a while, anyway.

In between all this domestic panic, I was working harder than ever with the band. David Walker made sure of that. His first big idea – the *Rockin' All Over the Years* greatest hits compilation in 1990, released to 'celebrate' our twentieth anniversary – was an enormous hit. The fact that it cost nothing to produce, because it was all old stuff, meant that the two million copies it sold worldwide brought in a huge dollop of cash for us. Always welcome at any time but much needed then, as our album the previous year, *Perfect Remedy*, had been a relative flop.

After that, whenever David came up with another idea it was hard to ignore him. 'You do want to sell records, don't you?' he'd ask sarcastically. Well, yes, we did. It was just the kind of records David wanted us to sell that got us down in the end. It was a long time before we got to that stage of the game, though. Meantime, I was having fun again. I know doing things like the 'Come On You Reds' single in 1994 with the Manchester United football squad made Francis squirm, to a degree, but I was in my element. After years of taking ourselves seriously, there was nothing wrong with having a bit of fun now and again. The fact that it actually went to Number 1 was the icing on the cake for me.

Other highlights from those days that I still recall with a smile include the Brits, of course, in 1991, where ripping off our dinner suits to reveal jeans and T-shirts underneath became the most talked-about thing of the show. Even more memorable for me, however, was the trip we made to Monaco in June that year to attend the World Music Awards. We were presented with the award for Outstanding Contribution to the Rock Industry by Prince Albert, which was amazing. An even bigger thrill for me, though, had occurred earlier that day when, as part of the entertainment, we were taken to see the Monaco Grand Prix! We got to watch the whole race from the VIP enclosure and, being a car nut, of course, I loved every noisy minute!

After the awards ceremony that evening there was a huge open-air banquet at the palace, hosted by Prince Albert. Everybody from the show was there: us, David Hasselhoff, Kylie Minogue, Britt Ekland, loads of other people. There was a big outdoor barbecue with people riding round on horses, giving the scene a faintly surreal quality. Then when we were leaving, me and our PR, Simon Porter, ended up sharing a limo back to the hotel with Sam Fox, Ursula Andress and Britt Ekland. We were all drunk and they were talking about whether their tits were real or not. In the end, I suggested, there was only one way to find out, and so all three lobbed them out for me and Simon to pass judgement on! I must say, they were all so nice in their different ways it took a while for us to decide and we had to study them quite closely . . .

It was at this point that me and Francis started to become bona fide showbiz personalities, appearing on things like the *Des O'Connor Show*, or hamming it up on *Hale and Pace*. We had been tabloid celebs since the eighties; now, in the nineties, we went completely mainstream. We had officially become loveable. Hence stuff like the waxwork dummies of me and Francis in Madame Tussaud's, or having our faces made into Royal Doulton mugs. It's all hugely flattering, of course, and wonderful to have achieved. Isn't this, after all, what we originally set out to do? To become mega-famous? And rich? In which case, mission accomplished on both counts . . .

In another sense, however, we made our beds at that point, and have been lying in them ever since. Once you make it on to the TV chat-show circuit you wave goodbye to so-called rock credibility for ever. Instead, we had become a British institution. Like egg and chips or the Blackpool Tower. Personally, I felt very comfortable with that. In fact, I loved appearing on TV with people like Terry Wogan and Cilla Black. I enjoyed working with Cilla, especially, because I was always a big *Blind Date* fan. And I got a kick out of hanging out on things like *The Aspel Show*. It meant we were more famous than ever, and that's the name of the game, whatever anyone says.

When it came to the music we now made, as far as I was concerned, it was simply a case of doing whatever it took to keep the band afloat. I wasn't thrilled by the idea of doing even one album of cover versions, let alone three! But in each case it was what either David or the record company wanted. There aren't any records worth putting out that your manager and record company don't want because they don't get behind them and they inevitably sink without trace. So it was a face-off. The first covers album, *Don't Stop*, in 1996, was a platinum album for us. So David and the record company were once again proved right. The trouble was they then wanted another and another . . .

We went along with it because it was the nineties and we were painfully aware of how much the game had moved on. Whether it was Nirvana and grunge, Oasis and Britpop, or the Prodigy and dance music, Quo had nothing to do with any of it any more. So we had to try a new tack. Several new tacks, as it turned out. David and Simon were always coming up with new angles to keep us in the news, like the Rock 'Til You Drop four-shows-in-one-day event in 1991. I look back on that now and think: never again! Because that really did nearly kill me. But it drew in all the world's press, radio and TV and was a hugely publicized success for us, not to mention raising over a quarter of a million pounds for charity. As long as all this stuff was working, and we were doing good at the same time, who was I to argue?

Besides, not all David's ideas were cheesy. In fact, I thought he'd pulled off a major coup when he persuaded the Beach Boys to sing backing vocals for us on our version of 'Fun, Fun, Fun' for the *Don't Stop* album. For someone like me, who grew up listening to their astonishing records, working with the Beach Boys was one of the highlights of my career. The first time they sang live with us, I was completely blown away! Like I was in a dream. The fact that Brian was there too just made the whole thing even more special.

The trouble was the albums of our own material weren't selling in anywhere near the numbers that the covers and compilation albums were. In truth, I don't think we were writing any great commercial hits, either, at that point. I hadn't written a new song for years. In fact, I lost the plot a little bit musically at this point. Not in my playing, but in my ability to actually sit down and write a song. I needed a spark to set me off but nothing was lighting my fire. I didn't want to write a 'Quo' song just to have something on the albums, I wanted to write something simply because I thought it was good, as I had done when I came up with 'Whatever You Want' or 'Again and Again'. But for some reason I just couldn't do it any more. I think it was laziness, as much as anything – and an over-eagerness, perhaps, to accept my lot. Francis and Bernie always had plenty of new songs and I was happy to go along with that.

My personal life, meanwhile, had become complicated again. After the first big bust-up with Patty, you might have thought I'd learned my lesson. Instead, I carried on secretly seeing Marietta even after she went back to Germany. Things between me and Patty had never been quite the same after the split; now we had begun arguing all the time. Finally, after yet another big fight, we let Silverdale go and Patty and Harry moved into a smaller rented house on a very nice private estate in Burwood Park, while I went back to living at the apartment in Key West.

Once the dust settled, we still saw each other, still stayed over at each other's places occasionally. We just no longer lived together. Maybe we would have got back together properly if I hadn't also carried on seeing Marietta on the quiet. I would drive all the way over to Germany – that used to chase the cobwebs out of the Merc, doing 150 m.p.h. down the autobahn – or she would fly over to stay with me at Key West for a few days. There were a number of problems between me and Patty, but that was the one that really drove the stake through the heart of our marriage.

Then Richard finished school and came to live at Key West, too. Now things got really complicated. I'd hang out at home with Richard, who was now a young man in his late teens, so we mainly talked about cars, birds and music – in that order. Then the next day I would drive down to Burwood Park to see Harry, who I still thought of as my baby boy but who was also now growing up fast. I never seemed to know the right things to say to him any more. He had his own private den now, with his own TV and CD player and stuff, and I remember complaining to Patty, saying he shouldn't be watching so much TV at his age. But as she pointed out, who was I to talk? If I wasn't out carousing or working with the band, I was sat at home in front of the telly. (Unlike Harry, I might add, who spent most of his time outdoors playing football, the telly only coming on at night.)

This went on for a couple of years. Eventually, though, my long-drawn-out affair with Marietta finally began to peter out. It began when I realized I just couldn't face any more eleven-hour drives to Germany. They say the road to a friend's house is never long, but after a while it just became impossible. That's when I began questioning the whole thing. Aside from the sheer impossibility of keeping a long-distance relationship going, life just felt very fragmented. Flitting between Patty and Harry in Burwood Park, me and Richard at Key West, and Marietta in Germany, the whole thing was just in pieces. I'd simply had enough of all the lies and, so, too, I suspect, had Marietta. She could see me drifting away and I was aware that she was allowing it to happen. We both knew things couldn't go on like that for ever.

It all came to ahead when I did another year out of the country as a tax exile between 1992 and 1993. I rented a place on Jersey, where Francis was also staying. Andy Bown came out for a while with Bernie Frost and we all did some writing together. Both Patty and Marietta had been out to stay with me, too, at different times during that year, but now the whole thing was really starting to get to me. I had already decided to stop seeing Marietta. I wanted us to stay friends, which I'm pleased to say we were able to do – she has a new life now in Miami and though we never really see each other any more, I still regard her as one of my best friends.

Now I decided to come clean with Patty and see if we could start again. Wipe out all the lies and start afresh. It sounded like a good idea on paper, anyway. I was allowed a designated number of days back in the country during the tax year and so I phoned Patty to tell her I was going to use one of them to come and see her. She seemed surprised but pleased. Then I flew to Heathrow, rented a Merc, and drove down to Burwood Park. I had made up my mind not to bullshit her any more. She deserved more than that. So as soon as I got there I sat her down and told her straight. Oh, dear . . .

For a moment, Patty sat there in shocked silence. Then it all began to sink in and she went into a terrible rage. I'd never seen anything like it before. She went absolutely mad! First she started screaming at me then she ran upstairs while I grabbed my coat and made a dash for the car. By the time I got there she had started throwing all this stuff out of the bedroom windows. Patty still had a lot of my clothes and things. Now it all came raining down on my head – shirts, jackets, trousers, shoes, anything she could lay her hands on.

At one point a pair of my old cowboy boots landed on the bonnet of the car and dented it. 'Mind the car!' I wailed. 'It's not mine!'

She wasn't listening, though. I scurried around collecting my things as more and more stuff came flying out of the window. I got as much of it as I could and threw it all in the back of the car, then got the hell out of there. What a scene! Once I was away from the place and could think straight again, though, I remember feeling relieved that I had at least told her. Until then I had been living this lie and it was poisoning everything. Now that at last it was all out in the open, I felt better.

Patty, however, took a different view on things. This latest indiscretion was simply too much for her and, far from wiping the slate clean, my confession signalled the end of our marriage. There was a long separation – during which she wouldn't even let me see Harry for a while – before we finally went to court, in August 1996. The judge ruled in Patty's favour and she was granted a £1.4 million divorce settlement. I also agreed to buy her and Harry their own home: a nice £250,000 four-bedroom place in Weybridge.

I was happy to do all those things. After all, it wasn't Patty or Harry's fault that I had been unfaithful. I did start to wonder, though, if maybe there was something wrong with me. That was twice I'd managed to fuck my marriage up just when things were going well. Was there a pattern emerging? I decided there was. The more I thought about it, in fact, the more certain I became, and that's when I learned something about myself, which is this: I simply cannot stay settled for long. As soon as the ocean is calm, I have to whip up a storm. I *have* to! And marriage isn't about that. Marriage is about *not* changing things. Not being able to come and go as I please, where I want, when I want and with whom I want – and I hate that.

Living back on my own again at Key West in the mid-nineties, not seeing either Patty or Marietta any more, was a great relief, in many ways. I had never been that bloke that comes home at night, has his dinner, watches telly, then goes to bed with the missus. It's nothing personal against Patty, or Marietta before her, it's just the whole convention of marriage. It doesn't suit me. It's a great day out, to get dressed up and get married and have a big party with all your friends afterwards. I did it on a whim both times. Had a great party both times, too. Then woke up the next day and began life as a married bloke, and just weakened and weakened . . .

Now, at long last, I was free simply to be me. I had a couple of different girlfriends during this period, but nothing heavy. For me, it was all about fun again. Escapism. Even being in the band seemed less of a chore. What with all the cover version albums and greatest hits compilations, we only seemed to make a proper new Quo album once every few years. We still toured as much as ever, but life in the band assumed a much more leisurely pace, creatively. Whereas in the seventies we had sweated blood trying to come up with two great new albums of original material a year, most of the stuff we made in the nineties, like the two '25th Anniversary Waltz' singles (which were a laugh) or the *Famous in the Last Century* album (which was so awful it almost made me cry), was basically just us coasting. Francis hated that fact; I went along with it. It wasn't that I was past caring; I still cared about Quo more than anything. I just didn't feel like I had the answers any more. To me, David Walker was the one with all the answers now . . .

Meanwhile, I had other concerns. Namely, my health. I've always had an amazingly strong constitution, but I would be turning fifty in 1998 and even I had started to notice signs of wear and tear. It was time to 'slow down' – two words that have never been part of my vocabulary. If I still needed a nudge in the right direction though, I certainly got one when, at end of April 1997, I collapsed at home one morning from what was later diagnosed as a severe angina attack.

I was on my own when it happened. There hadn't been any warning signs; I hadn't been feeling ill. I don't think I'd even been out the night before. We had just got back from a long tour of Japan, Australia and America, and were taking a break before starting again in the summer with some outdoor festivals around Europe, so I was taking it easy. I simply got up one morning and went upstairs (the bedrooms at Key West were on the ground floor) to the kitchen to make a cup of tea. I had just got to the top of the stairs when this massive lightning bolt of pain shot across my chest from one shoulder to the other! I had never felt such pain before, it literally put me on my knees! I thought I was dying ...

I don't know how long I lay there on the floor before the pain finally subsided enough for me to drag myself over to the phone. I didn't phone an ambulance, though, I phoned my doctor, who said he didn't like the sound of that and to come in and see him – only not that day, as he was busy, but the next morning. Then he told me to take two aspirin and lie down. I was relieved. By then I had dusted myself down and was starting to feel better. Maybe it wasn't such a big deal after all, I told myself.

But when I saw the doc the next day he sent me straight off to Wellington Hospital, in St John's Wood, for tests. I had a driver drop me off there and told him to wait until I returned. I thought I'd only be gone for a couple of hours. Then I went inside . . .

The smell immediately took me back to the day as a child when I'd nearly hacked my finger off in the garden gate. Suddenly the air was filled with foreboding. They took my clothes off, put me in a hospital gown and started doing their tests. Then they told me to lie down on this bed in a room on my own while we waited for the results. The next thing I knew I had a whole team of doctors scurrying around me saying they were going to keep me in and operate that night! An angiogram had revealed that the arteries in my heart were virtually closed and I would need immediate quadruple-bypass surgery. They said, 'If we don't operate on you tonight, you've got less than 24 hours to live.' Those were their actual words. I just sat there stunned.

There was a phone in the room. After they left, the first person I called was my mum. 'You're never gonna believe this,' I began. I tried to sound cheerful but that was a tough call to make. After that I phoned David. I don't know who else I phoned that day but I was talking for hours. They had given me a cocktail of tranquillizers and I was suddenly very calm and relaxed about things. They continued giving me more stuff to bring me further down as the afternoon and evening wore on. Then at eleven o'clock that night they wheeled me into the operating theatre. I was completely out of my tree by then. When they put the oxygen mask on and the doctor started to count backwards from four, I was out before he got to three . . .

The next thing I knew I was back in bed in the room. It felt like I'd closed my eyes for a second and when I opened them again I'd been transformed into the six-million-dollar man! I gingerly checked myself over. I discovered I had wires and tubes coming out of every possible orifice: things coming out of my chest, wires dangling from my stomach, tubes going up my nose and more tubes going down my throat. I'd got stuff in my arms and wrists, I'd even got a catheter up my knob . . . Awful! One of the most uncomfortable days of my life. Just trying to turn slightly to one side meant shuffling a whole network of wires and tubes into place. Total nightmare . . .

Apart from sawing open my chest, they had also taken the main London-to-Brighton line out of my left leg: chopping the main vein into four or five sections they then replanted in my heart. That was the most painful thing of all, the stitches that quickly turned to scabs all the way down my leg. Thankfully, they gave me a pain-relief button. When the pain became too bad, all I had to do was press the button to get another shot of whatever it was they had in that bottle. Needless to say, I felt no pain at all for several days. I pressed that button so many times they had to keep running off to get fresh supplies.

Once I was out of intensive care I was allowed visitors. My dad had died a few years before, but my mum and my Auntie Dot came to see me. Everybody was so nice. I got cards and flowers from Quo fans all over the world, plus some people in the biz I didn't even know cared. It was all very touching. Francis came by, too, one day and I sat up and smiled for the camera. I also remember both Marietta and Patty hovering around at different times. I think they all thought I was about to pop my clogs.

After intensive care, they got me up trying to walk a bit. You're still very unsteady, though, and it's bloody hard work. You can't believe how weak and fragile you have become, struggling along hanging on to a nurse. Thankfully, all the doctors and nurses at the Wellington were fantastic; they really worked hard to keep your spirits up. One doctor – meaning well but obviously not realizing who he was talking to – even told me if I fancied a drop of red wine I should have one because it was very good for the heart. Of course, he meant a *glass* of red wine. But I took him literally and started ploughing through bottles of the stuff. He didn't say anything about smoking but as soon as I started drinking again I started smoking too, standing there in the men's toilets, having a crafty fag and a glass of wine, this mobile coat-hanger standing next to me, trailing all my wires and tubes.

My powers of recovery have always been substantial, though. When I go and see my doctor now he says: 'Parfitt, I can't believe your scar!' Because he's had the same operation and it has left him with this long red welt down his chest, while my scar has all but disappeared. I've even fooled people by telling them I didn't really have the operation, it was all a PR scam, then baring my chest as proof. When I'm tanned, it's practically invisible.

As a result, I checked out of hospital just eleven days after the operation. They told me to go home and rest. There wasn't much else I could do. I moved between the bed and the sofa and that was it. After a week or so I attempted to take a walk down to the high street but I had to sit down halfway, then phone for someone to come and pick me up in the car. A few days later I tried again, this time with a walk over to Teddington lock. I was watching all the boats passing through when I realized with mounting alarm that I was about to sneeze. The doctors had warned me that sneezing might burst open my stitches and told me to hold a cushion to my chest if I felt one coming on. Of course, I didn't have a cushion to hand so I just crossed my arms against my chest and sneezed as gently as I could. I checked myself afterwards and I was still intact – no stuffing falling out the sides – so that was all right.

Sure enough, I recovered little by little, day by day. I had a couple of big nights, as they say, here and there, just to keep my spirits up. But, basically, I just took it easy and got myself together again, ready to return to the band. We discussed when I might be able to come back, and as we already had the show at Norwich City football ground, in August, pencilled in, I used that as my goal to aim for. (There's a pun in there somewhere but I'm not sure if it's intended or not.)

A month after the operation I was up and about almost normally again. I still got tired easily but I was definitely on the mend. By the time I walked on stage in Norwich six weeks later, I was raring to go. The only time I got seriously nervous was just before we went on. It's one thing to exercise; another thing entirely to do an actual gig, where you're running, skipping, jumping and playing your balls off for nearly two hours. The old ticker was going to be seriously road-tested for the first time and I decided it was either going to be a complete blinder or I was going to cause an even bigger sensation by dropping down dead after the third song. There was no point trying to hold back. Either I was going to be able to go full tilt as I always had done at a Quo gig, or I wouldn't be able to go at all. Fortunately, I felt fantastic throughout the show, and that was when I knew for sure that Rockin' Rick was back. It was such a great feeling; such a great night. I got a standing ovation just for being there!

After that, it was business as usual. The way I saw it, the heart operation was like a mid-life refit. I'd worn out the valves in the old engine, so I'd had some new ones put in, and now I was ready to take off down the road again. That's the way I still look at it. I just assume I'll live till I'm a hundred and any repairs I need to make along the way I will.

Of course, not everybody saw it that way. The doctor warned me after the operation: 'You can't live life as you used to. You've got to slow down now.' But did I? Did I hell! I was determined the whole thing wouldn't change me at all, and it didn't. In fact, I was back to my old ways the moment I came out of hospital. My first day home, I bought a gram of coke, a couple of bottles of red wine and forty cigarettes, then lay back on the couch and did the lot! I felt I deserved a treat after what I'd been through. How did it make me feel the next day? Fucking fantastic! Like I'd been given my life back again. That's the truth, whether people like it or not. I just lay down on the sofa the next day and didn't move again for a week . . .

Thankfully, my life did start to slow down after the operation. Not at first, while I was still trying to prove to everyone that it hadn't changed a thing. But gradually, over the next few years, as I got into my fifties, I simply found myself less and less enamoured of the whole business. Francis had knocked all the booze and drugs on the head a long time before, of course. With me it was much more gradual. Two divorces couldn't do it; a heart operation couldn't do it. In the end it was down to me, pure and simple. I was an older guy now and it just didn't hold the same appeal for me any more.

At first I simply downgraded and became a casual drug user, rather than a got-to-have-it-every-day man. If I had a free weekend with nothing to do I would get some in, maybe. A bit of Nikki Lauda, as I call it – i.e. powder. But even that started to lose its fun-factor. From there it was a gradual disenchantment which led me to where I am today: more or less completely drug-free, apart from the ciggies and the occasional gargle.

There was another reason, too, why I finally calmed down. It doesn't sound very rock'n'roll, but I was starting to miss ordinary family life again. Not marriage, as such, just the fact of being around my children, particularly Harry, who was still young and more in need of a regular dad than Richard, who was already finding his own way as a young man. Harry was ten in the summer of 1999 and it was around then that I first began making an effort to really try to get to know him again. After the long, painful years of separation from Richard – years I knew I would never be able to replace, no matter how hard I tried to make up for them now – I was desperate not to let the same thing happen to me and Harry.

After the divorce, I had been granted the usual meagre 'access' privileges. With Patty's blessing, however, I now began seeing Harry more often: meeting him from school sometimes and taking him out for pizza or a trip on the river, maybe. Because he was always talking about Patty, one day when we were going out I asked him if he wanted to bring his mum, too. Just to please him, really. So he asked Patty and she agreed to come, for the same reason as me, and suddenly we found ourselves going out together as a family again for the first time in years. We didn't do anything special, just cruised around in the car and got something to eat, but we had such a nice time together we did it again a few days later.

After that, it became a regular occurrence. Things became less formal and we went shopping together and even took a holiday together. Given the long history between us, I suppose it was inevitable that we would also start sleeping together again. But at first we actually managed to keep each other more or less at arm's length. Then, sometime in the early part of 2000, I invited Patty down to Brighton for a weekend away with me – our first time together on our own without Harry since he was born. I wasn't sure she'd accept but thankfully she did. We spent the weekend in Brighton together, and at last it felt right. After that, one thing led to another and before long we were taking turns to stay at each other's places again. There was no pressure, but little by little our lives were becoming fused again. The important thing was we'd become friends again first, then lovers. I thought to myself: what the fuck was so wrong with this the first time around? I must have been insane letting this go . . .

After all I've said about marriage, you might think the last thing I would have wanted right then was to become entangled again with the woman I had only just divorced a few years before. Seeing Patty wasn't like seeing other girls, though. There's always the excitement of being with someone new, but nothing can really match the intimacy you achieve with someone you have not only known for most of your life, but who you have also had a child with. There's something that exists between two people like that that goes to a place where words simply don't reach. We decided it was something worth holding on to.

There's also something else that will always hold me and Patty together. But I can't tell you what it is because it's far too personal, even for this book where I am truly baring my soul for the first time. I'm not just talking about sexual compatibility, either. This goes way beyond that. It's just something I've never had with anyone else; something so personal and special that it makes our relationship unique. More, though, I cannot say . . .

We had been living together on and off for nearly a year

when we decided to make it official and actually buy a new place together. Patty's house in Weybridge was now worth nearly half a million; Key West was worth about the same. We decided to sell both of them and put the proceeds towards buying one big place together: a beautiful penthouse apartment we had found in Teddington, just up the river from Key West, which we bought two years ago for just under a million. It's only got three bedrooms but what we like about it is it's very spacious and open plan, with twenty-foot-high windows overlooking the river. Every room has a door out on to the balcony and there are mezzanines on both floors. Just beautiful. We've since tried looking for somewhere further down the river in the countryside but we've never been able to find anywhere half as nice.

Harry also played a big part in our decision. We wanted him to have a proper, balanced background in order to safeguard his future; to have his mum and dad back together again, living with him under the same roof. He had asked us about it often enough when we were on our own with him, so we knew that was what he wanted too. The only thing I wasn't prepared to do again was get married. No disrespect to Patty, who I love and cherish dearly. Deep down inside, I think she would probably marry me again tomorrow. But I truly believe I'm past all that now. I do love her, though, and I worship Harry, and I like the idea of being together as a family again. I just don't ever want to be married again, that's all. That's one area where I really have learned my lesson.

Now that we've got all that straight, home life is fairly tranquil these days. I'm a bit of a claustrophobic in that I like to see a lot of space around me. But I like space with something going on in it. When I lived at Hydon Ridge with Marietta, I loved the idea of being able to sit on my back porch and look out over miles of uninterrupted views. But it was so panoramic, it never moved, never changed, except for the colours through the seasons, which was beautiful to behold but hardly made for gripping day-to-day viewing.

Looking out over a space like the Thames is a completely different scene. There's all the peace and tranquillity of the river but there are always things going on out there too. The river is always teeming with life; it never stops moving, from the different boats gliding past to the people on the riverbank going about their business. It's very leisurely, the whole culture that goes with living by the river, and I never want to live anywhere else ever again. I love getting up in the morning and having a cup of tea and my first cigarette of the day while standing on my balcony looking out over it all. It's absolutely the best time of the day: a feeling of freedom and peace. On hot sunny mornings the water glistens like a vast silver mirror. On cold, rainy afternoons it's as black as coal. It's such a beautiful thing to have going on outside your door each day. I even like it when the ferry-boats come past at night with big parties on board. Beautiful boats all lit up red, green and blue. It's so lovely to look at and I get off on the sound of the music and laughter wafting your way for a few seconds; it just transports you to another place.

My current boat is a Cessa: an Italian-made thirty-six-foot cruiser with twin bedrooms, kitchen, shower, two bathrooms; much the same as *Silver Sun* but even bigger. I named it *Piledriver* (or Piled River, if you prefer), after the first big Quo album. I bought it for £120,000 just after we moved in together in Teddington and we've had some great parties on it. I was going to upgrade it this year to a fifty-footer but then I changed my mind at the last minute. For once, I realized I was perfectly happy with what I'd already got. I really must be getting old . . .

The band, meanwhile, have also gone through some pretty drastic changes in the last few years. When David Walker died in 2001, at first I thought that might be the end of us, too. We'd certainly reached a crossroads. *Famous in the Last Century* – the last album we'd released with David, yet another collection of covers released to tie in with all the excitement over the millennium – was the worst Quo album ever, in my opinion. It was still a fair-size hit but that was where we really hit rock bottom, musically.

David died too young for it to be considered anything but a tragedy. But even if he'd lived, I wonder now if we'd have stayed with him for much longer. After he died, we thought we'd be free at least from having to make any more terrible cover version albums. When Francis came up with the novel idea of writing a bunch of new songs and putting them out as our next album – a cunningly simple plan David would never have condoned – I didn't need any persuading. When Simon Porter, who took over as manager, got us a new deal with Universal Records off the back of a new four-track demo we'd made, we were convinced our days of cover versions were behind us for good. Ha, ha . . .

We were halfway through making what became the *Heavy Traffic* album, in 2002, when we were told the bigwigs at Universal had decided they also wanted a covers album from us. At first, we were mortified. *Heavy Traffic* was shaping up to be the best Quo album since our heyday because it sounded like a Quo album should. The fact that we still do a couple of numbers from it in the live show today – the truest test there is of a song – demonstrates how strong it is. I even came up with a new number with Rhino that I was quite pleased with, called 'Creepin' Up on You'.

When we were told we would have to make another covers album, it really took the wind out of our sails. At first we fought the idea, but they made it clear it was a deal-breaker; that they saw it as their financial safety-net. They couldn't be sure how well our own album would do, but as long as they had a covers album to follow – a sure-fire hit, in other words – they were happy to get behind both records. Francis took the news very badly. We agreed to it in the end, though, because this band has to go on, it has to survive, and if that's the way it has to be, then that's the way it has to be.

If there was a positive to be taken from all this, it was that the resulting album – titled *Riffs* – didn't do half as well in the shops in 2003 as *Heavy Traffic*, our album of original material, had done the year before. A complete reversal, in fact, on where we'd been in the nineties. We didn't say we-told-you-so but to us we had finally proved the point.

Looking too far forward, though, is not my thing. I live in the here and now and the only tangible event I'm focusing on right now is our forthcoming fortieth anniversary year in 2005. Some people find the whole 'anniversary' idea a bit crass. David was the one who started it back in 1990 with his original idea for going back to Butlin's to celebrate the twenty-fifth anniversary of me and Francis first meeting, and we've been lumbered with it ever since. (We did manage to avoid a thirty-fifth anniversary hoo-hah by dint of the fact that it was in 2000 and David decided the millennium was a better bet to hang our campaign on that year.)

A fortieth anniversary, though, is pretty special. It's a bit like a batsman standing undefeated at the cricket crease on ninety-nine. He knows he's already won the match but he doesn't want to stop until he gets his hundredth run. That's how I feel about Quo's fortieth anniversary. We can't stop now, not with something like that in sight. Not that we intend to stop after that, either. But that's the target we're aiming for right now. There will be a new Quo album out as well by then, but all I can tell you about that is that Francis and I agree that if Quo is to survive into the twenty-first century, it has to go back to doing things the old-fashioned Quo way. Which is to make our own records and rely on that to get us through. After all, it's worked once or twice before . . .

When I look back on all the highs and lows of our career, I think you'd have to agree that, ultimately, we've always done what it says on the tin. We've worked it and we've done it, and we're very proud of that. To have come this far and for this long, well, neither Francis nor I could possibly have dreamed it when we first started. We thought we'd be laughing if we got four good years out of it, let alone forty! After the music, I think the reason we're still so popular comes down to a basic warmth people get off us: a family feeling. Which is why we now get people at our shows aged anywhere between eight and eighty! When I look out and see so many different types of people all enjoying themselves together at one of our gigs, that means more to me than anything.

These days on tour, I'm almost a monk. Really! We have such a strict routine laid down now that the whole day is mapped out for you. You just have to turn up. It's better that way because I've got my act together. Apart from wanting to be at your best at the show and not let the fans down, you don't want to let yourself down either. I might be fifty-five now but I don't feel it mentally, and physically I don't think I look it, and I'd like to keep it that way – at least for a while longer. Ian Wright, the former Arsenal footballer turned TV star, came to see us play in Brighton just before Christmas last year. After half an hour, he said to Patty, 'How long do they play for before they take a break?' She said, 'They don't take a break.' He was flabbergasted. I suppose he thought we should have half time and oranges in the dressing-room. (Just a joke, Wrighty!)

The point I'm trying to make is that even he, a former professional athlete, couldn't believe the energy coming off the stage. In order to achieve that we *have* to look after ourselves or we simply won't make it through the tour. It might not sound very rock'n'roll, but you tell that to the audience. Once we're on stage it becomes very rock'n'roll indeed because it allows us to be at our best every night. Something drugs never did.

I admit there are still times when I fancy a little blast. Just to show that I still can if I want to. I always pay for it the next day though, when I look and feel like shit. But then it's good to get carried away sometimes. Or carried out. And if it makes the papers the next day – well, it's all good publicity, isn't it? These days, I usually go out a couple of times a week for a drink, just to see what happens. It might turn into a big night, it might not. But I take Patty with me these days and we go out together as a couple.

The other thing I'm still mad about, of course, is cars. I'm not the big collector I once was, but I still have my moments. For example, when Francis and I started writing this book in the summer of 2003, my pride and joy was my Mercedes CL600; a beautiful piece of kit with lots of toys – radar, TV, all sorts. By the time we'd nearly finished the book in the spring of 2004, however, I'd sold that and bought myself the new Bentley Continental GT: an ultra-sleek machine with even more gadgets to make your head spin. It cost me

£117,000 and was only the fifth one off the production line; I believe Elton had the first two. It was capable of doing 200 m.p.h. and I was really looking forward to taking it out on the autobahn.

Then all at once I fell out of love with it. Don't ask me why, I'm just much more promiscuous with cars than I used to be. Love 'em and leave 'em, that's my philosophy now. It's a fantastic car but I'd only been driving it for about a month before I realized it wasn't really my cup of tea. Fortunately, I found someone who wanted to buy it. Because there's a two-year waiting list for the next batch, I even made £20,000 on the deal! Not that the money stayed in my pocket for long because I went out the same week and bought myself a new Mercedes CL65 bi-turbo, with the full AMG racing spec and all the bells and whistles. I paid £150,000 for it, which took all the profit from the Bentley and then some. But it was worth every penny. Hand-built by Uli Gruber, using F1 technology, it has 612 horsepower and goes from 0 to 60 in 4.1 seconds. You can't buy them, you have to commission Mercedes to make one specially for you: there are only eight in the whole of Britain. In other words, a car built with my name written all over it.

Standing next to it in the garage these days is Patty's Mercedes SL350, and I've still got the Range Rover for things like taking the dog out or going down the garden centre – in other words, all those journeys you *don't* want to use the other cars for. (I'm not having dog hairs all over my beautiful Merc!)

Ultimately, though, it's the driving that really turns me on, not the car. Last year I drove a race-speed Ferrari 360 around a circuit in England. I'd never experienced anything like it! It was such brilliant fun I decided to get my own racing licence so that I could race cars like that regularly. I'm sure the band and my family would rather I didn't, but you have far less chance of an accident zooming round a professional racetrack than you do out driving at so-called normal speeds on the public roads. I'm also pals with Damon Hill, the former Formula One world champion, who used to be my neighbour. He plays guitar and has his own band, the Six Pistons. They supported us when we performed a special show at Silverstone racetrack, as part of the after-race party at the British Grand Prix in the summer of 2003. Over 15,000 people stayed behind to see us and it was a great day. I'd like to get together with him again some time, just sit around, play guitars and talk motors . . .

So life right now is good. Harry is still at school and smart enough to be anything he wants to be when he grows up. Richard has now decided to try to forge his own career as a pop singer, and if looks and talent are anything to go by you could well be hearing more of him and less of me in future. Patty, meanwhile, continues to be the light of my life. We've been talking about buying a place abroad recently. Maybe a nice villa in Spain somewhere by the sea. It's all just talk at the moment, but I do fancy it. Waking up to the sun every day, the boat idling nearby. Like a sunnier version of what we've got now. Whether we would keep the London place on and divide our time between the two, or just sell up completely and go and live abroad for good, is debatable. Harry will be seventeen in 2006 and a lot will depend on what he wants to do.

Right now, for me at least, it doesn't really matter where we live because the band is going to be so busy over the next eighteen months I am not going to be at home often enough to enjoy one place, let alone two. Once the fortieth anniversary tour is out of the way, however, it opens the door to all sorts of possibilities. Lately, in fact, I seem to be flooded with ideas. I don't know what it is, if it has a name, but something is definitely happening to me. All of a sudden I'm becoming really creative again.

For example, this year I launched my own quiz game. It's called *Rick Parfitt's Name Game*. Slogan: Get the Name – Win the Game! I came up with the idea on another long journey on the tour bus once, just to keep myself and the others amused. I made up the rules as we went along and, before I knew it, I had the whole thing worked out. It led to me looking into the world of games over the last year or so, and what I've discovered is that it's almost as cut-throat as the music business. The biggest seller in 2003 was the *Bargain Hunt* game, spun off from the TV series starring David Dickinson. It seems like all the most successful games are now spun-off from a TV show, like *Who Wants to Be a Millionaire?*. This game, however, is completely original. No one has ever thought of it before, which is amazing as it's so simple! But then the best ideas often are.

Another idea I've had that I'm now developing is a fitness idea I had, which sprang from my desire to keep in shape but my general boredom at the thought of going to the gym. It's like a portable peck-deck. We've called it *Parfitt's Portable Pecker*. Slogan: the Natural Lateral Way to Firm Your Pecks. You can put it in your briefcase, exercise with it in hotel rooms or offices ... I can't say any more than that at the moment in case anybody steals the idea. But again, it's just so simple, I can't believe anybody hasn't thought of it before.

I just seem to be coming up with these things at the moment. So many, in fact, that I've formed a company specifically to handle them with my partner Mike Hrano, who also oversees the merchandizing on Quo tours. Most of my friends in the business don't call me Rick, they call me Rock, so we've combined the two names and called the company Rockano. Our latest idea involves Fender and how to revolutionize the look of their guitars, except I can't talk about that yet either.

Something I can talk about is my plan to open my own bar-restaurant on the river. I fancy the idea of being your genial host for the evening, sitting there on a bar-stool welcoming the regular patrons. Not every night of the week, obviously. But occasionally during those times when the band is off the road, maybe. I want to make it into the sort of place I would like to go myself of an evening. Funky but smart, and lots of lovely waitresses walking around. Well, they can't touch you for looking at the menu as long as you don't eat, as my old dad used to say.

The only area where all this newfound energy doesn't seem to be manifesting itself yet is in my music. Don't get me wrong, Quo has been number one in my life for so long now there isn't anything that could possibly take its place, and I would love to be able to recount how I just came up with a brilliant new song. But the fact is, I haven't come up with many of those for a while now. I still get lots of brilliant ideas, but as soon as I sit down and try and make them into something they turn to dust in my hands. The trouble is, you can't force these things – that leads to bad writing. I'd rather write no songs than bad songs.

Whether this new burst of ideas has actually *replaced* those musical impulses, though, I don't know. But it all just feels really fresh and new to me right now, very crisp in my mind, and I'm very excited about it all. I've always been capable of being more than just that bloke in that band, and now I seem to be getting the chance to prove it.

One thing I would love to have done, but unfortunately had to turn down, was when I was approached last year by the producers of *I'm a Celebrity – Get Me Out of Here!*, to see if I would be one of the celebs in the series that also featured Jordan, Peter André and Johnny Rotten. I was going to do it, too. I think it's a great show and was glued to the set every night when it was on.

The reason I didn't in the end was because they wouldn't let me take a few of what I regard as the absolute essentials – i.e. my guitar, which I could have gone without at a pinch, I suppose. But also my own pillow, which sounds like a silly thing but is something I always carry with me on the road. When they also said I would only be allowed ten cigarettes a day, I knew we were on shaky ground. (I honestly don't think I could survive on less than twenty!) The real deal-breaker, though, was over my sleeping tablets, which are prescribed for me by my doctor. I've been on them for such a long time now, it would be dangerous to suddenly stop taking them. But they were insistent I wouldn't be allowed to have them, at which point I said, 'Well, it looks like I won't be coming to the jungle then.'

A pity, because it is a great show – and I'd love to have met Lord Brocket and Johnny Rotten. I've heard Johnny was a Quo fan as a kid, and his Lordship certainly seemed a laugh-a-minute, helping wash Jordan. A proper gentleman, after my own heart . . .

In terms of Quo, the only vague plan after 2005 is to take a break. A journalist once counted up all the shows we had ever done and told us that, in effect, the band had been on the road constantly for almost twenty years! In other words, more than half the time we've been together has been spent entirely on the road. That's a staggering thought, even for me, who travelled all those thousands of miles with them. Therefore, I don't think a short break now would hurt us. If anything, it might help to keep us going even longer. I can just picture the fiftieth anniversary tour now. Francis will have no hair left at all by then, just the ponytail, and I'll be in one of those motorized wheelchairs, souped-up for me specially by Mercedes.

As for my own personal relationship with Francis, although we've obviously grown up and changed a lot since we first met as teenagers, in many ways we're still the same underneath. We may be joined at the hip professionally but we've always been different; always led separate lives away from each other when we weren't working together. In most cases, those differences are probably what has helped keep us together. If we'd been too similar and agreed on everything, Quo would have disappeared up its own arse years ago.

Just occasionally, however, those differences have caused friction between us. We've never actually come to blows, touch wood, but we've certainly had our altercations down the years. Francis so rarely shows any signs of real emotion, I sometimes think he's devoid of it. I know it's in him somewhere. You only have to see the warmth he exudes when he's surrounded by his wife and kids to know there's a gentle heart beating inside there somewhere. But would he ever willingly show it to you? Never. He keeps it all locked away inside. On stage he comes across as this carefree cheeky chappy, but he's a very different character off it. He's a creature of absolute habit, his whole day worked out to the second, to the point on tour where he'll pick up his guitar at exactly the same time every night. He can't just relax and do things spontaneously. He will not let go of this grip he has on himself. He likes to read it all ahead.

There's nothing wrong with that; it's another reason, I suspect, why the band has enjoyed such longevity – because Francis is always thinking three moves ahead. With me, though, it's a case of whatever's going to happen is going to happen. We've got this wonderful vessel called Status Quo, let's just ride the waves and see where it takes us. I prefer life that way because it's more exciting and colourful – and simpler! It's better not knowing what's going to happen next. Sometimes it's great; other times it's, oh no! Either way, you have to deal with it. Like driving a really fast car: you don't want to know every bend in the road because that would spoil all the fun. Never plan a party, that's what I say. In fact, that should be my epitaph . . .

Give Francis his due, though, whatever he does, it definitely works for him. He keeps himself in incredible shape on and off the road and he's utterly professional to work with these days. He's basically a lovely guy who thinks deeply about things. Maybe a bit too deeply sometimes. He's also quite secretive. But I've known him for nearly forty years now and I know what goes on in his mind. He thinks I don't, but I do.

We get on much better these days, too. The fact that I'm not the boozy drug-taker I used to be has obviously helped, but it's more than that. Since David died, we've been able to meet more halfway again. We're always going to be different as people – I still like going out on the town, looking the part; he'd still rather sit at home doing the crossword in his cardigan – but, hopefully, we're always going to be the same when it comes to Status Quo. Let's face it, it just wouldn't be the same without the two of us.

And we know that. Certainly we've never been more famous; way beyond anything we ever dreamed of in the sixties, when getting on the cover of *Melody Maker* was still regarded as the pinnacle. We're recognized pretty much everywhere we go in the world now. We're also richer than at any previous time in our careers, which is amazing considering the dire position we were in at one point. Being in Status Quo means far more to me, though, than just fame and fortune. The best thing about being in Quo is that it gives me a reason to get up in the morning; something to be part of and proud of. I love my job and how many people can say that?

Nevertheless, you're only human and sometimes things do get you down, no matter how well off you are. Some of the saddest, loneliest people I've ever met have also been some of the richest. In spite of the image we all help perpetuate of this zany, happy-go-lucky, alternative universe we all inhabit, the fact is the music business is one of the toughest professions in which to make it. Very few guys who start out as teenagers dreaming of pop stardom ever get as far as one hit record, let alone nearly forty years' worth like us.

That isn't something that happened by accident. We didn't win the lottery; we had to work hard for all those years. To endure the ups and the downs, the rough and the smooth. So when we go to work, we work hard. For a start, it's a twenty-four-hour day, and you don't get to go home at night. Not for months at a time. That can either be torture or it can be an adventure. Usually it becomes a mixture of both, depending on how long we're away for. We are in the bubble, as we call it, and that's where we stay until the tour is over. Even when we play Wembley Arena and we're just a few miles from home, we stay at a hotel. We daren't go home in case it bursts the bubble. I made the mistake once of going home when the tour hit London, and I felt like a lodger. On tour the only reality we recognize is the hotel, the tour bus and the stage. Nothing else is real.

Instead of using drugs to keep me distracted, these days I use the power of my imagination. I suppose I've always been a bit of a dreamer; it's probably one of the reasons why I became so attracted to drugs in the first place, because they allowed me to stretch my imagination even more. Now I try to put my dreams to better use, and all the time we're away on tour I keep a picture in my mind of the place I'm trying to get to, which I visualize as a desert island: the kind of idyllic setting where there's just you, a sandy beach, a blonde and a few palm trees swaying overhead. It's like I can see my little island just there on the horizon; all I have to do is keep swimming, chalking up the days in my mind until I get there. There are times when you get tired, so you lie on your back and kick your feet, but you keep going no matter what, until suddenly that island doesn't look so small any more. Until you're close enough, in fact, to climb out of the water and rest on it. To have made that long journey, to have got there in the end, the sun shining down and the hoola girls dancing – that's the best feeling in the world to me.

Whether it's another album or a tour, that's the way I look at all my adventures with Quo now. Like a distant tropical island I have to get to. Sometimes I can literally see it getting closer and closer; sometimes I can't see it for all the clouds. But I keep swimming, keep kicking my feet, and eventually I get there. And the water's always warm – or at least it is in my mind. When the water starts to turn cold, the sun stops shining and the hoola girls stop dancing, that will be the time for me to stop.

So far, though, the sky is blue, the sun is out and the water's still warm, and I can already see the next beautiful island starting to appear on the horizon. See you there, too, maybe . . .

2005

Hello again. Well, it's been a year since Rick and I finished writing this book. And so, with the publication of this new paperback edition, we thought it would be nice to bring you up to date with everything that's happened to us in the past twelve months.

I suppose the first thing I should say is how pleasantly surprised I was at how well the hardback version was received; everyone seemed to be very taken with it. Obviously, it was a much more truthful, much more revealing book than any we've ever put our names to before. But then this was always meant to be less a history of Status Quo and more an honest, warts and all, account of my and Rick's personal lives. Yet, despite being so personal, it seemed to draw everybody in, from long-time fans to people who wouldn't necessarily describe themselves as Status Quo devotees but who simply enjoy a damn good read. So in that sense I think both Rick and I are very proud of what we'd done. The fact that the book also went on to become one of the UK's bestselling music biographies of 2004 was also very gratifying to say the least. I've become used to seeing Quo's singles and albums going into the charts over the years, but to see a book go Top Five was definitely a wonderful moment for both of us.

In fact, the interest was much greater than we had dared hope and at first I think we were both rather taken aback by it all. When Rick and I embarked on a series of book signings, we couldn't believe how many people came to each bookshop – literally hundreds each time! Most of them, in fairness, were Quo fans, and very pleased we were to see them. But there were an awful lot of other people who came along who clearly couldn't be described that way. But something got them off on the book. We played a concert in Ireland the other day and some of the fans complained that we didn't do a book signing over there. You can't win, I suppose, but the whole thing did really well.

The annual winter tour which followed the release of the book was also our best attended for several years. In fact it was completely sold out! Another thing I was very pleased about was the single we put out at the same time as the hardback was published. It was called 'You'll Come Round' and I thought it was one of our best new songs for years. The Catch 22, from our point of view, was that it was one of those songs that grows on you – but we knew full well we'd never hear it played on the radio often enough for it to grow on anybody, which was a real shame as it has a great groove, I think, like something we might have come up with in the early seventies. It went straight into the Top 20, reaching number 14, but that's the thing about the band and the radio in the UK these days – we don't have time to put out records that grow on you any more.

It was the same with the next single, 'Thinking Of You' we released last Christmas, and which got to number 21. To me, it sounded like a classic slice of Quo but outside of the

Quo faithful hardly anyone knew it had come out because, as usual, the radio more or less ignored it. It's partly for this reason that the new single we're planning now, as I write, is something else again; probably the most outwardly commercial track we've released as a single since the eighties. In fact, it may even upset the more fanatical, hardcore Quo fans out there because it's *too* instant. It's called 'The Party Ain't Over Yet' and it's completely in your face from the very first time you hear it! A really top tune written for us by our mate John David (formerly of Dave Edmunds' Rockpile). It was John, of course, who also wrote 'Red Sky' and 'I Didn't Mean It', both of which were big hits for us back in the late eighties. But it's the first time we've worked with him since then and I have to say he's come up trumps.

It's actually a song we've had kicking around for a while but just not got around to recording. I really like John's songs and he seems to know what we're about and how we do things. In fact, we've just recorded two of his songs: 'The Party Ain't Over Yet' and 'All That Counts Is Love', and they're both fantastic! But what happens whenever we do something like that, and is probably the reason why we've held off recording them until now, is that we get accused of becoming a pop band all over again. It really does seem like we can't win, which is why I say, fuck 'em. If we can't please the hardcore fans without alienating the radio people and we can't please the radio stations without upsetting some of the hardcore fans, we might as well say to hell with it and just concentrate on pleasing ourselves.

Still, I don't want to sound as though I'm complaining, especially as this year has been all about celebrating our 40th anniversary together – how many rock or pop bands have been together that long?

Signing a new record deal since we completed the book – moving from Universal to Sanctuary – has given us the chance to take a really fresh look at things musically. As our first album of genuinely new material since *Heavy Traffic* in 2002, Bob and I were determined to come up with some really great new tracks. So much so, in fact, that we eventually ended up with over twenty-five new songs! Plus Rick came in with two or three really good songs this time as well, which is something he hasn't done for a long time. So we had plenty to sift through when we got back into the studio with the band.

Somebody said to me once; never mind the critics; as long as people can whistle your tunes, that's all that matters. I was in my early twenties at the time and I remember thinking: bollocks to that, I'm gonna change all that. Then 'Down Down' came out and loads of people came up to me and said how much their three-year-old kid loved it! My reaction was still the same: I didn't care how much somebody's toddler loved it, I wanted it to be approved of by the deep-and-meaningful brigade: the critics.

I realize now that that was a stupid thing for me to think, because in ten years' time a three-year-old will be a record-buying thirteen-year-old. I also realize now that if a small child likes a song it's almost certainly a sign of a really good, catchy tune. It doesn't matter whether it's the Tweenies or the Rolling Stones, little kids couldn't care less about what's cool, not when it comes to singing along to a song they love. They haven't had anything planted in their minds about what they should or shouldn't like. They only care about what sounds good to them. Now I take it as a great compliment whenever anyone says anything like that to me.

It's like the huge success that Tony Christie had with

'Amarillo' this year. It's got absolutely nothing to do with what's cool and what's not, it's just one hell of a great tune. I defy anyone who claims to have any interest whatsoever in pop music to tell me they don't hum along or tap their toes whenever it comes on the radio or TV. As far as I'm concerned, anybody who says they don't is a liar. The cool squad can knock it all they like. The fact is no one cares what they think, they just like the record regardless.

As I write, we're in the middle of our annual summer tour of outdoor venues in Britain and Europe. What with making the new album, we've been working fairly non-stop since we brought the book out. One of the great things about being in Quo is that whenever you get tired or burnt out, and start to think maybe you just can't face another day, you'll do a gig that will blow all that away and restore your faith in humanity again. We had a show like that the other night in Dublin. Bloody hell, I've not experienced a show or an audience as enthusiastic as that in a long time! Don't get me wrong, we're lucky to have some of the most loyal and exuberant fans in the world, but that night in Dublin really was something else. So now I'm all charged up again about the forthcoming tour of Britain this autumn.

We are definitely going to change the set for the winter tour, not just because we've got a brand new album to celebrate, but because, being our 40th anniversary, we feel we want to make it extra special for those fans who have been coming to see us for years. That said, there are some things you simply can't change – like the beginning of the show, which we've started with 'Caroline' for years now. That's definitely not going to change. We tried it once, on our 2003 UK tour, when we moved 'Down Down' to the beginning of the set and put 'Caroline' further down the set list.

But it was one of those change for change's sake things and it didn't really work. For some reason, 'Down Down' lost something by being the opening number, and 'Caroline' lost something for *not* being the opening number. Don't ask me to explain it, because I can't. I guess it all comes down to what they call chemistry. Some things just work and some things don't. Luckily, we had only done a few shows when Rick came to me and said he didn't think it was working, which was a relief as neither did I. It had sounded like a great idea when we first thought of it, but something that sounds great in your head doesn't always translate before a living, breathing audience. So we put 'Caroline' at the start of the set and 'Down Down' back to where it used to be later on and from thereon in everything went swimmingly.

I suppose, after forty years of doing this, we should know by now what works and what doesn't, but it's easy to get bored and start fiddling with things. 'Caroline' has been the opener of our show for years now for a good reason – because it's simply one of the best opening tunes there is. That said, there will definitely be surprises this year. I don't want to say what they will be, because then they wouldn't be surprises. Let's just say the stage will look completely different and, apart from those cornerstone moments in the show like 'Caroline', 'Down Down' and 'Rockin' All Over the World', it will be a completely new show for us.

One final thing I feel duty bound to comment on is this summer's much publicized Live 8 concert in Hyde Park. As soon as the show was announced people were asking me whether or not Quo would be appearing. I had to answer that I didn't know but that probably we wouldn't be doing it. Not because we didn't want to but for the simple reason that I don't honestly think the organizers wanted us to. Why?

Because we're not fashionable enough for them. I heard on the grapevine that they only wanted 'contemporary' groups on the bill, but how long have U2 been going for? Or Pink Floyd, Paul McCartney and Elton John?

It's a pity because ever since the show was announced and our names weren't on the bill, it was amazing how many media people started demanding we be included. The *Daily Mirror* was the first to make a big deal of it. Then the next thing we knew both Radio 1 and Capital Radio started going on about it. I ended up doing interviews on the Colin and Edith afternoon show on Radio 1, the Johnny Vaughn breakfast show on Capital Radio and about half a dozen other places. AOL actually conducted a poll, asking people to vote on whether they thought Quo should open Live 8. I'm told that over 15,000 people replied, out of which 90 per cent said yes, we should – and AOL are the main sponsors of Live 8! Then Gordon Brown was interviewed on GMTV, and even he said he thought Quo should open Live 8. Next thing we knew, Richard and Judy held a poll on their Channel 4 show, out of which 94 per cent said Quo should open Live 8!

It was all a bit weird, because we didn't open the show, nor were we asked to. Meanwhile, I notice that the recent documentary on Live Aid, made by Geldof's own TV company, was called ... *Rockin' All Over the World*.

The truth, in my view, is that it all came down to politics. Unlike the original Live Aid show in 1985, there seemed to have been a lot of vying for position this time round. When we were asked to open the bill at the 1985 show, it was mainly because the BBC thought that us doing 'Rockin' All Over the World' would be a great way to start, but it was also partly because no one else wanted that spot, they all thought opening the show would mean, in effect, being bottom of the bill. Then they saw what happened – us doing 'Rockin' All Over the World' was shown on all the TV and radio newsreels that day and is still shown when Live Aid is mentioned. So now everybody wants to open the show; let 'em. Unlike so many of these bands, we really didn't care where we appeared on the bill. Or even *if* we appeared on the bill. Contrary to some of the so-called experts I've seen waffling about this on the telly, Quo is doing very nicely indeed without needing to add to our profile by doing Live 8. But I do think they missed a wonderful opportunity by not letting us go out there and play 'Rockin' All Over the World' at some point in this year's show. Not only would it have linked Live 8 with Live Aid, but it's probably one of the only songs that would have been performed this year that the mums and dads, the grand-parents and non-fanatical music fans would actually have recognized.

There was nothing cool about the original Live Aid, it was all about old ladies phoning in offering their jewellery; it was about little kids giving their weekly pocket money; it was about forgetting what's cool and what's not and trying to do something more interesting and more valuable for one day. I wonder how many of this year's bands will be able to say that now the whole thing is over?

The bottom line is this: they did, at one point – after the *Daily Mirror*, Radio 1 and Capital Radio started asking too many questions about why we hadn't been invited this time – say we could have the 6 p.m. slot. But we couldn't do that as were due on stage in Ireland that night at roughly the same time, performing at a show we sold the tickets for long before anyone came up with the idea of Live 8. We offered to do any other time slot, even though it would have cost us a lot of time, money and energy to make it happen. But they said they couldn't do that – it would have meant re-jigging the whole bill. OK, fair enough. But if you ask me, if they had really wanted us to perform they would have helped us find a way. They just made the right noises about it whenever anyone with a microphone cornered them and asked about it.

Meanwhile, it seems as though we're not the only band who fell foul of the organizers in some way. The Stones were going to appear but they pulled out. Their excuse? That they're rehearsing. Surely they were rehearsing when they originally committed to appear. You ask me, they smelled a rat and got out. Oasis were in the same position. They were offered a slot, too, then decided, no, they didn't want any part of it. Their excuse? They were playing in Manchester that night, which is laughable but they decided, for whatever reason, that they didn't want to know. Something went wrong, I don't know what it was. But once Pink Floyd agreed to appear, my bet is there were a lot of noses bent out of shape over who would actually close the show. In the end Paul McCartney opened *and* closed it. I mean, what *was* going on? I don't know, but whether Quo performed or not had very little to do with us, or what the general public would have liked to see, that's my view.

As for the future, right now we're all really looking forward to the release of the new single and album in September, both of which are going to be called *The Party Ain't Over Yet.* For me, it's an album that could be the biggest thing we've ever done – or could be something that comes out and goes completely off the radar, except for the most dedicated Quo fans. Right now, I'm way too close to it to tell. It contains some of my and Rick's best songs for years – as well as those amazingly catchy songs by John David. For a band currently celebrating it's 40th anniversary, it's certainly some statement, put it that way.

I have also been working on a new solo album, which I'm planning to bring out sometime in 2006. Whether it surprises everybody by being a big hit or whether it just slips out and dies on its arse, I simply feel it's something I've really got to do. For the good of my own soul as a musician, I need to do stuff like that sometimes. At the same time, I must confess I'm looking forward to having a long break once this 40th anniversary year is over. I need to find myself in a place where I can just hole up and not go out at all for a while. Call it recharging the batteries, call it what you will, but after nearly two years non-stop, I think I have that coming.

As for looking any further into the future. Will there be any more chapters to this book? Watch this space . . .

2005

Looking back over the past twelve months, the main thing I feel now is just how quickly the time has gone. Which is good, in my book, as it's a sure sign good stuff has been happening to us. Time only seem to drag when things aren't going well.

Like Francis, I was pretty taken aback at how well the original hardback version of this book was received when it was published last year. Considering we also released a new single, a compilation album and a brand new career-spanning DVD at the same time, it could easily have got lost in the rush of product. Instead, of all those things, the book probably got the most attention. We had the most fantastic reaction to it. Everyone we spoke to who'd read it, from long-time fans to close personal friends, really seemed to enjoy it. We did a whole load of book signings and they all went really, really well, too. We didn't know how many people to expect, whether we'd only meet a few dozen or what, but we were getting over three hundred people along to each one, so that was amazing. It was also very gratifying to see the kinds of people who came along. You got the really obvious Quo fans, of course, but then you also got quite a few of what I would call civilians – i.e. people you wouldn't necessarily expect to come to the Quo gigs or even buy that many Quo records. They were obviously just ordinary book buyers, which was especially gratifying.

Then there were all the professionals who interviewed us about it, from appearing on *This Morning* on ITV 1 with Phil and Fern, to doing Frank Skinner on ITV 1 and the *Steve Wright Show* on Radio 2. Me and Francis were happy to talk about any of the stuff we had recently done but all anyone really wanted to know about was the book. As I say, it was all very gratifying indeed, especially as Francis and I had spent so long trying to get the book right and really tell it how it was, as opposed to a lot of these celebrity autobiographies you get where it's fairly obvious the person in question is being, shall we say, economical with the real facts of their lives.

But then, Francis and I had decided early on that this book should contain the real nitty-gritty; all the stuff we've never had the courage to tell before. As a result, the over-riding reaction we got from everybody was how honest the book was, and how down-to-earth and revealing about our personal lives. Everybody seemed surprised it was so candid, but I can't see it could have been any other way and done the job properly. My attitude has been: what's the point in trying to hold anything back? This was our chance, I always felt, to set the record straight once and for all. Just let it all out and see where it goes, sort of thing. Try and give the outside world a really deep insight into who we really are and how we tick.

The new single we released simultaneously, 'You'll Come Around', was also our biggest hit for some time, stopping just short of the Top 10; another gratifying notch on the belt, so to speak. Having said that, I didn't think it was the greatest record we've ever produced. But it was certainly all right, and of course it was good to have something out there that was fresh and new, as opposed to the greatest hits compilation we also released at the same time, which was fine and dandy but at the end of the day was exactly what it said on the tin: another greatest hits. The DVD was somewhat different, of course, and I enjoyed doing that, because, again, it's full of stuff most of our fans don't already know or own. But there's still nothing quite like putting out a brand new record and, from that point of view, both 'You'll Come Around' and the other new single we released after that, 'Thinking of You', which also got a dip into the Top 20, were both very pleasing. It all serves to keep things afloat, to keep wind in the sails, and that's very much what it's all about for us at this stage.

The UK tour following the publication of the hardback and the release of those records was our best attended for years. I believe something like 35,000 more people came along to that tour than had done in previous years, which is a hell of a result when you consider that all our recent UK tours have been big sellers for us. It seems to have carried over into all our tour dates this year as well, so that the 2005 tour looks to be shaping up as even larger than the 2004 outing. Why that should be, particularly, I really don't know. Rock music in general seems to be back in a big way, but then it's never really gone away. Maybe the book made a lot of people reconsider us, I don't know. But I'm very glad, whatever the reason. It's a hell of a thing to get to your 40th anniversary year as a band and find out that even more people are coming to your shows than ever before!

The only downside to all this activity, if you can call it a downside, is the fact that we have been busier than ever this year. It being our 40th anniversary year, we always planned to be busy, of course, but we really haven't stopped working, it seems, since we finished writing the book.

Apart from all the shows we've been doing, we've also made a new album – our first collection of all new material since *Heavy Traffic* was released three years ago. It's quite different for us but really good, too, I think; we're all very pleased with the way it's come out. We recorded it over three months in the spring of 2005 at a wonderful residential studio called Jacob's in Farnham. It was a great environment for us because there was no sidetracking, no distractions whatsoever. You're in the middle of a field in the middle of nowhere, so you've really got no choice but to get on with it. It's like being in a mini-bubble, no temptations to go running down to the pub or nipping off to the shops for a bit of retail therapy – there are no pubs or shops!

We shut ourselves up in the studio and got our heads down into making the album. We were armed with some really good songs, too. Francis and Bob had written over twenty new tunes on their own. I was also able to contribute a couple of songs this time. As I explained in the last chapter, I haven't found it easy over the past few years to come up with new material of my own. I've always had lots of ideas, but that's not the same thing as actually turning them into finished songs. This time, though, I managed to complete a handful of tunes I am really happy with. I had a couple of bits that I've been messing around with for quite sometime, but for the first time in a long time I was able to sit myself down and actually turn them into finished songs. The fact that I was so keen to submit them to the rest of the band for approval was a big thing, too. That has always been the acid test for me. I would never put forward any material for a

Quo album I wasn't absolutely 100 per cent about. So in the end I wrote three tracks for this album and had a hand in helping finish off another one, which is co-written with everybody in the band.

That said, I'm never quite 100 per cent happy with anything we do; I don't know why, but I never am. I always think this could have been just a little bit tighter, or that could have been just a little bit more polished or whatever. If and when the day finally comes that I am a 100 per cent happy with one of our albums, maybe that will be the day to knock it all on the head.

But this next album, for me, is definitely up there in the top 10 per cent of Quo albums. Ultimately, it's an album that's going to take a bit of listening to, I think. But given the effort I honestly think all our fans are going to like it, and maybe it will attract some new fans to the band as well. Personally, I really love it. There's at least a couple of tracks that if you didn't know it was Status Quo, you'd probably never guess just by listening to them. I think that's a good thing at this juncture in our career. It sounds a cliché, but there's definitely stuff to satisfy everyone on this album, some slower tracks, some deep and meaningful stuff, and plenty of all-out Quo rockers too – as you would expect from us. Definitely a good variation and a lot more commercial – a tad more pop-oriented, I think – than anything we've done for many years. As Francis says, both the John David songs we've done – 'The Party Ain't Over Yet' and 'All That Counts Is Love' – are very, very catchy. Both of them will be released as singles, I'm sure. The album was produced for us by Mike Paxman and he's done a wonderful job getting all the sounds just right.

As Francis and I are writing this update, the Live 8 show has just happened and, of course, Quo weren't there. We would have happily agreed to appear if they had actually asked us when they were originally setting the whole thing up. Because they didn't ask us – they only got round to that after the media all kicked up such a fuss about us not doing it – it seemed there wasn't room for us in the time slot we would have been able to work to.

It's a shame, I think, because Quo opening the original 1985 Live Aid concert is a big memory for most people who saw the show. Witness the amount of clips of us doing 'Rockin' All Over the World' at Wembley that have been shown on TV every time this latest concert was mentioned! And it's not like we weren't prepared to put ourselves out to do it, either. We actually had a concert on in Killarney scheduled for the same night. Nevertheless, we offered to put together two sets of roadies and equipment to help us do both that and the Live 8 show. It would have meant paying for our own helicopter in and out of Hyde Park, plus the cost of a private plane to fly us from London to Ireland – all of which we were happy to put our hands into our own pockets for.

The only thing we couldn't do was agree to the time slot they eventually offered us, which was at 6 p.m., because the Killarney show was scheduled to start at almost exactly the same time. We worked out the logistics and told the organizers we would be happy to do any slot they liked, as long as we could be away from the show by 3. But with the Live 8 show not actually starting until 2 that would have meant putting us on in the first hour and for some reason they weren't prepared to let us on then. We even offered to come on and do just one song – 'Rockin' All Over the World' – but again, no good. They just weren't having it.

So there you go. It's a shame, but what more could we

have done? Personally, I can't find any logical reason why we shouldn't have been on that bill but unfortunately the decision just wasn't ours. The tough part is that everywhere we went once the concert was announced people kept asking us if we were performing and if not, why not? It seemed as though the only people who didn't get it were the people actually putting the concert together. There was obviously a degree of backstage politics involved and that really is a shame, because at the end of the day it shouldn't have been about Quo or U2 or any other band, it should have been about the causes the concert was set up to espouse. It was irrelevant really who was on and who wasn't, as long as the aims of the concert were achieved. The first Live Aid concert was more like a bolt out of the blue and it just felt so natural the way the whole thing came together. This time round it seemed to have been more contrived, with more people jostling for position. The first Live Aid concert had a real magic about it that was always going to be be hard to duplicate.

Right now, I'm looking further forward to Quo's own plans for the rest of our anniversary year. Because of our new album, this autumn we will have a whole new stage show to bring to people – new set list, new stage show, it should be really exciting and different. And with both the single and the album called *The Party Ain't Over Yet*, I think it sends out just the right message about where me and Francis and the rest of the band are at now in terms of our lives and career. Because trust me, this party isn't over yet, not by a long chalk. And as anyone who knows me well will tell you, I do like my parties . . .

INDEX